The Land We Love:

The South And Its Heritage

By Dr. Boyd D. Cathey

The Scuppernong Press

Wake Forest, NC
www.scuppernongpress.com

The Land We Love:
The South And Its Heritage

By Dr. Boyd D. Cathey

©2018 The Scuppernong Press

First Printing

The Scuppernong Press
PO Box 1724
Wake Forest, NC 27588
www.scuppernongpress.com

Cover and book design by Frank B. Powell, III

All rights reserved

Printed in the United States of America

No part of this book may be reproduced or transmitted in any form or by any means, electronic or mechanical, including photocopying, recording, or by any information and storage and retrieval system, without written permission from the editor and/or publisher.

International Standard Book Number: ISBN 978-1-942806-19-6

Library of Congress Control Number: 2018962861

Dedications

To my father, Harry Sloan Cathey (1908-1999), Pvt. 1st Class, 101st Cavalry, U. S. Army, European Theater, 1942-1945

To my great-grandfather, Pvt. Henry Cathey (1827-1891), Company B, "The Ranaleburg Riflemen," 13th Regiment, North Carolina Troops, 1861-1865

To my great-grandfather, Pvt. Hill Ennett King (1847-1929), Company H, 67th Regiment, North Carolina Troops, 1864-1865

To my great-great-grandfather, Captain Marquis LaFayette Redd (1824-1871), Company E, "The Onslow Grays," 3rd Regiment, North Carolina Troops, 1861-1865

Nothing fills me with deeper sadness than to see a Southern man apologizing for the defense we made of our inheritance. Our cause was so just, so sacred, that had I known all that has come to pass, had I known what was to be inflicted upon me, all that my country was to suffer, all that our posterity was to endure, I would do it all over again.

— Jefferson Davis, Address to the Mississippi legislature, 1881

Truth crushed to earth is truth still and like a seed will rise again.

— Jefferson Davis, 1873

…forgive me if I have troubled you more than was needful and inevitable, more than I intended to do when I took up my pen proposing to distract you from your distractions. And may God deny you peace, but give you glory!

— Miguel de Unamuno, *The Tragic Sense of Life*

TABLE OF CONTENTS

Foreword by Dr. Clyde Wilson .... *v*

Preface and Acknowledgments.. *vii*

Introduction .... *xi*

Part I: In Defense of the South and Its History: 1

1. "A New Reconstruction: The Renewed Assault on Southern Heritage" 5
2. "The Land We Love: Southern Traditions and Our Future" 17
3. "Paladins of Christian Civilization: The Universality of the Confederate Cause" 35
4. "The Eternal 'Rebel Yell'" 43
5. "How the Neoconservatives Destroyed Southern Conservatism" 47
6. "How You Stand on the War Between the States: A Window into Your View of Western Christian Heritage"........................... 57
7. "Merchants of Hate: Morris Dees, the Southern Poverty Law Center, and the Attack on Southern Heritage" 63
8. "The Southern Poverty Law Center Expands its Tentacles … and is Still the Merchant of Hate" 79
9. "Robert Lewis Dabney and the Conservative Rout" 83
10. "The Historical Folly of 'Nothing but Race'" 87
11. "Secession and Catalonia: What is A Nation?" 93

Part II: Defending the Symbols and Monuments of Our History: 99

12. "A Letter from North Carolina" 101
13. "Was Lee A Traitor?" 105
14. "New Orleans: A People Without A Past Have No Future" 109

15. "Taking Down Our Monuments is Part of the Marxist Campaign to Transform America" 113
16. "Defending the Monuments: The North Carolina Case" 117
17. "Our Monuments: A Battle for Western Civilization and the South" 127
18. "'Silent Sam' and the Disaster Known as Public Education" 135
19. "Thoughts on Charlottesville and What It Means for Us" 139
20. "Charlottesville – One Year Later" 143
21. "Celebrating Lee Day, While Thousands of Women Go Marching Off to Hell" 147
22. "Leftist Crazies Don't Want You to Exist" 153

Part III: What the Nativity Says to Southerners: 159

23. "The Vigil of the Nativity: Reflections on the Hope that Came to us Two Millenia Ago" 161

Part IV: Eight Southern Heroes (and Two Demons): 167

The Heroes:
24. "Nathaniel Macon and the Origins of States' Rights Conservatism" 173
25. "What was Lost 152 Years Ago: James Johnston Pettigrew and His Notes on Spain and the Spaniards" 179
26. "Remembering President Jefferson Davis" 185
27. "Robert Lewis Dabney and His Attack on Progressivism" 189
28. "Mel Bradford and the Defense of Southern Conservatism" ... 201
29. "A Partisan Conversation: Interview with Eugene Genovese" . 205
30. "Rejecting Progressivism by Recovering the Fullness of the American Past: Senator Sam Ervin" 213
31. "The South Out West: Randolph Scott, the Man from North Carolina" 217

The Demons:
32. "On Abraham Lincoln and the Inversion of American History" 223
33. "Victor Davis Hanson: Demonizing the South to Purify the Nation" 229

Part V: Reviews and Review Essays: Film and Books: 235

34. Review essay, "Kirk Still Leading the Charge" 237
35. Review essay, "Classic Confederate Hollywood" 243
36. Review essay of John Ford's *The Sun Shines Bright* on DVD.... 247
37. Review essay of Dinesh D'Souza's Latest Film, *Death of a Nation* 251
38. Review of David Loy Mauch, *This Constitution Shall Be the Law of the Land* 255
39. Review of Howard Ray White, *Bloodstains: An Epic History of the Politics That Produced the American Civil War: Volume 4: Political Reconstruction and the Struggle for Healing* 259
40. Review of Charles A. Jennings, *Cultures in Conflict: The Union Desecration of Southern Churches and Cemeteries* 261
41. Review of Walter Donald Kennedy, *Rekilling Lincoln* 263
42. Review of W. David Waters (author) and Joseph I. Brown (technical consultant), *Gabriel Rains and the Confederate Torpedo Bureau* 267
43. Review of R. E. Mitchell, *Souls of Lions* 269

Part VI: A Final Essay and an Appeal to the Virtue of Hope: ... 273

44. "Reflections on the Future" 275

About the Author 281

FOREWORD

History is not a science, it is a story. A story has to be somebody's story, the remembered past. Otherwise it is just abstract speculation, useless and potentially destructive. We Southerners are blessed to have a rich story that is still powerful among us and also far beyond our borders. That history is envied and hated by postmodern Americans who have no story of their own and work to destroy the memory of ours. Defending our story is not backward and provincial but is a part of the defense of civilization as we have known it. Seldom has this defense been made by writers as eloquent and as vastly and broadly learned as Dr. Boyd Cathey. Herein he has erected a sturdy wall where we can gather to resist the barbarism of our time.

Clyde Wilson
Emeritus Distinguished Professor of History,
*   University of South Carolina*
The Dutch Fork, South Carolina, July 2018

Dr. Boyd D. Cathey

PREFACE AND ACKNOWLEDGMENTS

The idea for this volume of essays on the South and Southern tradition and heritage came about because of requests from some respected friends and authors whose opinions and suggestions I greatly value. The forty-four items collected here cover a time frame from Spring 1983 until August 2018, a span of thirty-five years. When I wrote my first piece for the old *Southern Partisan* magazine (about Russell Kirk, included herein), I was just a few years out of graduate school in Spain, having taught a couple of years on the college level, and then back at the North Carolina State Archives where I had interned and worked as a temporary and contract researcher during the summers, 1966-1975.

Writing was in my blood — my mother had been an English teacher who went back in her 50s to earn a degree in reading and return to teaching. Great literature and family lore were integral to me as I grew up: I read widely; I devoured old copies of *National Geographic* and *The State* magazine. As a family, we visited most of North Carolina's historic sites, and family genealogy and history were central to me — as they were to many of my friends back then. History and family heritage were very real and tangible.

My mother's family — Kings and Perrys — had figured, at times prominently, in North Carolina's history: one ancestor, John King, had been a provincial delegate at Halifax when the "Halifax Resolves" (April 12, 1776) were adopted, making the colony of North Carolina the first to call for independence from Great Britain. My father's people were some of the first settlers west of the Yadkin River, having come down the Great Wagon Road from Pennsylvania, where they reached these shores from Ulster, and earlier from County Ayrshire in Scotland. Branches of the family eventually made it to almost every Southern state, even to California during the Great Gold Rush of 1848.

On both sides of my family I had ancestors who served in Confederate ranks during the War for Southern Independence. On my father's side my grandmother actually was born in 1865 and lived until 1962 — she remembered vividly as a girl the years immediate after that war and Reconstruction, and when I was a boy, she recounted and passed on those memories and stories to me. And I was proud of my ancestors' service.

The Land We Love

All this served as something of a seedbed for me and an inspiration as I began my career and began to write and publish.

These essays range over several subject areas — longer essays about Southern heritage and history, pieces regarding the present assault on the symbols of that heritage, short semi-biographical items focusing on diverse figures who have played a role in Southern history (both positively and negatively), various reviews, and, finally, a couple of meditations on the Christian faith and hope that even yet nourish millions of Southerners.

Given the nature of this collection, there is much repetition, especially in the first section. I ask your indulgence in advance for that. It is hard to avoid, given the context and the close relationship that these topics have to each other, and the fact that the background and basis for one essay may also serve, in some way, as background for another essay. I would like to go back and rewrite some of the essays in this anthology, but that would defeat and undo the idea that these are all essays written in real time, at moments over the past thirty-five years. So, the repetition and material offered by those earlier pieces will just have to remain as written. Needless to say, I am a practitioner of the philosophy which states "if it is good enough to say once, then it is good enough to repeat."

These essays and reviews have appeared in print and online in: *Confederate Veteran, The Unz Review,* The Abbeville Institute, *The Remnant,* Communities Digital News, *The Southern Partisan, Southern Mercury, The Carolina Confederate,* Reckonin.com, and on my blog, *My Corner* by Boyd Cathey. My appreciation and gratitude to those publications and outlets which have featured my occasional pieces over the years.

I also must acknowledge several friends who have read what I have written and offered comments and suggestions. I must mention these two above all: Dr. Clyde Wilson, professor emeritus of history at the University of South Carolina and without doubt the South's pre-eminent historian; and Dr. Paul E. Gottfried, Horace Raffensperger Professor of Humanities (retired), Elizabethtown College in Pennsylvania, and one of the world's most significant political theorists. And then there are others who have over time made additional comments, including nationally syndicated columnist and longtime friend Patrick J. Buchanan; national columnist Ilana Mercer; and professor of philosophy and columnist Jack Kerwick of Rowan University in New Jersey.

Dr. Boyd D. Cathey

And I must not leave out editors and publishers of publications where my essays have appeared earlier: Ron Unz at *The Unz Review*, Brion McClanahan at The Abbeville Institute, Michael Matt at *The Remnant*, Frank Powell at *Confederate Veteran* magazine (and before that, *Southern Mercury*), Jacquie Kubin at Communities Digital News, Anne Wilson Smith at Reckonin.com, and Byron Brady at *The Carolina Confederate*.

And lastly, I must thank my editor and publisher Frank B. Powell of The Scuppernong Press for his advice, his good counsel, and his patience throughout this project. Frank and his dear wife Sara have been close friends for well more than twenty-five years. Frank is one of those rare individuals among professionals: both a superb editor and a dear friend.

This volume would have been impossible without him and Sara.

Boyd D. Cathey
September 1, 2018

Dr. Boyd D. Cathey

INTRODUCTION

The title of this little book, *The Land We Love*, is not original, but comes from a journal Confederate General Daniel H. Hill published in Charlotte after the War Between the States, dedicated to "the vindication of Southern history." In like manner, but with less expectation than General Hill's noble efforts, I offer this collection in hopes of vindicating more recent Southern history and, in some way, standing as my ancestors did against those who would take my heritage from me.

Over the past several years I had been writing essays for several publications and media outlets regarding Southern and Confederate history and heritage, and, in particular, about the growing assault on the symbols of that history and heritage. None of what I wrote — nothing I put into print — should have seemed that unusual or radical. My thoughts and observations could have been put down on paper fifty years ago — even thirty years ago — and I don't think they would have caused much of a stir or raised an eyebrow for most readers. Of course, much has changed in fifty years, and what was admired, revered, and considered normal then, is, in large part, considered controversial, even hateful, or subject to censorship and banning, now.

The Southland that I grew up in has, indeed, changed in many ways. There are millions of new residents, mostly transplants from the more northerly climes who find our climate, our low taxes, our more relaxed way of life, and our generally more friendly and accommodating people, to their liking. No doubt these newcomers, along with thousands of immigrants, legal and illegal, from south of the border, have effected changes in the South. Yet, I believe there is still what the late Southern historian, Francis Butler Simkins, once called "the everlasting South," a South — a land and a people — that subsists and continues to exist, even if at times occulted or not easy to grasp or experience, and even if under severe stress and assault from those who would purge it of its past and exile or extinguish its traditions handed down as a legacy from our ancestors.

The symbols of any society, of any culture — its flags and banners, its monuments to veterans and historical figures, its markers, its street and city names, the names of its schools, even its holidays, and so much more — are public manifestations not just of the history of that society, but represent visibly the beliefs and principles that culture has held

— and holds — most dear. In a real sense as well, they offer an aspirational guide to what the future will be, what will give it structure and sustenance, and what the offspring of this generation will bequeath to the next.

It is that way with any culture which remembers its history. As Mel Bradford once wrote, it is through "remembering who we are" that we come to comprehend how the fullness of that history, that heritage, that legacy have shaped us and given us a richness and distinctiveness of character that make us a people.

When I was doing doctoral work in Spain at the University of Navarra in Pamplona, I came across an observation by the subject of my research, the Spanish traditionalist writer and philosopher, Juan Vazquez de Mella (1862-1928), that I think is universal in its application:

Who has ever seen 'the individual,' if not defined by his family, his region, his profession, his language, his inheritance, his faith? Removed from these defining characteristics the individual is an abstraction, and a political system based on an abstraction must either end in despotism or revolution.

Show me a rootless society, point to a society where the sense of community has disappeared, a society deprived of its heritage and the inherited legacy of its customs, its literature, its heroes, its shared beliefs, all that lore passed down not just officially by the state, but from father and mother to son and to daughter — and you have a social anthill, a mass of humans as faceless cogs, reduced to the status of the aimless and amorphous mass of grunting pigs inhabiting George Orwell's dystopian fantasy novel, *Animal Farm* — and susceptible to the beckoning calls and tempting of the first demagogue who appears on the scene, or to the lunacy of an ideology that promises utopia here on earth, but ends in enslaving the inhabitants.

Southerners, among all Americans, have been the most resistant to such Siren calls. As in no other region of the country they have been aware of and suffered the hardships and cruelties of defeat in war, a war between the states which they understood philosophically as a war to preserve the original Constitutional system left to them by the Framers, many of whom were Southerners.

That Southern character and sense of community, if you will, was already in formation long before the bloody conflict of 1861-1865, as I discuss later on in this volume in examining the work of Professors

Mel Bradford, Richard Weaver and Richard Beale Davis (see chapters "The Land We Love: Southern Tradition and the Future" and "How the Neoconservatives Destroyed Southern Conservatism"). It manifested itself in the early colonial settlements and the creation of colonial communities of like-minded peoples. It derived much of its integrity and nourishment from the Old World, from Europe, and, in particular, from the British Isles, from settlers who brought with them their customs, their mores and religion, their songs and ballads, their legends, and their beliefs, to these shores. As David Hackett Fisher has indicated in his volume, *Albion's Seed* (1989), tracing transatlantic migrations from the British Isles, the early inhabitants of the South country came mostly from southern England, colonists who were more apt to have been Cavalier and Royalist supporters in the seventeenth century (and thus favorable to plantation culture), or from the borderlands, from Scotland and the far north of England or Ulster, fiercely independent, but also dedicated to agriculture and a rural way of life.

These cultures gave rise to a uniquely Southern society, a culture that while it would differ over the years about such political issues as representation (e.g., the Virginia Constitutional Convention of 1829, and the North Carolina Constitutional Convention of 1835) or internal improvements, still found much more in common than not. Southern Whiggery may have supported Henry Clay's "American (or national) system," but regional and, especially, communal and state identification were never far from the surface.

As Professor Bradford illustrates in his illuminating study, *Original Intentions: On the Making and Ratification of the United States Constitution* (1993), discussed later in several essays included in this volume, at the debates over the framing of the Constitution the Framers basically created a document and a resulting new nation which reflected Southern states' rights views, a national executive which was in no way like the increasingly centralizing power that emerged in 1865 after four years of war. And, in fact, that regionalist view was generally held by many national political and intellectual leaders, not just by those from below the Mason-Dixon Line.

It was not so much a radical transformation of Southern thinking and views which propelled the nation on a course to eventual conflict. While it is certainly true Southerners and their perspectives on what was occurring in the Union hardened and sharpened in intensity in the years leading up to the outbreak of the War Between the States, it must be argued that intensity was occasioned as a response to increasing assaults, both political and, finally, violent, by their brethren north of the Mason-Dixon, and in particular, from the descendants of those largely Puritan New Englanders. As such historians as Paul Conkin (*Puritans and Pragmatists*) and Perry Miller (*The Life of the Mind in America* and *The New England Mind*) have documented, the intellectual and eventually political influence on America, at least the northern portion of it, by the latter-day inheritors of Puritanism was immense and wide-ranging. And it ran up against a South that, for its part, would undergo what liberal historian, Louis Hartz in his classic volume, *The Liberal Tradition in America* (1955), called somewhat despectively, a "reactionary enlightenment," a time of doubling down on those "original intentions" and beliefs that increasingly Southerners felt to be under attack.

It is impossible, of course, to ignore slavery and its effects in the Southern states. The coming of the African slave to American shores would become an important factor both culturally and socially, and eventually, politically in the life of the American republic. Yet, the modern concentration on race and slavery, to the exclusion of all other factors, as the all-important — and often only — determinant in Southern history, both misreads the fullness of that history and turns it, too frequently, into an ideological cudgel with which to damn all of Southern heritage and culture. As Professor Davis has detailed in his massively-documented three-volume work, *Intellectual Life in the Colonial South, 1585-1763* (1978), a Southern character — a distinctive Southern personality — was already maturing before the presence African slavery figured as a disquieting note in Southern history and long before it became an issue debated widely on the national level.

Certainly, the questions surrounding slavery and the existence of a growing mostly servile black population in a dominant white society would become more visible in the first half of the nineteenth century. The rise of abolitionist sentiment in the northern states, brought on as a kind of zealous evangelical afterbirth of the Puritan tradition, and the pressure to end the slave trade and attempts by Christian reformers either to ameliorate the condition of slaves or advocate for their emancipation, had their effects. Indeed, Southerners, themselves, grappled with the issues, as Professor Eugene Genovese has shown in his various studies, including *The World the Slaveholders Made*, and more significantly, *The Mind of the Master Class*. And none more deeply and profoundly than perhaps the greatest of the antebellum theologians of the

South, James Henley Thornwell. (See later in this volume, "A Partisan Conversation: Interview with Eugene Genovese").

Slavery in the antebellum South was not an earlier version of Auschwitz or the Gulag, which is clear and evident from a close examination of the abundant historical record. As Robert Fogel and Stanley Engerman in their path breaking study *Time on the Cross* (1974) have demonstrated, employing extensive research and careful statistical and economic analysis, "many slaves were encouraged to marry and maintain households, they were given garden plots, the dehumanizing practice of slave breeding was virtually non-existent, the quality of their daily diets and medical care were comparable to the white population, and many trusted slaves were given great responsibility in managing plantations." In short, the antebellum South was much more akin to a traditional patriarchal society than to a modern totalitarian state.

White Southerners understood that slavery and the presence of a large black population were part of their culture. With that understanding and the historical reality of natural inequality and a "master class," Southerners dealt with that fact generally honestly according to the best of their comprehension and abilities within the context of the age, as Professor Genovese explains. That the response was not of the moralizing kind of our modern age should not be a surprise to anyone.

Southerners — those who thought deeply about the question — understood that although Almighty God had created all human beings and therefore endowed them with a certain spark of divinity and a certain dignity, human equality of status and opportunity on this earth was chimerical and non-existent. Even the famous words of the Declaration of Independence that "all men are created equal" were never intended by the Founders for literal domestic consumption, but rather directed at the parliament in England. The Founders intended that document as a statement of grievances against the Mother Country, and not a charter of natural rights which could and would entail the future aims of egalitarians.

All through the eighteenth century thousands of white folks were brought to the new world as indentured servants, as well. In many cases, that servitude was entered into involuntarily, as a forced arrangement, and one can argue that in some ways its parameters, like other systems of servitude, resembled slavery. Indeed, slavery, and not just of the African kind, existed throughout the world in colonial times. Historic Christianity, as Thornwell and others pointed out, countenanced its existence, but also with the strict admonition for humane treatment by slaveholders that mirrored the immemorial traditions and teachings of the church, and with the goal of possible future manumission.

In the more than two centuries during which slavery existed not only in what became the Confederate States of America, but in other parts of the nation, slaves were acculturated and made contributions to the country. They were absorbed by that country, as they, in turn, absorbed the European culture and traditions on which it was founded. No longer were they Africans, but Americans — and Southerners. Thousands were eventually manumitted and became "free persons of color," sometimes landholders (according to census statistics) and even electors in some instances if they held property, as I documented in a thesis presented to the Graduate Faculty of the University of Virginia in June 1971 ("Race, Representation, and Religion: The North Carolina Constitutional Convention of 1835"; see: https://libra2.lib.virginia.edu/public_view/zs25x853s) — And all of this before the War Between the States.

In a hierarchical society, as the old South was, both black and white inhabitants lived and existed on various levels, some politically and culturally powerful, others not; some exercising the franchise, but most (blacks and whites), not. And some as slaves, and others not. Yet, even among the servile population there had developed a love and appreciation for the land they lived and worked on, and for their white masters and neighbors. And when war finally came, the overwhelming majority of blacks, freeman and slave alike, resisted the opportunity to take advantage of the situation, and engage in civil insurrection.

I can cite here, as personal examples of this, several letters from my great-great grandfather, Captain Marquis LaFayette Redd, stationed at Aquia Creek, Virginia, along the Potomac in 1861, to his wife, Emily Ann Sidbury Redd, in Onslow County, North Carolina. She was there alone with her young children, surrounded by slaves — but completely trusting and, indeed, secure. Captain Redd, in his correspondence, always finishes his missives declaring: "My love to all my family, both white and black." The meaning and sincerity — and the bond he felt — are palpable and real, and they were repaid by the entirety of his household. (See, Marquis LaFayette Redd Papers, 1798-1895, PC. 1635, North Carolina State Archives, Raleigh, North Carolina)

Indeed, thousands, perhaps as many as 30,000 black men, and probably many more, enlisted in Confederate ranks during the war, and not just as auxiliaries but fully integrated into regiments, often times voted in, as I touch on in the first essay in this volume, and as is examined in detail by such authors as Ervin Jordan, Jr. in *Black Confederates and Afro-Yankees in Civil War Virginia* (1995), and Charles Kelly Barrow, J. H. Segars, and R. B. Rosenburg in *Black Confederates* (2001), and more recently researched by North Carolina Museum of History historian and curator, Earl Ijames (See, for example, information on his in depth investigations, "NC history museum curator to speak at Civil War Roundtable," The *Kinston Free Press*, March 18, 2016, link: www.kinston.com/news/20160318/nc-history-museum-curator-earl-ijames-to-speak-at-civil-war-roundtable)

Without the war, would slavery have eventually disappeared, succumbing to the great economic currents and pressures of the later nineteenth century? I think so, and I believe the former slaves, given that evolution and natural development economically and internationally, would have found their way into a welcoming Southern society, not due to the abrupt results of an incredibly disastrous war or well-intentioned but largely misguided Federal legislation, but rather because of the natural bonds of affection which were already existent and the Christian charity that characterized Southern folk.

When war finally came it not only molded Southern volunteers into an exceptionally fine fighting force — they were, after all, fighting for home and hearth — but brought together Whigs and Democrats, plantation slave owners in the Tidewater and around Natchez and Charleston with small yeoman Scotch-Irish farmers from the Piedmont, most without slaves, but all dedicated to state sovereignty — a concept even an uneducated backwoodsman could fathom. As even historian James McPherson, not necessarily a partisan of the Confederacy, revealed in his extensive survey of war time letters and diaries of nearly a thousand Union and Confederate soldiers, *What They Fought For, 1861-1865. The Walter Lynwood Fleming Lectures in Southern History* (1994; and later, *For Cause and Comrades: Why Men Fought the Civil War*, 1997), most soldiers felt a keen sense of patriotic and ideological commitment and attachment to a cause. And for Southerners it was the cause of protecting their rights under the old Constitution, the rights of their states and of their communities and families, which they believed to be imperiled by an aggressive executive, mad with power and a desire to destroy that Constitution.

Much has been written, probably far too much, about the War Between the States. Needless to say, what has been occurring in recent years has as its antecedent that conflict and subsequent history since then. Through it all, through "Reconstruction and Reunion," through the period during the middle of the twentieth century when it appeared the South was finally "back in the Union" and its traditions appreciated by all Americans, and later, during the Civil Rights Revolution of the 1960s and beyond when the South became the object, again, of scorn and disapprobation, of Federal authorities once more enacting a "new Reconstruction," and with new immigration and social changes, and the effects of national television and such items as the automobile that increased mobility and eliminated distances and, to some degree, differences between communities — through it all there remained the South of our memory and our childhood, on the defensive but still there, still visible, yet capable of sustaining its citizens if they would only seek it and accept its legacy and its inheritance … and defend it against those who wish to extinguish it.

I am reminded of another great Spanish writer and traditionalist, Marcelino Menendez y Pelayo (1856-1912), who warned Spain at the end of the nineteenth century that it was in danger of forfeiting its very credal identity. At that time, in the midst of dissolution that seemed to be affecting his country, he wrote:

Spain, evangelizer of half the world; Spain, hammer of heretics, light of Trent, sword of Rome, cradle of St. Ignatius — this is our greatness and our unity; we have no other. The day it is lost, Spain will return to the anarchy of the tribes and barbarians or the satraps of the Caliphs. To this end we are traveling more or less rapidly, and blind is he who will not see it.

Menendez y Pelayo's words could apply analogously to the contemporary South. We have only one enduring body of tradition which has characterized us and sustained us, and it seems to be disappearing before our eyes, almost daily. Yet, there remains a South to love, a South to defend. There is still an incredibly rich wellspring of history, of literature, in the arts and music and folklore, in regional cuisine, in language, in customs, in so much that binds us and has held us together since colonial times: it is worth our best efforts and our undying commitment.

There is a wonderfully evocative passage by the novelist William Faulkner which encapsulates the vision the contemporary son of the South must possess:

For every Southern boy fourteen years old, not once but whenever he wants it, there is the instant when it's still not yet two o'clock on that July afternoon in 1863, the brigades are in position behind the rail fence, the guns are laid and ready in the woods and the furled flags are already loosened to break out and Pickett himself with his long oiled ringlets and his hat in one hand probably and his sword in the other looking up the hill waiting for Longstreet to give the word and it's all in the balance, it hasn't happened yet, it hasn't even begun yet, it not only hasn't begun yet but there is still time for it not to begin against that position and those circumstances which made more men than Garnett and Kemper and Armistead and Wilcox look grave — yet it's going to begin, we all know that, we have come too far with too much at stake and that moment doesn't need even a fourteen-year-old boy to think This time. Maybe this time with all this much to lose than all this much to gain: Pennsylvania, Maryland, the world, the golden dome of Washington itself to crown with desperate and unbelievable victory the desperate gamble.... (from Intruder in the Dust, 1948).

It is that same spirit — that same dedication — that same inextinguishable hope — that fuels our commitment, and through all the turmoil and sense of loss and anguish, allows us to smile and even relate a funny tale to a friend and still enjoy a fine plate of barbeque and fried chicken, grits and country ham, and greet our neighbors and help them cut down that low-hanging white oak which endangers their work shed.

It is the same spirit that motivated the once-reviled president of the Confederacy to declare after the end of the War to a visitor who remarked the cause of the Southland was lost and history had passed us by, that, despite defeat on the field of battle, "the principle for which we contended is bound to reassert itself, though it may be at another time and in another form."

And, I trust, it is the same spirit and commitment that informs these meditations, these essays written concerning the challenges we now face and of how some of our ancestors met them, and their legacy and beliefs, and what they mean and should mean for us.

Dr. Boyd D. Cathey
Wendell, North Carolina
September 1, 2018

PART I

IN DEFENSE OF THE SOUTH AND ITS HISTORY

The eleven essays on the South and its heritage in this first section are items written for *Confederate Veteran* magazine (print), the Abbeville Institute (online), *Southern Mercury* magazine (print), *The Unz Review* (online), *The Remnant* (print), *The Carolina Confederate* (print), Communities Digital News (online), and for my blog site, *My Corner* by Boyd Cathey. They offer a discursive survey of the history, background, and some of the more fashionable and dominant assaults made currently against Southern tradition and the legacy of the South's Confederate heritage. The first three, longer essays are: "A New Reconstruction: The Renewed Assault on Southern Heritage," "The Land We Love: Southern Traditions and Our Future," and "Paladins of Christian Civilization: The Universality of the Confederate Cause." The first two were written specifically for *Confederate Veteran* magazine, and the third is based on a speech given on the occasion of Confederate Flag Day in Louisburg, North Carolina, March 19, 2017, and then published in the *Confederate Veteran*. All three have been reprinted several times since their initial publication, and where available, an Internet reference is provided.

The following seven essays —"The Eternal 'Rebel Yell,'" "How the Neocons Destroyed Southern Conservatism," "How You Stand on the War Between the States: A Window into Your View of Western Christian Heritage," "Merchants of Hate: Morris Dees, the Southern Poverty Law Center, and the Attack on Southern Heritage," "The Southern Poverty Law Center Expands its Tentacles … and is Still the Merchant of Hate," "Robert Lewis Dabney and the Conservative Rout," and "The Historical Folly of 'Nothing but Race'" — explore in more specific detail these aspects of the assault on Southern traditions and heritage.

The essay "How the Neocons Destroyed Southern Conservatism" repeats observations contained in some of the other essays, and I beg the indulgence of the reader for this obvious repetition. For this essay details how the once-highly-regarded strains of Southern conservatism have in large part been exiled by the modern conservative movement. Yet, it is important to repeat in some way these comments in that context if we are to understand what has happened to the Southern political tradition and the contempt in which modern conservatism now holds those symbols of Southern heritage that still dot the Southern landscape, and which are under severe attack and extreme duress in our time.

Following that entry is a shorter item, "How You Stand on the War Between the States: A Window into Your View of Western Christian Heritage," which attempts in few words to correct some of the calumnies directed at the Confederacy, while distinguishing between Southern heritage and its inherited legacy and the forces that wish to extinguish it.

The next essay, "Merchants of Hate: Morris Dees, the Southern Poverty Law Center, and the Attack on Southern Heritage," was commissioned as a major research investigation of the controversial operations of the professional "anti-hate" organization, the Southern Poverty Law Center (SPLC), based in Montgomery, Alabama, and headed by Morris Dees. The SPLC has for some time been engaged in efforts to ban Southern heritage and frequently attacks Southerners who defend that inheritance. This long, heavily footnoted article was based almost entirely upon information provided and publicized by Left-leaning and non-conservative sources, long before the current criticisms of the SPLC had much currency. The essay appeared first in the short lived *Southern Mercury* magazine (July-August 2003) and was then reprinted several times, by Dr. Samuel Francis and the Council of Conservative Citizens, by E. Michael Jones' magazine *Culture Wars*, and elsewhere. It also got me into hot water, as Dees's response to my investigation and to its verifiable repercussions was to label me a "hatemonger" and one of whom he called "40 to watch" on his web site. I realized that when that counter-attack happened any chance that I might have to return to academia at any major college or university had ended. An interesting aside in this little episode came when a group titled the "Skinheads of America" publicly complained that I did not deserve to be on Dees' "hatemonger" list as I had not really engaged in any real hate, and that there were many others far more deserving of that honor!

More recently, I followed up that 2003 exposé with a shorter piece in July 2018 on my blog site, *My Corner* by Boyd Cathey. The title is "The Southern Poverty Law Center Expands its Tentacles … and is Still the Merchant of Hate," and I include that essay next as a kind of postscript.

Although I include the essay, "Robert Lewis Dabney and the Conservative Rout," in this section, a biographical essay on Robert Lewis Dabney is included later in this collection, and it offers more details and information about this remarkable writer and postwar critic. Readers may wish to consult it as they examine this earlier piece quoting Dabney included in this volume.

The last essay in this section, "Secession and Catalonia: What Is a Nation?" is included as it addresses a question which has been central to American history and over which a war between the states was waged. In examining the effort of the historic Catalonia region of Spain to secede an analysis of what has occurred assists us to see similarities between that effort in the Iberian Peninsula, but also some rather distinct differences, and the situation in the American nation in 1861.

A New Reconstruction: The Renewed Assault on Southern Heritage
↷ *Chapter 1* ↶

In June 2015, after the depraved shootings in a Charleston, South Carolina, black church, a frenzied hue and cry went up and any number of accusations and attacks were made against historic Confederate symbols, in particular, the Confederate Battle Flag. Monuments, markers, flags, plaques, street and school names, everything memorializing anything associated with the Confederacy have come under severe attack. Even grave sites and cemeteries have not been exempt from this onslaught. It is, as one writer wrote, "a new Reconstruction," and, in fact, an attempt to eradicate the very existence of Confederate heritage.

Let us briefly examine these attacks and offer some responses.

First, the demand was made that the Battle Flag must come down. In South Carolina, Alabama, and other states, governmental authorities, reacting to loud voices and the pressures of political correctness, have removed flags from places of prominence and from public property. They declare that the flag needs to be banned and suppressed because it is a "symbol of hate" and "was carried by racists," that it "flew over a racist country."

This argument ignores much of the history of that banner. The Battle Flag, with its familiar Cross of St. Andrew, was a square ensign carried by Southern troops during the War Between the States. It was not the national flag of the Confederacy, but, rather, was carried by Southern soldiers, a large majority of whom came from non-slaveholding families. And of those soldiers from slaveholding families, the overwhelming number came from families with half a dozen or fewer slaves who lived and worked with their families, attended the same churches and were treated by the same doctors. (Interestingly, regiments of the Union army from Delaware, Maryland, Kentucky, and Missouri included slave holding soldiers in their ranks; indeed, General Grant's wife, Julia Dent Grant, owned slaves throughout the war).

As Professor James McPherson — certainly no defender of the Confederacy — has carefully documented in his study, *For Cause and Comrades: Why Men Fought in the Civil War* (Oxford University Press, 1997), the vast majority of Confederate soldiers — men who carried the Battle Flag — believed they were fighting for liberty. After examining

574 manuscript collections and nearly 30,000 letters, diaries, and journals in twenty-two archival repositories, he wrote: "Southern recruits waxed most eloquently about their intention to fight against slavery than for it ... that is, against their own enslavement to the North." (pp. 19-20) "Confederates professed to fight for liberty and independence from a tyrannical government." (p. 104)

By contrast, the United States flag, the "Stars and Stripes," not only flew over slavery for seventy-eight years, it flew over the brutal importation, the selling and the purchase of slaves, and the breaking up of slave families. Additionally, the Stars and Stripes flew over the infamous "Trail of Tears," at the Sand Creek massacre of innocent Native Americans, later at the Wounded Knee massacre, and over the harsh internment of thousands of Nisei Japanese American citizens in concentration camps during World War II.

Although there are some zealots who suggest doing away with the United States flag because of these connections, it is highly unlikely that most of the inside-the-Washington-Beltway pundits, including many on Fox News, and several Southern Republican governors who have clamored for banning the Battle Flag, would join them in that demand. Yet, if the history of both banners is closely examined from the radically changing contexts which are used to attack the one, should not there be a focus on the history of other, as well? And, if only a particular snapshot context is used to judge such symbols, is any symbol of America's diverse history safe from the hands of those who may dislike or despise this or that symbol?

Second, a comparison has been made between the Battle Flag and the Nazi flag (red background, with a white circle and a black swastika centered). Again, this comparison demonstrates a lack of historical acumen on the part of those making it: the Nazi flag was created precisely to represent the Nazi Party and its ideology. The Battle Flag bears a traditional Christian "saltire," the St. Andrew's Cross, which has deep historical roots in Scotland, Spain, Burgundy, Russia, and in Christian iconography.

Third, the charge has been made Confederate symbols must be banned because they represent "treason against the Federal government." That is, those Southerners who took up arms in 1861 to defend their states, their homes, and their families, were engaged in "rebellion" and were "traitors" under Federal law.

Again, such arguments fail on all counts. Some writers have suggested that Robert E. Lee, in particular, was a "traitor" because he violated his solemn military oath to uphold and defend the Constitution by taking up arms against the Union. But what those writers fail to note is Lee had formally resigned from the US Army and had relinquished his commission before undertaking his new assignment to defend his home state of Virginia, which by then had seceded and re-vindicated its original independence.

And that brings us to point four: the right of secession and whether the actions of the Southern states, December 1860-May 1861, could be justified under the U.S. Constitution.

One of the better summaries of the prevalent Constitutional theory at that time has been made by black scholar, professor, and prolific author Dr. Walter Williams. Here is what he writes in one his columns:

"During the 1787 Constitutional Convention, a proposal was made that would allow the federal government to suppress a seceding state. James Madison rejected it, saying, 'A union of the states containing such an ingredient seemed to provide for its own destruction. The use of force against a state would look more like a declaration of war than an infliction of punishment and would probably be considered by the party attacked as a dissolution of all previous compacts by which it might be bound.'

"In fact, the ratification documents of Virginia, New York and Rhode Island explicitly said they held the right to resume powers delegated should the federal government become abusive of those powers. The Constitution never would have been ratified if states thought they could not regain their sovereignty — in a word, secede.

"On March 2, 1861, after seven states seceded and two days before Abraham Lincoln's inauguration, Sen. James R. Doolittle of Wisconsin proposed a constitutional amendment that read, "No state or any part thereof, heretofore admitted or hereafter admitted into the union, shall have the power to withdraw from the jurisdiction of the United States."

Several months earlier, Reps. Daniel E. Sickles of New York, Thomas B. Florence of Pennsylvania and Otis S. Ferry of Connecticut proposed a constitutional amendment to prohibit secession. Here's a question for the reader: **Would there have been any point to offering these amendments if secession were already unconstitutional?"** [emphasis added]

An examination of the ratification processes for Georgia, South Carolina, and North Carolina in the late 1780s, reveal very similar discussions: it was the independent states themselves who had created a Federal government (and not the reverse, as Abe Lincoln erroneously suggested), and it was the various states who granted the Federal government certain very limited and specifically enumerated powers, reserving the vast remainder for themselves (see Professor Mel Bradford, *Original Intentions: On the Making and Ratification of the United States Constitution*. University of Georgia Press, 1993). As any number of the Founders indicated, there simply would not have been any United States if the states, both north and south, had believed that they could not leave it for just cause.

During the Antebellum period there was little political support for denying the right of secession or for the Constitutional right to suppress it. Of the pre-war presidents, it is true, Andrew Jackson threatened South Carolina in 1833 over Nullification of the "Tariff of Abominations," but that crisis was resolved through compromise. Even staunch anti-slavery unionist President John Quincy Adams advocated secession over the annexation of Texas, and in his April 30, 1839, speech "The Jubilee of the Constitution," commemorating the 50th anniversary of George Washington's inauguration as the first American president, he affirmed:

"... if the day should ever come, (may Heaven avert it) when the affections of the people of these states shall be alienated from each other; when the fraternal spirit shall give away to cold indifference, or collisions of interest shall fester into hatred, the bands of political association will not long hold together the parties no longer attracted by the magnetism of conciliated interests and kindly sympathies; and far better will it be for the people of the disunited states, to part in friendship from each other, than to be held together by constraint."

In his address to Congress in January of 1861, lame duck President James Buchanan, while deploring secession, stated frankly he had no right to prevent it: "I certainly had no right to make aggressive war upon any State, and I am perfectly satisfied that the Constitution has wisely withheld that power even from Congress." Former President John Tyler served in the Confederate Congress, and former President Franklin Pierce, in his famous Concord, New Hampshire, address, July 4, 1863, joined Buchanan in decrying the efforts to suppress the secession of the Southern states:

"Do we not all know that the cause of our casualties is the vicious intermeddling of too many of the citizens of the Northern States with the constitutional rights of the Southern States, cooperating with the discontents of the people of those states? Do we not know that the disregard of

the Constitution, and of the security that it affords to the rights of States and of individuals, has been the cause of the calamity which our country is called to undergo?"

More, during the antebellum period William Rawle's pro-secession text on Constitutional law, *A View of the Constitution of the United States* (1825,) was used at West Point as the standard text on the US Constitution. And on several occasions the Supreme Court, itself, affirmed this view. In *The Bank of Augusta v. Earl* (1839), the Court wrote in an 8-1 decision:

"The States...are distinct separate sovereignties, except so far as they have parted with some of the attributes of sovereignty by the Constitution. They continue to be nations, with all their rights, and under all their national obligations, and with all the rights of nations in every particular; except in the surrender by each to the common purposes and object of the Union, under the Constitution. The rights of each State, when not so yielded up, remain absolute."

A review of the Northern press at the time of the Secession conventions finds, perhaps surprisingly to those who wish to read back into the past their own statist ideas, a similar view. As historian William Marvel explains in his volume, *Mr. Lincoln Goes to War* (Houghton Mifflin Harcourt Publishers, 2006, pp. 19-20), few Northern newspapers took the position that the Federal government had the constitutional right to invade and suppress states who had decided to secede. Many favored peaceful separation. Indeed, were it not the New England states in 1814-1815 who made the first serious effort at secession during the War of 1812, to the point that they gathered in Hartford to discuss actively pursuing it? And during the pre-war period various states asserted in one form or another similar rights.

One last comment regarding the accusation of "treason" after the conclusion of the War, the Southern states were put under military authority, their civil governments dissolved, and each state had to be re-admitted to the Union. But, logically, a state could not be "re-admitted" to the Union unless it had been out of it. And if it were out of it, legally and constitutionally, as the Southern states maintained (and some Northern writers acknowledged), then it could not be in any way guilty of "treason."

The major point that opponents of Confederate symbols assert is that the panoply of those monuments, flags, plaques, and other reminders honoring Confederate veterans represent a defense of historical slavery. Slavery was the cause of the war, they say, and since American society has supposedly advanced progressively in understanding, it is both inappropriate and hurtful to continue to display such memorials.

Again, there are various levels of response. Historically, despite the best efforts of the ideologically-driven Marxist historical school (e.g., Eric Foner) to make slavery the only underlying cause for the War Between the States, there is considerable evidence — while not ignoring the significance of slavery — to indicate more varied and profound economic and political reasons why that war occurred (cf. writers Thomas DiLorenzo, Charles Adams, David Gordon, Jeffrey Hummel, William Marvel, Thomas Fleming, et al). Indeed, it goes without saying when hostilities began, anti-slavery was not a major reason at all in the North for prosecuting the war; indeed, it never was a major reason. Lincoln made this explicit to editor Horace Greeley of *The New York Tribune* a short time prior to the Emancipation Proclamation (which only applied to states in the South where the Federal government had no authority, but not to the states such as Maryland and Kentucky, where slavery existed, but were safely under Union control).

Here is what he wrote to Greeley on August 22, 1862:

"My paramount object in this struggle is to save the Union, and is not either to save or destroy Slavery. If I could save the Union without freeing any slave, I would do it, and if I could save it by freeing all the slaves, I would do it, and if I could save it by freeing some and leaving others alone, I would also do that. What I do about Slavery and the colored race, I do because I believe it helps to save this Union, and what I forbear, I forbear because I do not believe it would help to save the Union."

The Emancipation Proclamation (January 1, 1863), issued just three months after Lincoln's communication to Greeley, was a desperate political ploy by Lincoln to churn up sagging support for a war which appeared stalemated at the time. Indeed, Old Abe had previously called for sending blacks back to Africa and the enforcement of laws which made Jim Crow look benign. He knew fully well "freeing the slaves" had little support in the North and was not the reason for the conflict.

In the Southern states, the issue of slavery as the *raison d'etre* for secession (and for war) is more complex. Clearly, the secession of North Carolina, Virginia, Arkansas, and Tennessee (and the attempted secession of Kentucky and Missouri) was chiefly a response to Lincoln's call for troops to suppress the states of the Deep South and incursions by

Federal troops (e.g. the Federal occupation of St. Louis and invasion of Missouri, and the tyrannical suppression of *habeas corpus* in Maryland). The overwhelming view in those states, as elsewhere in many areas of the Union, was the Federal government did not have the right to coerce a state that had seceded, and such action was a flagrant violation of the Constitution.

In January of 1861 North Carolina voted by a healthy margin to remain in the Union. The other states in the northern tier where slavery existed initially resolved to do the same thing. However, the demand by the Lincoln administration that the states supply troops to participate in an attack on South Carolina was met by widespread revulsion. Tar Heel Governor John W. Ellis's famously replied to this summons: "You can get no troops from North Carolina!" Zebulon Vance, a leader of the state's Whigs and an adamant unionist, and future war-time governor, recounted that he was on the stump when the news of the Federal demand came: "When during my oration my hand went up I was a staunch Unionist, but when it came down, I was a diehard secessionist." In the North Carolina debates over secession in early May 1861 slavery was hardly mentioned, and the state's representatives voted unanimously in convention to secede on May 20, 1861.

In several of the Deep South states, declarations of grievances did mention slavery as a reason for severing connection with the Federal union. And it is true a defense of the "peculiar institution" forms one of several justifications for the secession of Texas, Mississippi, South Carolina, and Georgia. The Federal government appeared increasingly incapable or unwilling to secure property rights and insure civil order for those states. Still, for them slavery was subsumed in the overriding question of constitutionality and the perceived impression that the Federal government could no longer be depended upon to defend the Founders' Constitution.

But as an issue slavery was overshadowed by the severe and immediate hit that Southerners were threatened with economically through the imposition of the Morrill Tariff, which raised the average tariff rate from 15 percent to 37.5 percent (and eventually to 47.5 percent) and greatly expanded the list of taxable items. Abraham Lincoln had campaigned vigorously on a platform of strong support for the Morrill Tariff and increased economic protectionism — extreme protectionism that threatened to completely cripple the economies of the import-dependent Southern states. As noted economist Frank Taussig detailed in his classic study, *Tariff History of the United States* (Augustus M. Kelley

Publishers, 1967 edition), the tariff was the chief revenue source for the Federal government, and the South would be paying nearly 80 percent of the tariff, while most of the revenues were spent in the North.

In his famous "cornerstone speech" to the Georgia legislature, November 13, 1860, Senator Robert Toombs, laid bare these Southern grievances and explained why they would provoke secession and war:

"... *the Northern States evinced a general desire and purpose to use it [the Constitution] for their own benefit, and to pervert its powers for sectional advantage, and they have steadily pursued that policy to this day. They demanded a monopoly of the business of ship-building, and got a prohibition against the sale of foreign ships to citizens of the United States, which exists to this day.*

"They demanded a monopoly of the coasting trade, in order to get higher freights than they could get in open competition with the carriers of the world. Congress gave it to them, and they yet hold this monopoly. And now, to-day, if a foreign vessel in Savannah offer[s] to take your rice, cotton, grain or lumber to New-York, or any other American port, for nothing, your laws prohibit it, in order that Northern ship-owners may get enhanced prices for doing your carrying.

'This same shipping interest, with cormorant rapacity, have steadily burrowed their way through your legislative halls, until they have saddled the agricultural classes with a large portion of the legitimate expenses of their own business. We pay a million of dollars per annum for the lights which guide them into and out of your ports.

'The North, at the very first Congress, demanded and received bounties under the name of protection, for every trade, craft, and calling which they pursue, and there is not an artisan . . . in all of the Northern or Middle States, who has not received what he calls the protection of his government on his industry to the extent of from fifteen to two hundred per cent from the year 1791 to this day. They will not strike a blow, or stretch a muscle, without bounties from the government.

"No wonder they cry aloud for the glorious Union . . . by it they got their wealth; by it they levy tribute on honest labor. Thus stands the account between the North and the South. Under its . . . most favorable action . . . the treasury [is] a perpetual fertilizing stream to them and their industry, and a suction-pump to drain away our substance and parch up our lands.

'They will [under Lincoln] have possession of the Federal executive with its vast power, patronage, prestige of legality, its army, its navy, and its revenue on the fourth of March next. Hitherto it has been on

the side of the Constitution and the right; after the fourth of March it will be in the hands of your enemy. What more can you get from them under this Government?" [emphasis added]

In his first inaugural address, delivered Monday, March 4, 1861, Lincoln threw down the gauntlet. After declaring that "I have no purpose, directly or indirectly, to interfere with slavery where it exists ... I believe I have no lawful right to do so, and I have no inclination to do so," he warned: "The power confided in me will be used to hold, occupy, and possess the property, and places belonging to the government, *and to collect the duties and imposts*." [emphasis added]

Professor Thomas DiLorenzo sums up this volatile economic and constitutional tinderbox:

"Whatever other reasons some of the Southern states might have given for secession are irrelevant to the question of why there was a war. Secession does not necessitate war. Lincoln promised war over tax collection in his first inaugural address. When the Southern states refused to pay his beloved Morrill Tariff at the Southern ports [monies that supplied a major portion of Federal revenues], he kept his promise of 'invasion and bloodshed' and waged war on the Southern states."

The inability to find compromise in late 1860 and early 1861 must be laid squarely at the door of the Lincoln administration, as William Marvel has detailed. Various attempts at finding a compromise (e.g., Crittenden Compromise) and avoiding war were repeatedly undermined by the administration. "It was Lincoln, however, who finally eschewed diplomacy and sparked a confrontation," writes Marvel. "[H]e backed himself into a corner from which he could escape only by mobilizing a national army, and thereby fanning the flames of Fort Sumter into full-scale conflagration." (p. xvii)

Thus, it was the intransigence of the Lincoln administration which literally provoked war, and not the cause of "freeing the slaves."

In fact, in the Southern states during the years previous to the outbreak of war there had been discussion about "the institution," its future, and its continuing role in the American nation. Even in South Carolina, probably the most famous and brilliant theologian of the antebellum South, James Henley Thornwell, struggled with the issue for years. While staunchly defending the institution of slavery biblically with solid arguments, he, nevertheless, continued to search for an all-encompassing and just solution to the question, but a solution that the South, working by itself without outside interference, might find. The late Professor Eugene Genovese, perhaps the finest recent historian of the antebellum South, has written Thornwell attempted "to envision a Christian society that could reconcile — so far as possible in a world haunted by evil — the conflicting claims of a social order with social justice and both with the freedom and dignity of the individual." The outbreak of war abruptly halted such discussion, making a peaceful solution practically impossible.

Late in the conflict (March 13, 1865) the Confederate government authorized the formation of black military units to fight for the Confederacy, with manumission to accompany such service. According to several research studies (see Ervin Jordan, Jr. *Black Confederates and Afro-Yankees in Civil War Virginia*. University of Virginia Press, 1995; Charles Kelly Barrow, J. H. Segars, and R. B. Rosenburg, *Black Confederates*, Pelican Publishing, 2001), thousands of black men fought for the Confederacy, perhaps as many as 30,000. Despite the earlier declarations of some Deep South states, would a society ideologically committed to preserving in *toto* the peculiar institution as the reason for war, even in such dire straits, have enacted such a measure? Did the thousands of black men who fought for the Confederacy believe they were fighting for slavery?

It is, of course, easy to read back into a complex context then what appears so right and natural to us now; but it does a disservice to history. Understanding the intellectual struggle in which many Southerners engaged over the issue of slavery, Professor Genovese cautioned readers about rash judgments based on politically correct presentist ideas of justice and right, and in several books and numerous essays defended those leaders of the Old South who were faced with difficult decisions and a nearly intractable context. And more, he understood as too many writers fail to do today, that selecting this or that symbol of our collective history, singling it out for our smug disapprobation and condemnation, may make us feel superior temporarily, but does nothing to address the deeper problems afflicting our benighted society.

For an overwhelming majority of contemporary Southerners the Battle Flag is a symbol of regional pride and an honorable heritage. In recent years it has been used universally as a symbol of liberty against oppression, including atop the Berlin Wall in 1989 and by the ethnic Russian freedom fighters in eastern Ukraine; it has nothing to do intrinsically with "hate" or "prejudice." Concerning Dylann Roof, the disturbed lone gunman responsible for the Charleston shootings, the proper response should be: if a lone rabid fox comes out of the woods and bites someone, you don't burn the woods down, you stop the fox.

But in the United States today we live in a country characterized by what historian Thomas Fleming has written afflicted this nation in 1860 —"a disease in the public mind," that is, a collective madness, lacking in both reflection and prudential understanding of our history. Too many authors advance willy-nilly down the slippery slope — thus, if we ban the Battle Flag, why not destroy all those monuments to Lee and Jackson? And why stop there? Washington and Jefferson were slaveholders, were they not? Obliterate and erase those names from our lexicon, tear down their monuments, also! Fort Hood, Fort Bragg, Fort Gordon? Change those names, for they remind us of Confederate generals! Nathan Bedford Forest lies buried in Memphis? Dig him up and move him to obscurity! Amazon sells *Gone with Wind*? Well, to quote a writer (June 2015) at the supposedly "conservative," Rupert Murdoch-owned *New York Post*, it should be banned, too!

It is a slippery slope, but an incline that in fact represents a not-so-hidden agenda, a cultural Marxism which seeks to take advantage of tragedy to advance its own designs which are nothing less than the re-making completely of what little remains of the Founders' Old Republic. And, since it is the South that has been most resistant to such impositions and radicalization, it is the South, the historic South, which enters the cross hairs as the most tempting target. And it is the Battle Flag — true, it has been misused on occasion — which is not just the symbol of Southern pride, but becomes the target of a broad, vicious, and zealous attack on Western Christian tradition, itself. Those attacks, then, are only the opening salvo in this renewed cleansing effort, this new Reconstruction, and those who collaborate with them, good intentions or not, collaborate with the destruction of our historic civilization. For that they deserve our scorn and our most vigorous and steadfast opposition.

(Abbeville Institute, November 19, 2015, at: www.abbevilleinstitute.org/review/a-new-reconstrution-the-renewed-assault-on-southern-heritage/; originally printed in the *Confederate Veteran* magazine, November/December 2015)

The Land We Love: Southern Tradition and Our Future
◆ *Chapter 2* ◆

Forty years after the end of the War Between the States, Confederate Lieutenant General Stephen D. Lee addressed a group of wizened old veterans and members of a new organization, the Sons of Confederate Veterans, assembled in reunion in New Orleans on April 25, 1906. His address is important in that it lays out in few words a monumental "charge" not just to the descendants of those veterans, but to all Southerners.

By 1906 the remaining veterans were old men, and the growing desire was that the memory of the great Iliad of 1861-1865 not pass away, that its true history be written and passed on to future generations — and also, that the principles of those who had fought be defended, preserved, and advanced.

Here is the Charge General Lee gave to those men — and also to future generations of Southerners:

"To you, Sons of Confederate Veterans, we will commit the vindication of the cause for which we fought. To your strength will be given the defense of the Confederate soldier's good name, the guardianship of his history, the emulation of his virtues, the perpetuation of those principles which he loved and which you love also, and those ideals which made him glorious and which you also cherish."

General Lee charges the inheritors and recipients of Southern tradition with the task of not just defending and "vindicating" the cause for which the Confederate soldier fought, but also of defending — the "perpetuation" of — the "principles" and the "culture" of the Southland: a set of beliefs, customs, traditions, a way of life.

What were these "principles" General Lee refers to? He does not discuss them in any great detail in his commentary. But that does not mean those men in New Orleans did not have some understanding of what he was talking about — indeed, most Southerners of the period would have had some understanding of what he meant.

For another half-century, the South went forward, more or less secure in the assurance that its history and traditions would continue to inform its existence, and those principles and beliefs held dear by it would continue to give it sustenance.

Perhaps it was too much to hope for, given the radical changes and transformations in the world in general, and in the United States in particular. Indeed, after World War II and especially since about 1960 or so, Confederate Southern heritage — its very history, and cultural and social manifestations — has endured constant, overwhelming, and severe attack. What once was held generally to be honorable and worthy of respect was now disparaged and, in many cases, banned or consigned to dusty museums as an antiquated symbol of a dark and forgettable past.

Yet, although we constantly experience this denigration of our heritage, just how many times do such attacks cause us to reflect on what these our symbols actually mean and should symbolize for Southerners? Do today's descendants of the heroic soldiers of 1861-1865 really understand the principles those warriors fought and died for and General Lee certainly meant when he addressed that assembly in 1906? Do the inhabitants of the land which produced Thomas Jefferson, James Madison, John C. Calhoun, John Randolph, Robert Lewis Dabney and Nathaniel Macon comprehend the profound ideas that motivated them and, consequently, gave life to the early American republic, as well as to the abortive Confederate nation?

For Southerners interested in understanding their heritage, it is instructive to discuss the basic principles which underlie that heritage and give greater detail and substance to them. These principles — these foundational elements of what I would call a "Southern philosophy" — are fundamental to our understanding of what it is be a Confederate Southerner and why we oppose not just the Leviathan and managerial "big government" state that has been thrust upon us, but just how we differentiate ourselves from folks in the rest of the Federal union.

In this brief discussion, I rely upon the observations, insights, and research of several distinguished authors, historians, and noted Southern apologists, some well-known, others not so well-known (but who should be). In addition to the classic writings of Jefferson Davis, Robert Lewis Dabney, Nathaniel Macon and Albert Bledsoe, I acknowledge several modern masters.

First, perhaps the most impressive and profound study of the formation of the Southern consciousness in the American colonial period is historian Richard Beale Davis' three-volume *Intellectual Life in the Colonial South, 1585-1763*. (1) Davis, it seems, has read everything from the Colonial period: letters, diaries, newspapers, court records. His treatment is encyclopedic. He demonstrates conclusively that from its beginnings the South had a civilization which was unique, remarkably different from that of New England and the northern states. Although by no means in conflict with its inherited British heritage, as were the Puritan settlements and traditions to the north, the South did over the years modify its rich English patrimony, adjusting to distance, circumstance, climate, the presence of Indians, and the mixture of additional folk from other European countries, with their customs and traditions. The result was quantifiable conservative and localist.(2)

A second, and incredibly fecund, source for understanding the Southern cast of mind and the development of a Southern philosophy can be found in the writings of Tar Heel author and long-time University of Chicago professor, Richard M. Weaver, a writer that noted historian Eugene Genovese has called one of the most impressive intellects that America produced in the 20th century. (3) Weaver, in his classic study, *The Southern Tradition at Bay* (4) and in any number of essays (many republished in volume-form), including most notably "Two Types of American Individualism," explores what he called "the 'social bond' individualism" and rooted traditionalism that distinguished the South from New England.(5)

Lastly, I can think of no better guide than the late Professor Mel Bradford, who for many years was professor at the University of Dallas. About thirty years ago Dr. Bradford published a series of his essays under the title *Remembering Who We Are: Observations of a Southern Conservative*.(6) Summed up in the first part of Dr. Bradford's short title is an imperative command for Southerners. That is, we cannot hope to preserve our traditions, our beliefs, and our symbols — we cannot hope to survive as a people, if we do not know — if we do not remember — who we are and what defines us as a people. Bradford does this impressively in *Remembering Who We Are* and in a large body of other essays in which he incorporates the insights of Weaver, Richard B. Davis, and other Southern writers. Most of his writings have been subsequently published in collections. (7)

In his essay "Is the American Experience Conservative?" Bradford states eloquently the overarching basis for our Southern philosophy: "That man is," he writes, "a social being, fulfilled only in the natural associations built upon common experience, upon ties of blood and friendship, common enterprise, resistance to common enemies, and a common faith."(8) It is this communitarian tradition, inherited intact from our ancestors from the British Isles, from Germany, Ireland, and France, that permitted us to develop a belief in a decentralized republicanism that is at the same time both hierarchical and democratic, social and individualistic. It was our Christian religious orthodoxy, whether Presbyterianism in the Southern Piedmont, Anglicanism in Tidewater areas, or historic Catholicism in Louisiana and Maryland, that first annealed our infant colonial society, dictated social relations and an accompanying cohesiveness, and, during the hard days of the great war and afterwards, provided a much-needed explanation for suffering and defeat. Our ancestors settled in Virginia, the Carolinas, and along the Catawba and Yadkin Rivers, not to create some paradise on earth, not to build a "City on a Hill"— like the Puritans in New England — but to establish freeholds, to farm and raise families, to create self-governing communities, and to give order to the New World. Our ancestors were thus "traditionalists" and "republicans" before there was even a United States.

So, paramount among those principles to which General Lee made reference would be the following: (1) a decentralized republicanism, (2) a religiously grounded society, (3) a firm attachment to shared traditions, and (4) a strong feeling of community and kinship, rooted in the land, in a common history, and in custom. Certainly there are others, but these seem to be the most significant.

Those who have seen Ron Maxwell's epic movie *Gettysburg* will remember the scene when the captured Tennessee troops are interrogated by the C. Thomas Howell character, Joshua Chamberlin's brother. He asks the Tennesseans why they are fighting, and they respond: "For our rights" — Howell can't understand their accents, and asks them again — "rights" sounds like "rats" to him. And they respond again. They are fighting for their God-given rights — inherited rights, and because the Lincoln administration has usurped the powers of the states by waging war against them. Indeed, in the upper South, in states like North Carolina, Tennessee, and Virginia, in particular — it was Lincoln's unconstitutional call for troops to suppress the new Confederacy of the lower South which transformed unionist pluralities into overwhelming secessionist majorities.

The first "principle" the South stood for, then, and has continued to some degree to stand for, is classical republicanism. Often times we use the term "states' rights," but the idea of states' rights is too limited. If we are to understand what united men as diverse in political views as North Carolina Governor Zebulon Vance, Robert E. Lee, Jefferson Davis, and Edmund Ruffin — if we are to comprehend what brought both Southern Whigs and Southern Democrats, unionists and secessionists together in the bloodiest and most eventful conflict of our history, then we must understand the classical republicanism that Southern society of 1860-1861 had received and inherited from the Founders and from statesmen like Nathaniel Macon and later John C. Calhoun.

It was this principle which was elaborated upon at length in the remarkable memoirs of Confederate leaders such as President Jefferson Davis in his *The Rise and Fall of the Confederate Government* and by Alexander Stephens in *A Constitutional View of the Late War Between the States*. The South's faithfulness to the republicanism of the Founding Fathers as carried forth in the Southern Confederacy is a constant theme in such post-war defenses of the South as Albert Taylor Bledsoe's *Is Davis a Traitor?* and Robert Lewis Dabney's *A Defense of Virginia, and Through Her of the South*. It was the Federal violation of this principle embodied in our Constitution which unleashed the war in 1861.

What did Southerners mean by classical republicanism? Most importantly, it had to do with how they viewed the Federal union, which they saw as a compact, freely entered. The Constitution guaranteed the power of the Federal government would not exceed the authority granted to it by the respective states. For the first eighty-five years of American history the statement that "all politics is local" was abundantly clear in hundreds of hamlets and communities across both the South *AND* the North.

In 1861 it was the consensus of practically all in the South, despite various differences, that the Federal government had not the power to coerce a state as Lincoln intended. As President Davis explained twenty years later in *The Rise and Fall of the Confederate Government*: "The invasions of the Southern States for the purpose of coercion were in violation of the written Constitution, and the attempt to subjugate sovereign states under the pretext of 'preserving the Union,' was alike offensive to law, to good morals, and the proper use of language. The Union was the voluntary junction of free and independent states; to subjugate any of them was to destroy the constituent parts, and necessarily therefore, must be destructive of the Union itself."(9) The Republican Party was seen as a vehicle not so much for direct emancipation which was never in its platform and initially not a war aim, but as a means of overturning the original understanding of the Federal union and asserting the supreme power of the central state, and with that economic and political dominance of North over South. Thus, Southerners of all stripes in the South in 1861-1865 fought for what they knew to be the Founding Fathers' understanding of "true republicanism" — a decentralized commonwealth, a compact based on subsidiarity, which was Jefferson's idea of the only kind of republicanism consistent with liberty. Or, as Albert Taylor Bledsoe explains in his defense of the South, our ancestors were, he states, "perfectly loyal to truth, justice, and the Constitution of 1787 as it came from the hands of the fathers."(10)

This is not to suggest there weren't Northerners troubled by the Lincoln administration's usurpations, as well. Indeed, we can cite instances in the North where constitutional opposition to Lincoln and the Republicans was fierce, but as time went on, it was mostly tamed and overawed by force, cajolery, violation of *habeas corpus*, and more subtle forms of suppression. It was in the South that constitutional republicanism became coterminous with Southern identity.

Just what are the essential ingredients of the Southerner's classical republicanism?

First, there is what we call subsidiarity — that is, the belief that things *CAN* be resolved on a lower level of government or of justice, *SHOULD BE* resolved on that level and *NOT* adjudicated on some higher level. Thus on the community level, the community itself should be the judge of local law enforcement and of most taxation, and not faraway bureaucrats in Washington, DC. And even before that, the family — as the primary God-given component of society — should be the first judge and primary master of our children's education, not Washington or Raleigh.

Second, and closely related to subsidiarity, is autarky — which we can define as the ability to run one's life and affairs more or less self-sufficiently, independently of foreign and governmental intrusion. As early as 1810s we see this principle in the speeches and letters of men such as Nathaniel Macon and John Randolph. In 1818 Macon, with reference to the impending Missouri crisis, wrote to Congressman Bartlett Yancey: "Add not to the Constitution nor take therefrom," he states. "Be not led astray by grand notions or magnificent opinions. Remember you belong to a meek state and just people, who want nothing but to enjoy the fruits of their labor honestly, to lay out the profits in their own way," (11) and to be left alone by government to do it.

But this autarky does not isolate the individual, does not separate him from his immediate community or communities which help define him and shape him. Richard Weaver develops this principle of autarky further when he distinguishes between what he terms the "social bond individualism" of the old South, personified and exposited by John Randolph, comparing it with the "cold" dialectical New England individualism championed by Henry David Thoreau. While Thoreau's individualism practically strips "man" of all external links and communal bonds, exposing him eventually to the direct influence and machinations of a faraway government, Randolph, the acute observer of his Southern society and the great defender of the dignity and autonomy of local rights, insists that battles must be fought within the community, and that such efforts do not deny all political organization. As Weaver states,

"... Randolph never lost sight of the truth expressed in Aristotle's dictum that man is a political animal. His individualism is, therefore what I am going to call 'social bond' individualism. It battles unremittingly for individual rights, while recognizing that these have to be secured within the social context." (12)

Thirdly, Southern republicanism is anti-egalitarian. While our ancestors believed in the right, duty, and opportunity of their fellow citizens to work hard and achieve to the best of their abilities, by no means did they believe that every man was endowed by his Creator with equal gifts or talents, nor did he have some unqualified right to participate in or rule over the commonwealth. Participation in government was not based on the modern concept of "one man, one vote."

Our ancestors believed in limited suffrage, and throughout our history favored age, race, sex, and educational qualifications for exercising the franchise. Egalitarianism for them was a leveling view of society which meant an enforced standardization and the same rights for all, and they rejected this outright. Consult such primary examples as the famous debates at the Virginia constitutional convention of 1829 or the North Carolina constitutional convention of 1835, and you will have to look long and hard to find any believers in egalitarianism.(13)

Let us add here, in discussing anti-egalitarianism, a word about slavery. Millions of gallons of ink have been spilt on this topic. Many historians would have us believe Southern history and our Southern way of life are wrapped up uniquely in issues of race and the always-present history of slavery. Slavery for them is the issue which explains literally everything about the South and its history. Even sympathetic historians like Eugene Genovese suggest our distinctiveness as a region and the principles we profess grew out of and were sustained by the social arrangements implicit in the slave system and cannot be separated from slavery.(14)

I would suggest a somewhat different view, one that, I believe, is more reflective of historical reality. I would maintain the South's anti-egalitarian beliefs can be — and are — somewhat distinct from the system and history of slavery. I would argue that for many, perhaps most Southerners, the question of slavery was subordinate to their belief in the sanctity of property and in the necessity for social hierarchy within their autarkic society. Here I owe much to the insights of authors David Gordon and Charles Adams, and most significantly, to the work of Professor Richard Beale Davis.(15)

Davis, in the two-thousand pages of his *Intellectual Life in the Colonial South*, lays to rest the interpretation of Southern history and character which attributes everything to the presence of slavery. As Professor Bradford, commenting on Davis, makes precise:

"The South thought and acted in its own way before the peculiar institution was much developed within its boundaries. Colonial Southerners did not agonize in a fever of conscience over the injustice of the condition of those Negroes who were in bondage among them. Contrary to popular misconception, intense moral outrage at slavery was almost unheard of anywhere in the European colonies in the New World until the late eighteenth century, and was decidedly uncommon then. The South embraced slavery in its colonial nonage because Negro slavery seemed to fit the region's needs — and because the region, through the combination of its intellectual inheritance brought over from the England of the Renaissance with the special conditions of this hemisphere, had reached certain practical conclusions."(16)

Commenting on the recent tendency to attach an overriding importance to slavery in the earlier development of Southern culture and character, Davis adds "… it is difficult to see that in the slave colonies any consistent rationale if indeed any at all developed in defense of the peculiar institution, simply because there was not sufficiently powerful attack upon it to warrant or require a defense." (17) The development of a natural and innate conservatism of the South predates the furor over slavery.

Most significantly, in both slavery and post-slavery times it was not so much race, but rather a desire to preserve the social order— hierarchy and balance in society — which motivated most thinking

Southerners. Just consider the moves by the Confederate government to manumit slaves at the end of the war if they would serve under the Confederate flag. Would a society concerned only about preserving slavery have considered such a program?

Interestingly enough, University of Virginia Professor Gary Gallagher, commenting on his study, *The Union*, which examines in detail the views and mentality of Northerners during the War Between the States, offers a kind of confirmation from north of the Mason-Dixon line. Gallagher states unequivocally: "Abundant evidence leaves no doubt that, first to last, most loyal [Northern] citizens would have said the overriding goal of the war was restoration of the Union." (18) In neither the South nor the North was slavery seen as the reason for the conflict. Questions about race would, indeed, arise and plague the South after the war and since; but their influence on the formation of a Southern character was not critical.

Southerners have understood perforce that the races must live and work side by side, and hopefully harmoniously, but that did not imply legal and social equality for all, either black or white. The key here has been Southerners' religion. Our Southern society is an outpost of Western Christian civilization; Southerners have traditionally been both tolerant of and hospitable to others as long as that understanding has prevailed.

The South as a religiously based society thus forms another major principle General Lee would have us defend. Much indeed has been written about Southern religious faith and belief, and the role of the church in Southern life. Let us recall that classic re-statement of Southern belief — *I'll Take My Stand* — and in particular the fascinating essay on Southern religion by Allen Tate. We are, to paraphrase Flannery O'Connor, a "Christ-haunted society." Just as whole Scots-Irish and German communities pulled up stakes and left the old country together, and settled together in the new, bringing with them their customs and mores when they crossed the Atlantic, so they brought their faith and the church. In the South orthodox Trinitarian and Incarnational Christianity, in its various forms, has been and still is central to and pervasive in our society. This fact cannot be emphasized enough. While third and fourth generation Puritans of New England and various groups in New York and Ohio, began to veer into Unitarianism, transcendentalism, and heretical millenarian cults, the South's popular orthodoxy inhibited deviations and heterodoxy. As historians such as Louis Hartz have indicated, in the 1840s and 1850s the South was becoming more orthodox and religious, while the religious fervor in the North was translated into social gospel and secularist movements, such as abolitionism and prohibition. (19)

There are no better examples of this widening religious divide than some of the favorite hymns sung by Southern and Northern armies during the War of Southern Independence: In the North, Julia Ward Howe's violently secularist words, combined with the music of "John Brown's Body," gave us the millenarian "The Battle Hymn of the Republic," in which the "coming of the Lord" has unleashed a "terrible swift sword" and a "fiery Gospel" to "make men free." In the South soldiers sang orthodox hymns like "Amazing Grace" and "How Firm a Foundation," which assured them "when through fiery trials thy pathways shall lie, my grace, all sufficient, shall be thy supply." It was "How Firm a Foundation," this hymn of consolation, divine hope, and quiet strength General Robert E. Lee had sung at his funeral.

Who cannot but be impressed with the immense outpouring of faith in the Southern armies during the war? This faith did not evaporate after the war, as the South remains a religiously-grounded society, and this consuming religious belief remains central to its identity.

Growing out of the reality of their religiously-grounded society, Southerners were — and still are — self-consciously "traditionalists." It was their defense of the legacy of their fathers — the customs, mores, usages, language, and values they had inherited, as much as the economic warfare unleashed by the North — which propelled them to secession in 1860-1861. The South, despite its regional variations, partakes in a shared tradition, a shared identity, which is hard to quantify, but is there just the same, in its historical consciousness, in its literature, in its shared experiences, its beliefs and myths. The war of 1861-1865 cemented this solidarity and re-enforced it spiritually.

The fourth principle, shared community and kinship, is intimately related to the Southerner's lived traditionalism. I think it was Jefferson who used the term "kindred community" when talking about his fellow Virginians and Southerners. Above all other Americans, Southerners have maintained a unique sense of community and rootedness in time and place — and in the land they love. The family forms the bedrock basis of this community life, and indeed up until recently it was the extended family — parents, children, grandparents, uncles and aunts — that served as the primary "schoolhouse" for our children, instilled values and a sense of deference, passed on customs and etiquette, and imparted the first instructions in religion in our offspring.

During the Colonial Period and leading up to the War for Southern Independence, the migration of Southerners from the four or five original Southern colonies westward was characterized by "familial movement," that is, the movement of entire communities of families in groups, and, indeed, in some cases communities of families that had lived in close proximity since before arriving on American shores in the late 17th or early 18th centuries. Thus, for example, Robert W. Ramsey in his seminal study, *Carolina Cradle*, chronicling the migration southward and settlement of Scots-Irish pioneers who had first landed in Pennsylvania, illustrates how lands were platted in old Rowan County, North Carolina, at the end of their "Great Wagon Road" journey to the Carolina Piedmont. The same family surnames which show up in Ramsey's volume later appear in the records of various communities in Mississippi, Arkansas, east Texas, portions of Missouri, and even, after the 1848 gold strike, in the Sierra Nevada of California. Correspondence exists, of course, between brothers and sisters, children and parents in the Atlantic South and those gone west to seek new lands and a possible fortune.(20) Thus, there was a kind of familial blood unity already firmly planted on the eve of the outbreak of war in 1861 that tied such geographical outliers as Texas and Missouri to older communities in North Carolina and Georgia, and it was a virtual certainty that kinfolk in the Carolinas would not make war on their kindred in the west, and vice-versa. In my own extended family, of the 248 males who served during the War of 1861-65, all came from ten Southern states (except Florida and Virginia) and all of them wore gray. For many Southern families it would be the same.(21)

While this process went on in some areas of the North, it was only in the South that community and kinship unmistakably shaped a common outlook and were, in turn, shaped by privation in war and hardship in defeat. We find this evoked with eloquence in the great works of the Southern novelists and poets, and in the continuing consciousness we all share.

After the war and Reconstruction there had developed an unwritten "understanding" between North and South. While the old Confederacy rejoined the federal union and acknowledged Northern victory, the North, after 1877, more or less left the South alone to manage its own internal affairs, to celebrate its heroes, and eventually to write its history. This arrangement continued up to the 1950s and 1960s. During this period Southerners went about their business, remembering their history and heritage, largely through commemorative events, through maintaining cemeteries, through special reenactments, and through the passing on of oral histories, fathers and mothers to sons and daughters. The media and Hollywood more or less cooperated, with films which paid tribute to the nobility of the South and the Confederate Southern warrior. Universities and academic texts reflected this arrangement as well.

But this understanding began to break down in the 1950s and 1960s. The decisions of the Supreme Court, the triumph of the "civil rights" movement which in some ways was a frontal attack on constitutional republicanism and the rights of property, and the triumph of political correctness and cultural Marxism, all signaled the beginning of a "Second War of Northern Aggression" aimed at totally reshaping and restructuring our culture and at rejecting the principles and beliefs of our ancestors.

Through education, or better named, through indoctrination in the public schools; through manipulation by and through the entertainment media; through virtual control of both political parties so that even those candidates for office who *SHOULD* be favorable to our heritage are afraid to even give us a slight nod; through uncontrolled immigration policies favored by both political parties that dilute and submerge our native population; through the surrender to modernism by most mainline churches — through all these things, and the cowardice and retreat from the battlefield of many who should be our allies — our Southern way of life has come under increasing attack.

One hundred and thirty years ago Jefferson Davis warned all Southerners that the conflict between the South's beliefs and victorious Northern modernism had not ended with Appomattox. Perceptively, he foresaw what would come with Northern victory. Two decades before Stephen D. Lee's "Charge," Davis wrote in his memoirs: "The contest is not over, the strife is not ended. It has entered upon a new and enlarged arena; there the champions of constitutional liberty must fight until the government of the United States is brought back to its constitutional limits."(22)

Today it is paramount Southerners realize there can be *NO* memory, *NO* commemorations, *NO* expression of our heritage, if the very culture in which we live is hostile to us and to our inherited legacy and our beliefs. It is not just a question of the attack on our monuments, or the incremental attempts to reduce and eventually eliminate every symbol of our Confederate past. The attempts by our enemies are more profound — they seek to suppress our very Confederate Southern identity, our way of thinking, and our defining principles.

Perhaps the major opponent we face in the battle for our Southern and Confederate principles is the apathy and even hostility of a large portion of our own people. During the past fifty years we have witnessed the subversion of one, perhaps two entire generations, via the entertainment and news media, via an educational system which destroys our values and exiles our heritage, and via a political system that is intolerant of our views and beliefs. While the Democratic Party, the traditional home for most Southerners, has turned its back on those who used to provide it with huge electoral majorities, fully accepting the standards of "political correctness," many Republicans are not much better, demonstrating little loyalty to place or to our traditional culture. We have seen how politicians and groups who claimed to be on our side ended up being the pivotal difference in securing victories for our opponents.

Where does that leave the traditionalist Southerner? And what does that mean to those who are determined to conserve and defend our traditions and our culture as they confront powerful enemies on all sides?

All across the South diverse signs of resistance have arisen in recent years. Organizations like the Sons of Confederate Veterans, the League of the South, and various heritage groups have had perforce to respond, to return to and draw once again upon those principles that animated our ancestors. But too often this resistance is ill-informed, lacking in coordination, woefully underfunded, and without the means of getting a coherent message out to the general public. If we are to succeed in defending our history and our birthright, this resistance — a "second war for Southern rights"—will require much more dedication and much more sacrifice.

Not only are we facing the apathy and hostility of many of our fellow citizens, and the vigorous opposition of powerful pressure groups in the United States, but the very cultural and political environment of contemporary American Society is unfavorable to our cause. As the black writer Shelby Steele has written in the *Wall Street Journal*,(23) American standards of what is good and right have been so transformed in the public consciousness that even to speak the language we know — of heritage, of tradition, of honor and memory — is met with, at best, incomprehension, and at worst with active hostility. In today's America to be an orthodox Christian who believes in the traditional family is bad enough. To be also a Confederate Southerner and actively involved in defending Southern and Confederate heritage has become an impermissible contemporary sin.

To sum up: the task is not going to be easy. But we do have hope, and there are things that we can do.

One major effort must be in the courtroom, where litigation must be employed to defend the rights of Confederate Southerners and to protect the symbols of our heritage. We need batteries of pro-heritage attorneys ready to stand in the breach. And we must support and encourage efforts to counter heritage violations, organize parental and student groups, and work with (or against) local and state officials.

Our symbols are visible reminders of something much deeper. Monuments, flags, battlefields, historic buildings, named streets and parks, mascots — all these and more — represent a lived history which recalls for us a living past, artifacts of our continuous existence as a people and the land we love and our ancestors once died for. To forsake and give up these symbols — these remembrances — is akin to fossilizing our heritage, banning it, or, at best, locking it up behind closed doors, to be viewed only by the curious academic as a relic of a bygone age. A vibrant and living culture must deposit its monuments and leave something of itself to mark the march of its history. In a real sense, the symbols of our culture denote a series of living customs and mores that envelope and nourish our people, and without which our identity is radically altered or extinguished.

Secondly, in addition to legal defense, Confederate Southerners must become more effectively involved in the political arena, employing Federal code political action committees (such as 501(c)4 and 527 category groups) and funding them adequately. For far too long, perhaps due to the natural conservatism of Southerners and innate reluctance to "stir the waters," we have ceded the field of modern politics to the savvy PR consultant and to outside Political Action Committees. But the cultural war thrust upon us is also a rough political one, and will not abide inaction. There must be a practical union between "defending our heritage" and "defeating our enemies" at the ballot box. We must become truly effective in influencing public opinion and, yes, elections. We have seen what can be achieved in heritage battles if we are well-organized and well-funded, and our small victories can be repeated, if we are dedicated and smart.

Thirdly, Confederate Southerners need to become media and communications savvy, in particular, in perfecting the use of the Internet.

I will go further. A central problem we have faced for the past fifty or sixty years has been the open hostility of the entertainment industry to anything favorable to our Confederate and Southern history. It was not always this way. Just consider some big budget Hollywood productions in the past, not just *Gone With the Wind*, but such pro-Southern films as *Jesse James* (in 1939, with Tyrone Power), *Belle Starr* (with Randolph Scott), *Rocky Mountain* (with Errol Flynn), John Ford's lyrical *The Sun Shines Bright* (in 1953), not to mention Disney's *The Song of the South* or the television series of the late 1950s *The Gray Ghost* on the exploits of Mosby's raiders. Could any of those productions be produced today — except through a vigorous and independent, and probably non-Hollywood, financial outlay?

Part of the problem has to do with the career choices young Southern men and women made beginning in the 1960s. When I was in graduate school at the University of Virginia most of my Southern friends were studying business and economics, very few concentrating on communications, the arts, or film. In a real sense, we largely ceded those fields by default to the 1960s leftists, who are now producing and directing the films and television our children watch, and the news that we hear and see.

Additionally, in the 1960s the old Hollywood film Board of Review system — the so-called Breen Board — was dismantled, practically ending the ability to regulate excessive sex and violence in films. It's been a downhill slide ever since.

A love for and interest in the visual arts, in our great literature, in both great classical and folk music that we have received as a legacy, and in film, should and must be a part of the battle we wage for our culture. We should encourage our children to read, to sing, to listen, to perform, to write, and to dream. For it is only through the arts, which are deeply rooted in our history as a people, that we can actually remember and redeem our traditions and our culture.

Fourthly, Confederate Southerners must become serious educators. Across the Southland we have recently seen some small efforts in this direction, the Abbeville Institute, the Sam Davis Youth Camps, the Southern Military Academy, and a few proudly Christian colleges standing out as good examples. But can we not envisage a day when Southern parents will organize and sponsor a patchwork of independent grammar and high schools all across the South? And just as traditionalist Catholics have established orthodox colleges to educate young minds, so Southerners need to begin establishing colleges, to replace the Vanderbilts and Sewanees, to provide higher education for our children.

What we are talking about here is survival, for it is surviving we must do before we can actually be victorious. We need to learn from our enemies, who have worked patiently but consistently for decades to achieve their goals. The American cultural environment is arrayed against us, which makes our task all the harder.

That is why we must truly come to fathom the theological virtue of hope and what it means for us, collectively and individually. For, even if we believe and have a firm faith, without the supernatural gift of hope to embolden our resolve and help us confront this age which is so contrary to everything we hold dear, the temptation to compromise or give way is simply too great. We must combine hope inspired by our orthodox Christian faith with the imagination and dreams of our great Southern poets and writers.

Let us recall the title of Professor Bradford's book, cited earlier, *Remembering Who We Are*. In it he summons us to remember our ancestors and the reasons they fought 150 years ago. Bradford beckons us to maintain high their principles, to renew the covenant offered to them by Our Lord, and to redeem the time.

Our Confederate and Southern culture still lives, but our generation may be the last when the opportunity to turn the tide in its favor is truly possible. And victory will be won only through sacrifice — through sacrificing our time, our talents, our finances, and perhaps even our friends and reputations. But the alternative is far worse.

NOTES:

(1) Richard Beale Davis. *Intellectual Life in the Colonial South*, 1585-1763. 3 vols. Knoxville: University of Tennessee Press, 1970.//
(2) See Richard Beale Davis, volume III.//
(3) See Eugene Genovese, *The Southern Tradition: The Achievement and Limitations of an American Conservatism* (Cambridge, MA: Harvard University Press, 1993), for Genovese's high appreciation of Richard Weaver, M. E. Bradford, and other Southern traditionalist writers.//
(4) Richard M. Weaver. *The Southern Tradition at Bay: A History of Post-Bellum Thought*. New Rochelle, NY: Arlington House, 1968.//
(5) See Richard M. Weaver, "Two Types of American Individualism," reprinted in *Weaver, Life Without Prejudice* (Chicago: Henry Regnery & Company, 1965), pp. 65-97.

(6) M. E. Bradford. *Remembering Who We Are: Observations of A Southern Conservative*. Athens, GA: University of Georgia Press, 1985.
(7) See the Bradford bibliography in Clyde N. Wilson (ed.), *A Defender of Southern Conservatism: M. E. Bradford and His Achievements* (Columbia, MO: University of Missouri Press), pp. 152-185.
(8) "Is the American Experience Conservative?" reprinted in Bradford, *The Reactionary Imperative* (LaSalle, IL: Sherwood Sugden & Company, 1990), p. 140.
(9) Jefferson Davis, *The Rise and Fall of the Confederate Government* (New York: D. Appleton and Company, 1881), vol. I, p. 439.
(10) Albert Taylor Bledsoe, *Is Davis A Traitor? or Was Secession a Constitutional Right Previous to the War of 1861?* (Baltimore: Innes and Company, 1866), p. v.
(11) Nathaniel Macon to Bartlett Yancey, April 15, 1818, *Bartlett Yancey Papers*, Southern Historical Collection, University of North Carolina, Chapel Hill, NC.
(12) Weaver, "Two Types of American Individualism," p. 71.
(13) See the excellent survey of constitutional conventions in the 1820s, Merrill D. Peterson (ed.). *Democracy, Liberty, and Property. The State Constitutional Conventions of the 1820s*. Indianapolis: The Bobbs-Merrill Company, 1966; for North Carolina, in particular, see Boyd D. Cathey, "Race, Representation, and Religion: The North Carolina Constitutional Convention of 1835," M.A. thesis in history, The University of Virginia, Charlottesville, Virginia, 1970.
(14) See, for example, Eugene Genovese, *A Consuming Fire. The Fall of the Confederacy in the Mind of the White Christian South*. Athens, GA: University of Georgia Press, 1998.
(15) See, generally, David Gordon (ed.). *Secession, State & Liberty*. New Brunswick, NJ: Transaction Publishers, 1998; Charles Adams. *When in the Course of Human Events*. Lanham, MD: Rowman & Littlefield, 2000; and Richard Beale Davis, *Intellectual Life in the Colonial South, 1585-1763*.
(16) Bradford, "Where We Were Born and Raised: The Southern Conservative Tradition," lecture given at the National Humanities Center, Research Triangle Park, North Carolina, April 1985; reprinted in Bradford, *The Reactionary Imperative*, p. 118.
(17) Richard Beale Davis, p.1630.
(18) Gary Gallagher, "Required Reading" (Interview), *The University of Virginia Magazine*, Fall 2011, p.65.

(19) See Louis Hartz. *The Liberal Tradition in America*. New York: Harcourt, Brace & Company, 1955.

(20) See Robert W. Ramsey, *Carolina Cradle: Settlement of the Northwest Carolina Frontier, 1747-1762* (Chapel Hill: University of North Carolina Press, 1965) and the various census records of the more western Southern states in 1850 and 1860. Even today, many of the same Scots-Irish surnames that appear in Ramsey's volume show up in east Texas and counties of Mississippi, Arkansas, Tennessee, and other Southern states. Various private collections at the North Carolina State Archives, Raleigh, and at the Southern Historical Collection, University of North Carolina at Chapel Hill, offer correspondence between relatives in the Southern states.

(21) Alice Ann Berry Klingler (ed.). *Confederate Soldiers with the Last Names "Cathey" and "Cathy"* (Albuquerque: privately published, 1987) pp. 15-19.

(22) Jefferson Davis, vol. II, p. 294.

(23) See Shelby Steele's piece, "Yo, Howard!" in the *Wall Street Journal*, November 13, 2003.

(*Confederate Veteran* magazine, March/April 2012)

Paladins of Christian Civilization: The Universality of the Confederate Cause
⇾ *Chapter 3* ⇽

Thank you. I appreciate that kind introduction. I always like being over in Franklin County. You see, my mother was a "Perry," and although my branch remained up in Perquimans County for about eighty years after the first Perrys came to this part of North Carolina, I have been assured by family genealogists and by my own research that I'm kin to most of the folks with that last name in this area. So, in a way, I'm a Franklin County boy, and I also count many good folks out this way as dear friends.

Today is a special day, and it is special not just for the citizens of Franklin County. It is special because here — right here in Louisburg — 156 years ago, the first Confederate flag was designed and flown. Here, on this spot, began the epic of Americans attempting not only to keep and preserve the republic handed down to them as a legacy by their grandfathers, but also the effort by force of arms to repel the broader attempt by what Europeans have called "the Revolution," or, what I call global progressivism, to overcome and defeat one of the last remnants of true Western Christian tradition. That remnant was the Confederate South.

Let me explain with some historical context.

I begin with the French Revolution. The intellectual currents which produced that upheaval were already percolating during the early 18th century. In its eventual aims that revolution was not just a violent effort to destroy the French monarchy. No, its intellectual leadership and its practical executors were intent on dethroning the power of religious tradition and, in effect, rejecting the belief in a God Who was Lord of all Creation. In His place they would enthrone what they called "the goddess of Reason" in the heart of Paris, in Notre Dame Cathedral.

Of course, these were the extremists; not all the revolutionaries would go quite so far or advocate such radical measures. But all of those who soon denominated themselves as "liberals" would accept the primacy of reason and place man at the center of the universe, in effect, displacing God. I think we should keep that fundamental point in mind as we look at subsequent history on into the 19th century.

It is true the Founders of our American republic were familiar with the French radicals, and, although a few read them and expressed a mild enthusiasm for a few of their ideas, most of the Founders of our old republic rejected the radical democracy and the extremely destructive ideas of that revolution. In a real sense the formerly loyal colonists left Great Britain and declared their independence to vindicate their traditional rights and duties as patriotic Englishmen. That is, to use the words of the great historian, Bernard Bailyn, ours was a "revolution averted, not made."

Our Constitution was configured as a very conservative document. The paramount rights of the various states were fully recognized. And what we might call "liberal democracy" and across-the-board equality were avoided.

What do I mean by that?

First, the Founders set up a system which was balanced, based deeply in English law. Three branches of government were established as check-and-balance safeguards against tyranny. Only those citizens who really had an interest in the new commonwealth would have a real voice in its governance. It was up to each state to decide the qualifications for voting and for holding public office. And most states had a religious qualification for elected office holders. For instance, in North Carolina up until 1868 you had to be a Christian to hold elective office. As for voting, most states required voters to hold some kind of property — that is, they had to have some actual and real interest in the country. Our forefathers figured only if you had an interest — an involvement — could you be truly trusted to cast a vote.

Let me point out, parenthetically, that the Supreme Court never declared such conditions and qualifications illegal or unconstitutional in the 19th century. Only in our benighted modern era have such decisions been made. But it is equally evident and clear the Founders had no intention whatsoever to in any way impede religion or the states' establishing Christianity in their respective territories. To make that assertion is to reveal an abysmal ignorance of history.

Let us jump forward to 1860. Up until that time the general consensus had been that the old republican system established by the Constitution of 1787 was and should be the basis for American life. But beginning early in the life of our republic there were a few voices — not many, but a few — who advocated greater centralization and more radical changes. Even in the Northern states, those voices were a minority for most of our antebellum period. Yet, those voices who thought that way were loud and boisterous.

Certainly, the issue of slavery entered this discussion, beginning in 1820 with the debates over the Missouri Compromise. But even then, the issue for most members of Congress was not slavery itself, but the power, both economic and political, of the states. It was the great Nathaniel Macon, North Carolina's only Speaker of the House of Representatives, who saw clearly what was brewing. For him the issue boiled down to the power of the Federal government to dictate to the states the disposition of their property. If the Federal government could do that, he said, then a war between the states — that is, between those who believed in states' rights and those who did not — would be the eventual result.

In 1861 North Carolina very reluctantly left the Federal union, but only after the Lincoln administration had demanded troops to invade South Carolina. As members of the North Carolina Secession Convention declared, if a free state, a former colony, had freely entered the Federal union, then it could, with justice, freely leave that union if there were serious and grave reasons. Indeed, several of the original thirteen colonies actually said so in the acts of joining the union.

When North Carolina seceded on May 20, 1861, it did so on the anniversary date of its 1775 Mecklenburg Declaration of Independence. Our state declared the bond of union was dissolved and as a free people we were re-vindicating our rights as citizens under the original American Constitution and not the one abused and scorned by the Lincoln administration.

Now let us return to my earlier discussion of what I termed "the Revolution." And let's examine how the actions taken in 1861 and our Southern crusade were viewed worldwide. The efforts of the Southern Confederacy on the battlefield, 1861-1865, were seen by many traditionalists in Europe as part of a global counter-revolution — the resistance — against the revolutionary poison unleashed by the French Revolution.

When I studied in Spain for my doctorate and later in Switzerland, I began to read and examine documents in various archives detailing the enthusiastic support many persons, writers, even sovereigns, in Europe gave to the Confederacy. Thousands — yes, thousands — of volunteers came to the South to fight for the Confederacy.

Let me give some fascinating and incredible examples.

First, probably very few Americans know anything about the old Kingdom of Naples. It ceased to exist in early 1861, after the forces of the liberal Kingdom of Piedmont-Savoy defeated it, thereby establishing the modern Kingdom of Italy. The Kingdom of Naples was hated with a passion by European liberals. For them it was backward, too bound to tradition and custom, too undemocratic, too hierarchical. After an heroic fight the last Neapolitan army was defeated in February of 1861.

And then, guess what happened? As many as perhaps 2,000 of those soldiers of the old, traditionalist Kingdom of Naples got on boats and sailed for New Orleans to volunteer to fight for the new Confederacy. Many of them formed the Italian Brigade which fought valiantly in Louisiana, along the Mississippi, and most notably at the Battle of Mansfield. Many lie buried in Southern soil, honored by our SCV compatriots down in Louisiana and Mississippi. Some returned to Italy.

Back in 1977 I visited a museum and revered historic site outside the city of Naples. There, over the hallowed memorial to Neapolitan Confederates, flew side by side a Third National Confederate Flag and the Royal Standard of the old Kingdom of Naples — gone maybe, but not forgotten.

That story is not well known, but it is not unique. In Spain I discovered as many as 1,000 Spanish Traditionalists, or Carlists, who rose up against Liberalism in their own country under the motto, "God, Country, our Regional Rights, and our King," and then came to Texas to volunteer for the Confederacy. They came by way of Mexico and fought in Confederate ranks at Sabine Pass and at other battles. According to Spanish military historian, David Odalric de Caixal, some enlisted in the Louisiana Tigers. Others found their way as far afield as the 34th and 41st Tennessee regiments. A few even ended up in the Army of Northern Virginia, where General A. P. Hill called them "his rough, tattered lions sent by Providence."

In Spain one of my dearest friends, the Baron of Montevilla, had an ancestor who traveled to Texas to fight for the Confederacy. When his ancestor returned to Spain, an acquaintance asked him: "How can you justify fighting for two lost causes?" To which my friend's ancestor replied: "A lost cause is never really lost if the fight is for what is true and what is right."

Additional volunteers for the Confederate cause came from France and other European countries. We all should remember the great Prussian officer, Johann Heros von Borcke, who rode gallantly with General J.E.B. Stuart and distinguished himself throughout the war. Returning to Prussia after the war, he continued to fly our flag at his estate until his death. And who can forget Major General the Prince Camille de Polignac, from an old and noble traditionalist French family, who came and on the death of General Alfred Mouton, assumed command of Mouton's division at the Battle of Mansfield? Among his troops were Texas frontiersmen, and apparently many of them could not pronounce his last name. So they called him "Gen'ral Polecat." But they loved him just the same, and would have followed him to the gates of Hell. Interestingly, the Prince de Polignac was the last surviving Confederate major general, passing away in 1913.

In recent years it has been our Battle Flag which has flown as the people of East Germany tore down the Berlin Wall. And today in the centuries-old Russian-speaking area of Ukraine — the Donbas — as those valiant people attempt to secede from an oppressive, centralized and imposed Ukrainian state, they fly a replica of our Battle Flag as a sign of the defense of their liberties and their belief in their Christian and Russian heritage.

What I am saying, my friends, is that our cause, the cause of the Confederacy, the cause symbolized by that flag which flies here today, was and is a cause that has universal meaning.

In the eyes of European traditionalists the Southern Confederacy represented the finest of Western Christian heritage. They could identify with leaders like Lee, Beauregard, Jefferson Davis, Stuart, and others. Of course, most of those European supporters were Catholic, not Protestant, but they shared a fundamental world view of an order under God, a belief in Divine and Natural Law, an understanding that society is composed of families in communities, and an allegiance to the idea of states' rights, which they called subsidiarity. That is, what can be done on a lower level of government, very simply should be done on that level closer to the people, and not on a higher level.

But those Europeans also saw the heroic virtue of the South, and it was an heroic virtue based in the chivalry and honor of Christian tradition. It was opposed to the growing Liberalism in the North. That Liberalism advanced a progressivist view that history was an unfolding evolution of human perfectibility, throwing off older beliefs and what they called the "myths" and chains of tradition. Whether those boys in butternut and gray who sank deep in the cold mud trenches at Petersburg completely realized it or not, they were defending Western Christian tradition against Liberal Modernism. And thus they stood with their traditionalist brothers in Europe and elsewhere who also rejected the progressivist vision of history.

My friends, for 152 years we have watched as the results of Southern military defeat have metastasized like a voracious cancer. Sixty years ago many Southerners felt we had reached a real understanding with the Progressivists. We were mostly left alone; we had a thriving literature with America's greatest writers in our midst. Hollywood made films which treated us at least with some sympathy. Our colleges taught real history. Although still suffering the deep economic consequences of military defeat, our people had made giant strides of recovery.

All that changed beginning in the 1960s. Since then, not only here in our beloved Southland, but in America generally, the Progressivist revolution has taken aim, and the targets are many: our politics — our entertainment industry — our educational system — and our churches. It is as if a giant infection and subversion have taken place. Indeed, I would assert they have taken place, and, sadly, most of our fellow citizens have been lulled by the false victories by politicians who promise us one thing, but once in office, go along to get along with a powerful progressivist establishment. And that establishment will accept no dissent.

We are at ground zero in this cultural and political war. And although our particular conflict concerns basically our Southern heritage, our legacy, and our symbols, it also involves, as I said earlier, a broader battle for Western Christian civilization, itself.

When I was in Spain pursuing graduate studies, my good friend called the Southern soldiers who gave their lives at Gettysburg, Bentonville, and other battle sites — he called them "Paladins of Christian Civilization." I think that is very true.

Remember fifty years ago when Raleigh's Channel 5, WRAL-TV, would sign off by playing "Dixie?" The times have changed radically. The Revolution has made a lot of progress since then. Now our flags and precious relics are hidden away in dusty museums, our songs are banned, our symbols are labeled as "hateful."

So it is for us, under that flag, to redouble our commitment to those principles that our ancestors held dear and for which they bled and died. That may mean we lose friends or even lose positions. It may even mean we must spend years, perhaps decades, in a kind of dark catacomb. But if we are faithful to those principles and to that memory — if we are faithful to the precious inheritance we have received — if we are faithful to that flag and what it stands for — then we shall have done our duty.

For our principles are timeless and they only fall if we relinquish the field of battle. We cannot and must not.

As I grow older, the words of my Spanish friend's ancestor resound constantly in my ears: "A lost cause is never truly lost if the fight is for what is true and what is right."

That is our obligation before the long shadow of our ancestors and before the judgment of Almighty God. We can and should do no less.

Thank you, and God bless the South!

References:

David Odalric de Caixal, in the Spanish journal, *La Santa Causa*. Accessed online at: www.geocities.ws/boinasrojas/impresa.html

M. M. Estella, "Un historiador investiga la presencia de carlistas en la Guerra de Secession," *Diario de Navarra* [Pamplona], December 9, 2011. Accessed online at: www.diariodenavarra.es/noticias/navarra/tierra_estella_valdizarbe/un_historiador_investiga_presencia_carlistas_guerra_secesion_57393_1006.html

"Flag of Novorossiya," Accessed online at: https://en.wikipedia.org/wiki/Flag_of_Novorossiya

"Italians in the Confederate Army." Accessed online at: http://2italy.blogspot.com/2007/11/italians-in-confederate-army.html

Jeff Matthews, "Fighting for Two Souths" (2009). Accessed online at: www.naplesldm.com/confedbourb.php

See various biographical accounts, including Wikipedia, for information on Johann Heros von Borke and Prince Camille de Polignac.

(*Confederate Veteran* magazine, September/October 2017; originally speech for Confederate Flag Day, in Louisburg, NC, March 19, 2017)

The Eternal 'Rebel Yell'
❧ *Chapter 4* ❧

Recently, a friend sent me a link on the Smithsonian website to a 1930 video clip in relatively good sound of some aged Confederate veterans demonstrating how the famous "Rebel Yell" had sounded some 65 years earlier. All those men were at least in their late 80s, most in their 90s. But their remarkable spirit still showed through.

History and time can play tricks on us. As a boy I can remember, if vaguely, when the last Confederate and Union veterans passed away. More recently, I can recall when the last Confederate widow "crossed over the Jordan into Promised Land." My grandfather Henry Johnson Perry (1880-1962) on my mother's side vividly recounted to me in 1960 how he stood as a young apprentice in respectful silence when the Jefferson Davis funeral procession went up Fayetteville Street in Raleigh back in 1893, before continuing on to Richmond. On my father's side, my grandmother was born in 1865, and lived until 1962. I recall her telling me that as a girl she remembered an old gentlemen in Mecklenburg County, North Carolina, who was then 100 years old, who was born before the Revolution, and who remembered George Washington's "Southern Tour" stop in Charlotte in 1791!

Our ancestors are ever present in our memory, as long as we have not abandoned or forsaken it or them. They remind us, as the late Mel Bradford once wrote, of who we are, or, at the least, who we have been. They offer high standards of conduct, indeed — standards that, alas, too many in the post-World War II and post-Vietnam generations have rejected, either implicitly, or more callously, explicitly.

Unlike the centennial of the War Between the States fifty years ago, the observances for the sesquicentennial seem less palpable to many of our fellow citizens ... we cannot spend too much time commemorating, you see, as we might miss the latest installment of *Survivor* or *America's Got Talent*. Our schools, media, and pusillanimous political class encourage historical amnesia, that is, except as long as Martin Luther King, Rosa Parks, Malcolm X, and the freeing of the slaves (you know, "what Lincoln did") remain central to the remaining and terribly mangled historical American narrative.

In 2015, the "remembered past" seems too often to intrude on our petty concerns and small-minded lives of angst and boredom. Many of our fellow citizens, when not creating and accepting a made-up politically-correct "past," just simply ignore it, since it gets in the way.

And concomitant with this process, parallel to it, we witness the wallowing in defecation of what is left of a once proud nation. "America is a great nation, an exceptional nation," to hear various politicians and pundits say. "Exceptional," you say? "Exceptionally off its hinges," I would respond. "Exceptionally engulfed in a 'culture of pornographic filth' and aborted death," I would reply. "Exceptionally intrusive in imposing all our evils on the rest of the world, whether they wish them or not," I would retort.

Certainly, there are those men and women, those good families, who remain steadfast, who hold high the banners of sanity and Faith they have received from their fathers and ancestors, but that number is dwindling, not increasing. And those who dominate this decrepit nation, who run its politics, who conduct its foreign policy, who dictate rules and regulations from their managerial offices in Washington (or in Raleigh, Atlanta, or Columbia), are the faceless bureaucrats, the automatons, the cogs in the onrushing triumphant tide which represents the antithesis of what our ancestors believed, and what we, too, still hold paramount.

As I viewed the short video of those veterans, I recalled the sacrifice of our ancestors, their deprivations, their valiant fight for the beliefs and principles they held dear, so dear indeed that they left their homes, farms and families to go off to suffer mightily for four years, many never to return.

Once again, today, the call must go out for us to renew their struggle. This weary nation, eaten away by cancerous and alien philosophies — feminism, same sex ideology, egalitarianism, pseudo-"civil rights," "liberal democracy," statist centralization, and so on — will not survive as we have known it. With the millions of illiterate illegals both Obama and the Establishment GOP, at the behest of the Chamber of Commerce and big business, are letting in (you know, those future "bloc voters" who will take their places on the same modern, Leftist plantation where most blacks now reside), the almost total corruption of our colleges and educational system, the utter evil of the entertainment industry, and the collapse of most real opposition to the rampant radicalism — with these contagions continuing to gnaw away at an even more rapid pace, we must be prepared for the final end of this "exceptional American experiment," we must survive, even in the catacombs, to re-emerge when the weakened walls finally come tumbling down … and pick up the pieces, methodically separating our communities, our respective states, from the worst corruption and infection.

In the decaying America of 2015, at times it seems the truths our ancestors so valiantly defended have disappeared, consigned to museums, banned, or declared "politically-incorrect." But as history confirms, they are not really gone; if we cling to them long enough and maintain them fearlessly — yes, even in the catacombs — they will re-emerge. Then shall we raise up once more the flags of our ancestors, the flags they fought and died for, and those flags shall fly proudly, representing our dedication to the traditions which once again shall flourish and give rebirth to our culture.

(Abbeville Institute, March 26, 2015, at: www.abbevilleinstitute.org/blog/the-eternal-rebel-yell/)

How the Neoconservatives Destroyed Southern Conservatism
⇾ Chapter 5 ⇽

No discussion of Southern conservatism, its history and its relationship to what is termed broadly the "American conservative movement" would be complete without an examination of events which have transpired over the past fifty years and the pivotal role of the powerful intellectual current known as Neoconservatism.

From the 1950s into the 1980s Southerners who defended the traditions of the South, and even more so, of the Confederacy, were welcomed as allies and confréres by their Northern and Western counterparts. William F. Buckley Jr.'s *National Review* and Dr. Russell Kirk's *Modern Age*, perhaps the two leading conservative journals of the period, welcomed Southerners into the "movement" and onto the pages of those organs of conservative thought. Kirk dedicated an entire issue of *Modern Age* to the South and its traditions, and explicitly supported its historic defense of the originalist constitutionalism of the Framers. And throughout the critical period which saw the enactment of the Civil Rights and Voting Rights Acts, Buckley's magazine defended the "Southern position," arguing forcefully on constitutional grounds that the proposed legislation would undercut not just the guaranteed rights of the states but the protected rights of citizens.

Southern authors like Mel Bradford, Richard Weaver, Clyde Wilson and James J. Kilpatrick lent their intelligence, skill as writers, and arguments to a defense of the South. Yet by the late 1980s, that "Southern voice" had pretty much been exiled — expelled — from major establishment conservative journals. Indeed, friendly writers from outside the South, but who were identified with what became known as the Old Right, that is, the non-Neoconservative "right," were also soon purged from the mastheads of the conservative "mainstream" organs of opinion: noted authors such as Bradford (from *National Review*), Sam Francis (from *The Washington Times*), Paul Gottfried (from *Modern Age*) and others were soon shown the door.

What had happened? How had the movement which began with such promise in the 1950s, essentially with the publication of Kirk's seminal volume, *The Conservative Mind* (1953), descended into internecine purges, excommunications, and the sometimes brutal triumph of those — the Neoconservatives — who only a few years earlier had militated in the cadres of the Marxist Left?

To address this question we need to examine the history of the non-Stalinist Left in the United States after World War II. And we need to indicate and pinpoint significant differences between those — the so-called Neocons — who made the pilgrimage from the Left into the conservative movement, and those more traditional conservatives, whose basic beliefs and philosophy were at odds with the newcomers.

In this traversal I utilize the insights of a long list of writers and historians, including the late Richard Weaver, Russell Kirk and Mel Bradford, and more recently, Paul Gottfried and Gary Dorrien — plus my own experiences in witnessing what I term "the great brain robbery of the American conservative movement." That is, what can only be described as a subversion and, ultimately, radical transformation of an older American "conservatism" and pattern of thinking by those who, for lack of better words, must be called "leftist refugees" from the more globalist Trotskyite form of Marxism.

Shocked and horrified by the recrudescence of Stalinist anti-semitism in the post-World War II period and disillusioned by the abject economic failures of Stalinism and Communism during the 1960s and 1970s, these "pilgrims away from the Communist Left"— largely but by no means completely Jewish in origin — moved to the Right and a forthright anti-Communism. Notable among their number were such personages as Norman Podhoretz and Irving Kristol, both of whom had sons who figure prominently amongst the current Neocon intellectual establishment.

At first welcomed by an older generation of conservatives, and invited to write for conservative publications and participate in a panoply of conservative activities, they soon began to occupy positions of leadership and importance — and most significantly, to transform and modify historic views associated with conservatism to mirror their own vision. For, in fact, even though shell-shocked by the effects of Soviet Communism, yet they brought with them in their pilgrimage an overarching framework and an essential world view which owed much to their previous militancy on the extreme left. And they brought, equally, their relentless zeal.

Often well-connected financially, with deep pockets and the "correct" friends in high places, within a few years the "Neocons" had pretty much captured and taken control of most of the major "conservative" organs of opinion, journals, think tanks, and, significantly, exercised tremendous influence politically in the Republican Party (and to some degree within the Democratic Party, at least during the presidency of Bill Clinton).

This transformation — this virtual takeover — within conservative ranks, so to speak, did not go unopposed. Indeed, no less than the "father" of the conservative intellectual movement of the 1950s, Russell Kirk, denounced publicly the Neocons in the 1980s. Singling out the intellectual genealogy of major Neocon writers, Kirk boldly declared (December 15, 1988): "Not seldom has it seemed as if some eminent Neoconservatives mistook Tel Aviv for the capital of the United States."

Essentially, the Neoconservatives were "unpatriotic" in the sense they placed their zealously globalist values of equality and liberal democracy ahead of their allegiance to their country, or, rather, converted their allegiance to their country into a kind of "world faith" which trumpeted disconnected "ideas" and airy "propositions" over the concrete history of the American experience, itself. America was the "exceptional nation," unlike all others, with a supreme duty to go round the world and impose those ideas and that vision on other, unenlightened or recalcitrant nations. To use the words of author Allan Bloom (in his *The Closing of the American Mind*): "And when we Americans speak seriously about politics we mean that our principles of freedom and equality and the rights based on them are rational and everywhere applicable." We Americans must engage in "an educational experiment undertaken to force those who do not accept these principles to do so." (Quoted in Paul Gottfried, *War and Democracy*, 2012, p. 110)

Although he won few friends among the newly transformed conservative establishment, Russell Kirk's demurrer and the opposition of luminaries like internationally-recognized historian Paul Gottfried and author-turned-politician Patrick Buchanan starkly demonstrated the differences between the Old Right and the increasingly dominant Neocons.

In these so-called "conservative wars" Southern conservatism, when not sidelined by the Neocon ascendancy, found itself fighting side-by-side with the dwindling contingent on the Old Right. And that was logical, for the Old Right had — during the previous decades — treated the South and Confederacy with sympathy, if not support, while the Neoconservatives embraced a Neo-Abolitionism on race, liberal democracy, and, above all, equality which owed more to the nostrums of historic Marxism than to the historic conservatism that Kirk championed.

The late Mel Bradford, arguably the finest historian and philosopher produced by the South since Richard Weaver, also warned, very presciently in the pages of the *Modern Age* quarterly (in the Winter issue, 1976) of the incompatibility of the Neocon vision with the inherited traditions and republican constitutionalism of the Founders and Framers. In his long essay, "The Heresy of Equality," which was just one installment in a longstanding debate he had with Dr. Harry Jaffa of the Claremont Institute, Bradford laid bare the abundant intentions of those who came together to form an American nation, while giving the lie to the Neocon narrative that the republic was founded on universalized notions — those "ideas"— of equality and liberal democracy. Those notions, he pointed out perceptively, were a hangover from their days and immersion in the globalist universalism that owed its origin to Marx and Trotsky, and to the Rationalist "philosophes" of the 18th century, rather than to the legacy of kinship and blood, an attachment to community and to the land, and a central religious core that annealed this tradition and continued to make it viable.

What Bradford revealed in his researches, ultimately distilled in his superb volume, *Original Intentions: On the Making and Ratification of the American Constitution* (Athens, GA, 1993) and later confirmed in the massive research of Colgate University historian Barry Alan Shain (in his *The Declaration of Independence in Historical Context: American State Papers, Petitions, Proclamations, and Letters of the Delegates to the First National Congresses*, 2014) was that our old republic was not founded on abstractions about "equality" or "democracy," or some fanatical zeal to "impose our democracy and equality" on the rest of the world, or that we were "the model for the rest of the world," to paraphrase Allan Bloom.

North Carolinian Richard Weaver aptly described the civilization which came to be created in America, most particularly and significantly in the Old South, even a century before the Declaration of Independence and the Constitution, as one based on a "social bond individualism." By that he meant those transferred communities from Europe brought with them a communal conformity which offered certain enumerated liberties to each of its members, or at least to the heads of households of families within those communities. There was a degree of autarky that existed; but in many respects those little communities brought with them inherited mores and beliefs they had held in the old country, and those beliefs were based essentially in ties of blood and attachments to the soil, to the land.

As historian Richard Beale Davis has demonstrated conclusively in his exhaustive history, *Intellectual Life in the Colonial South, 1585-1763* (Knoxville, 1970; 3 vols.), it was in the South where a distinctive communitarian individualism developed which distinguished it almost from the beginning from other regions of America. From the earliest landings at Jamestown and the settlements in South Carolina and Georgia, the Southern colonies developed differently from those of New England. Although by no means in conflict with its inherited British heritage, as were the Puritan settlements and traditions to the north, the South did over the years very gradually modify its rich Anglo-Celtic patrimony, adjusting to distance, circumstance, climate, the presence of Indians, and the mixture of additional folk from other European countries, with their customs and traditions. The result was quantifiably conservative and localist.

Professor Davis equally lays to rest the interpretation of Southern history and character which attributes everything to the presence of slavery. As Professor Bradford, commenting on Davis, makes precise:

The South thought and acted in its own way before the "peculiar institution" was much developed within its boundaries. Colonial Southerners did not agonize in a fever of conscience over the injustice of the condition of those Negroes who were in bondage among them. Contrary to popular misconception, intense moral outrage at slavery was almost unheard of anywhere in the European colonies in the New World until the late eighteenth century, and was decidedly uncommon then. The South embraced slavery in its colonial nonage because Negro slavery seemed to fit the region's needs — and because the region, through the combination of its intellectual inheritance brought over from the England of the Renaissance with the special conditions of this hemisphere, had reached certain practical conclusions. (Bradford, "Where We Were Born and Raised: The Southern Conservative Tradition," National Humanities Center, Research Triangle Park, North Carolina, April 1985, reprinted in *The Reactionary Imperative*, p. 118)

Commenting on the recent tendency to attach an overriding importance to slavery in the earlier development of Southern culture and character, Davis adds "it is difficult to see that in the slave colonies any consistent rationale if indeed any at all developed in defense of the peculiar institution, simply because there was not sufficiently powerful attack upon it to warrant or require a defense." (Davis, p. 1630) The development of a natural and blood-and-soil conservatism of the South predates the furor over slavery.

Let me give a personal, and I think representative example: my father's family is of Scottish origin. Actually, after leaving ancestral homes in Counties Argyll and Ayrshire, then passing about fifty years in County Antrim in Ulster, they made the voyage to Philadelphia, arriving in 1716-1717, and settled initially in what is now Lancaster County, Pennsylvania (as deeds show). Their object was cheap and good land on which to raise their families; they were already able to practice their faith in County Antrim, just as they were able to do in Lancaster. And the same "liberties" they had in the old country they also had in Pennsylvania.

Seeking newer and fresh lands, whole families picked up in the later 1730s and made the trip southward along the Great Wagon Road to Augusta County, Virginia, and then, by the 1740s to Rowan County, North Carolina. And what is truly fascinating is from Scotland (in the early 1600s) to Ulster, to Pennsylvania, to Rowan County, North Carolina, it is the very same families in community, the very same surnames and forenames one finds in the deed and estate records. Robert W. Ramsey, in his path breaking study, *Carolina Cradle: Settlement of the Northwest Carolina Frontier, 1747-1762* (Chapel Hill, 1964), platted the land grants of those pioneers in Rowan County, and more than 90 percent of the family names are the same as those we find in Ulster a century earlier and in the parish registry books of Scotland before that.

And perhaps more striking is this pattern continued on for another century and more; collateral members of my father's family made the trek to California in 1848-1849, enticed by promises of gold and new, unploughed lands. There is a community still known as "Catheys Valley" (near Yosemite Park) where they settled, and as late as the 1950s, the same old surnames in the telephone directory still predominated.

But not only do we find the geographical movement of entire families and communities, in the existent correspondence that we do have there is, almost without exception, no word about traveling west or crossing the ocean to seek "freedom" or "equality" or to "create a new nation founded on [globalist and egalitarian] principles."

Our ancestors were not seeking to establish a "Shining City on a Hill" like the New England Puritans and their descendants, or "create a new people," but rather to preserve and enhance the old. When those settlers wrote about their experiences, if at all, it was about their respective families and communities having a better life, about cheaper and virgin farm lands, and about conserving the inheritance and traditions they took with them. In other words, the 18th century philosophy of Rationalism, and the ideas of "equality" and "democracy" we are too inclined to attribute to them, don't really appear on nearly any level.

And this, at base, practical and communal individualism is reflected in the deliberations preceding the Declaration and then, even more so, by the Framers in 1787— as both Bradford and Shain have convincingly shown. The documentary evidence in every form confirms that. The "right to equality" enshrined in the Declaration is an "equality" viewed from the Colonies across the Atlantic to the English Parliament, equality as to the "rights of Englishmen," not to social or economic revolution in the former colonies.

Those deliberations in Philadelphia were the product of a community of states, each with their own peculiarities, their own communities of families, with traditions inherited from Christian Europe (largely from the British Isles), and the desire to both preserve that inheritance while co-existing and collaborating with other communities and states in the creation of the American republic, where those traditions and that inheritance would be protected and respected, and could prosper as its families and communities prospered.

And in large part that result was the product of great Southerners, Virginians and Carolinians. It was a result which functioned well for eighty years. The legacy of Northern victory in 1865 was the overthrow of the original republic created by those men, which, in effect, paved the way for the present-day success of the Neoconservatives and the triumph of what the late Sam Francis called the managerial state … and what we now call the Deep State.

Given this history and this context, both the War Between the States and subsequent American history after that conflict, and with the modern displacement by the Neocons of the traditional (and Southern) conservatives and their opposition to the growth in government and to the destruction of those bonds and traditions which characterized the country for centuries, the results we observe around us do not augur well for the future. While the hardcore cultural and political Marxist Left continues its rampage through our remaining inherited institutions, those self-erected Neocon defenders accept at least implicitly, many of the same philosophical premises, the intellectual framework of argument, and the long range objectives of their supposed opponents.

Ironically, although they may appear at times in major disagreement, both the hardcore multicultural Left and the Neocon "Right" share a commitment to the globalist belief in American "exceptionalism." In explaining this exceptionalism, they use the same language — about "equality" and "democracy" and "human rights" and "freedom," its uniqueness to the United States, and the desirability to export its benefits. But, then, the proponents of the dominant Left and of the establishment Neocon Right will appear variously on Fox or on MSNBC, or in the pages of *National Review* or of *The Weekly Standard*, to furiously deny the meaning given by their opponents ... but all the while using the same linguistic template and positing goals — in civil rights, foreign policy, etc. — which seem remarkably similar, but over which they argue incessantly about the "means."

Thus, in their zealous defense of the "civil rights" legislation of the 1960s and their advocacy of what they term "moderate feminism" and "equal rights for women" (now extended to same sex marriage), the Neocons mirror the ongoing revolution from the Left and accept generally its overarching premises, even while declaring their fealty to historic American traditions and historic Western Christianity.

It is a defense — if we can call it that — which leads to continuous surrender, if not betrayal, to the Revolution and the subsequent acceptance by those defenders of the latest conquest and advance by the Left, and their subsequent attempt to justify and rationalize to the rest of us why the most recent aberration — same sex marriage, or "gender fluidity"— is actually conservative. Or, that it is critically necessary to send American boys to die in faraway jungles or deserts to "establish democracy," that is, prevent one group of bloodthirsty fanatical Muslims from killing off another group of bloodthirsty fanatical Muslims — this latter group, of course, willing to do our bidding economically and politically. And all in the name of spreading —mostly we should say imposing — global "equality" and "freedom" and the "fruits of American exceptionalism."

Neither the leftist Marxist multiculturalists nor the Neoconservatives reflect the genuine beliefs or inheritance left to us by those who came to these shores centuries ago. Both reject the historic conservatism of the South, which embodied that inheritance and the vision of the Founders.

They offer, instead, the spectacle of factions fighting over the increasingly putrid spoils of a once great nation which becomes increasingly weaker and more infected as they assume the roles similar to that of gaming Centurions at the Crucifixion.

The election of Trump threw them — both the cultural Left but also the establishment Neoconservatives — off stride, at least temporarily. And the history of the past year and a half has been a continuous sequence of their efforts to either displace the new administration (by the hard Left and some Never Trumpers) or surround the president and convert him, or at a minimum neuter his "blood and soil," America First inclinations (by many of the establishment Neocon and their GOP minions).

Who wins this battle, who wins this war, will determine the future of this nation and whether the dominant Deep State narrative, shared by both the establishment Left *AND* the establishment conservatives, will complete its triumph.

(Abbeville Institute, May 2, 2018, at: www.abbevilleinstitute.org/blog/how-the-neocons-destroyed-southern-conservatism/?mc_cid=3615d8ca09&mc_eid=8639a6a6ea)

How You Stand on the War Between the States: A Window into Your View of Western Christian Heritage
↣ *Chapter 6* ↢

You can tell a lot about a person by his actions and how he justifies them. And you can intuit much about how someone thinks on one topic by how he thinks on other, related topics. This surmise is not true in every case, but, I think it applies in a great majority of situations. Tell me what a person — a distinguished author, a political or military leader, a cultural icon — believes, his perspective on this or that significant historical event, how he acts in a particular situation — and you can usually gather a valid impression of his worldview and overarching philosophy.

A few years back I created my own set of measures, my own test, as it were, to determine on which side of immense and fundamentally unbridgeable divides various writers and authors, politicians, and others come down on. It seemed to me that we could take, historically, several major conflicts and wars, that fundamentally shaped not only subsequent history, but also, indelibly, the consciousness, thinking and cultural outlook of succeeding generations, and utilize them as markers.

I came up with the following five:

1) The English Civil War, 1642-1651;
2) The French Revolution, 1789-1799, also including the Napoleonic Period, 1799-1815;
3) The War Between the States, 1861-1865;
4) The Communist Revolution, 1917-1920; and
5) The Spanish Civil War, 1936-1939.

I won't dwell at length on my reasons for selecting these conflicts as measures except to say I believe how we think about them clearly illustrates where a person stands in relation to the accumulated inheritance — that great continuum — of Western and Christian tradition. They — each one of them — represent watershed events in the past 500 years of our Western European civilization.

I could have selected — but did not — World War I, for example, but even though a preponderance of evidence now indicates the outcome of that conflict was a disaster for Europe, that much (not all, certainly) of the blame for its initiation resides in Paris and in Whitehall (and not as much in Vienna or Berlin), I recognize there are yet persons of intelligence and devotion to the Christian West who differ. So, I do not include it.

Respond correctly on all five that I list (as I see it), and you are a staunch defender of Western European heritage and most probably have been able, in some fashion, to understand the fundamental connection those conflicts have in the context of our civilization and our willingness to defend it.

Obviously, for most self-described "conservatives," there are at least two "giveaways" in my list, that is, two of the five questions they would very likely answer correctly: about the French Revolution and the Communist Revolution. Most "conservatives," if queried, would have certainly opposed them. There are some, nevertheless, who are more positive about Napoleon, but I aver that it is impossible to understand the "little Corsican"— that "thief of Europe," to use William Pitt's classic appellation — and his actions outside his relationship to the French Revolution, and his normalization of much of its result, and, more seriously, the fact his tenure unleashed essentially the forces of liberal revolution which would threaten and undermine Europe for a century.

It becomes harder after that, and, I suggest, even more critical to a determination. Not many current "conservative" writers or politicians are intimately familiar with the history, causes, and issues surrounding the English Civil War. Yet, I would assert vigorously issues debated then were, in microcosm and incipiently, some of the issues we continue to debate today, and a faithful and thinking defender of the continuity of Western tradition must, necessarily, come down on the side of the Royalists, as opposed to Oliver Cromwell's faulty experiment in authoritarian democracy. King Charles I, for all his mistakes and bad decisions, nevertheless, represented the traditions of his country and, as he stated at his famous trial, represented "more the people of England" than the rump "democratic" dictatorship of the Cromwellians and Roundheads. (There is an excellent, historically-based BBC television series, *By the Sword Divided*, which showed up in part on American television about twenty years ago — the segment dedicated to King Charles' trial is taken verbatim from the recorded transcript of the process, and fully confirms that view.)

Back in the 1960s, back when William F. Buckley's magazine, *National Review*, and Russell Kirk's journal, *Modern Age*, were arguably truly conservative, the question concerning the Spanish Civil War would have, likewise, been a giveaway. Almost all conservatives would have viewed that conflict in the light of a much larger, universal conflict between international Communism and those forces opposed to it, and this despite the fact the anti-Republican Nationalist forces led by Francisco Franco did receive some support from Fascist Italy and Hitler's Germany (while the Soviet Union not only supported the Republic, but eventually via the Spanish Communist Party eliminated most of its opposition in Spanish Republican ranks).

But not today; indeed, many of the dominant "conservatives" of 2018 — the Neoconservatives — come down passionately on the side of the socialist Republic, and, employing the linguistic armor of the Left, they attack the Nationalist, Catholic and traditionalist forces which fought against the Republic, as "fascists." Thus, a few years ago, on the ostensibly "conservative" NationalReviewOnline, writer Stephen Schwartz let the cat out of the bag:

"To my last breath, I will defend Trotsky who alone and pursued from country to country and finally laid low in his own blood in a hideously hot house in Mexico City, said no to Soviet coddling to Hitlerism, to the Moscow purges, and to the betrayal of the Spanish Republic, and who had the capacity to admit that he had been wrong about the imposition of a single-party state as well as about the fate of the Jewish people. To my last breath, and without apology. Let the neofascists and Stalinists in their second childhood make of it what they will." [see Paul Gottfried's commentary onTakimag.com, April 17, 2007]

Schwartz's view can be multiplied tenfold in Neoconservative ranks.

Finally, there is the War Between the States, and, by far, how a person views that conflict determines much about his vision of the American republic, both its history and its future. It is here, in this case, where we indeed can separate the true traditionalist conservatives who comprehend and accept the continuum of Western Christian civilization, its virtues, and its authority, and those who have, in reality and to varying degrees, severed themselves from that continuity. It is here we can range on one side those who accept and participate in that "great chain of being"— that fundamentally religious and hierarchical structure of all matter and life, decreed by God, Himself, and present in our historical consciousness, and those who do not in varying degrees accept it.

For support, in some form, of the Confederacy becomes that crucial measure which determines not just a political outlook about states' rights and the original meaning of the American Constitution. It also demonstrates an understanding of reality and of our existence as human beings created by and subservient to God as part of an organic whole, a Creation which must continually be protected and defended against those who would seek to puncture it, or distort its meaning, if not, eventually, to subvert or destroy it.

Certainly, there are those of good will, and let us call it "invincible ignorance," who have been educated to think the primary issue in 1861 was slavery, and Abraham Lincoln was simply reacting to those "rebels" who wished to destroy "the sacred bonds" of Union, while advancing the great humanitarian cause of "freedom." So much for the caliber and character of our contemporary educational system, not to mention Hollywood's ideologically tendentious (and mostly successful) attempts to influence us.

Yet, that mythology surrounding the Southern Iliad of 1861-1865 will not stand serious cross-examination.

Consider these popular myths and shibboleths:

"The War was about slavery!" Not really accurate: the war aims cited repeatedly by Lincoln and Northern publicists consistently during the years 1861-1863, even afterwards, were that the War was to "preserve the Union." Indeed, if abolition of slavery had been declared as the principle war aim in 1861, most likely a great majority of Union political leaders, not to mention Union soldiers, would have recoiled, and the Northern war effort would most likely have collapsed. It was difficult enough to gain wide support in the North, as it was. Remember, Lincoln was elected with less than 40 percent of the vote in 1860, and barely gained pluralities in most Northern states.

"Lincoln freed the slaves!" Not so; Lincoln freed not one slave. His Emancipation Proclamation, issued first on September 22, 1862 and formally on January 1, 1863, supposedly "freeing the slaves," only applied to those areas not under Union military control or occupation, that is, territory of the independent Southern states. It did not apply to the "slave states" within the Union or controlled by the Union military, including Delaware, Maryland, Kentucky, and Missouri. Thus, Lincoln's proclamation "freed" slaves where his action had no effect, but left it untouched where he could have freed them. Not only that, exactly one month prior to his initial proclamation he had been interviewed by Horace Greeley, editor of *The New York Tribune*, where he forthrightly stated: "If I could save the Union without freeing any slave, I would do it … What I do about Slavery and the colored race, I do because I believe it helps to save this Union…." [August 22, 1861] The amendments to end slavery came after the conclusion of the war and after the death of Lincoln.

And most recently this charge: "**Robert E. Lee and other Confederate military leaders who were in the US Army committed treason by violating their oaths to defend the Union, and Confederate leaders were in rebellion against the legitimately elected government of the United States.**" Somehow critics forget to mention Lee and the other Confederate leaders resigned their commissions in the United States Army and from Congress prior to enlisting in the defense of their home states and in the ranks of the Confederate Army, or assuming political positions in the new Confederate government. They did not violate their oaths; their states had formally left the union, and, thus, the claims of the Federal government in Washington had ceased to have authority over them.

Nevertheless, this accusation has become the ultimate weapon of choice for today's fierce opponents of the various monuments which honor Robert E. Lee, Stonewall Jackson, P. G. T. Beauregard, Jefferson Davis, and other Confederate military and political leaders, and for the belief they should be taken down. And most especially, it is spewed forth as unassailable gospel by many Neoconservative writers, publicists, pundits, and their less distinguished camp followers in the elites of the Republican Party.

It must be opposed with courage and determination, not only because of what its triumph would mean for the Southland and its history, but for the sake of the old Republic and our Western and Christian inheritance.

(My Corner by Boyd Cathey, July 9, 2018, at: http://boydcatheyreviewofbooks.blogspot.com/2018/07/july-9-2018-my-corner-by-boyd-cathey.html)

Merchants of Hate: Morris Dees, the Southern Poverty Law Center, and the Attack on Southern Heritage

✣ Chapter 7 ✣

In the late 1990s what is perhaps the most powerful and professional "anti-hate" civil rights pressure group in the United States — the Southern Poverty Law Center (SPLC) — began targeting and attacking the Sons of Confederate Veterans, its leaders, and initiatives. In "exposés" published in the SPLC's quarterly journal *Intelligence Report*, in training courses offered to hundreds of law enforcement agents across the nation, and in its self-erected position as a "source" for "background" on "hate groups" to national media outlets such as CNN, ABC, and CBS News, this powerful group began lumping the SCV together not only with other respectable heritage organizations (such as the League of the South), but with "the Klan" and skinheads. The SCV was, said the SPLC, increasingly dominated by "neo-Confederates." The SCV's campaign, for instance, to retain the CSA Battle Flag atop the South Carolina capital building the SPLC termed "sometimes ugly" and various SCV leaders were called "racists" or "white supremacists." (1)

Why has the Southern Poverty Law Center unleashed these attacks? Just what is this powerful "civil rights" group, and who is its controversial leader, Morris Seligman Dees? Why is the SPLC so highly regarded by law enforcement? Members of the Sons of Confederate Veterans and open minded citizens need to understand and answer these questions. And educators and the news media should closely examine their reliance on the SPLC for "facts" or "background" when reporting stories relating to Southern and Confederate heritage.

First, a little history is in order.

In 1906 Confederate veteran General Stephen D. Lee addressed the national convention of the Sons of Confederate Veterans in New Orleans, placing before them what would be known henceforth as the "charge," summarizing the purposes and goals of the Sons (then a relatively new organization only ten years old). Those brief words of General S. D. Lee bear repeating:

To you, Sons of Confederate Veterans, we will commit the vindication of the cause for which we fought. To your strength will be given the defense of the Confederate soldier's good name, the guardianship of his history, the emulation of his virtues, the perpetuation of those principles which he loved and which you love also, and those ideals which made him glorious and which you also cherish.

For the first seventy-five years of its existence, the SCV was mostly concerned with memory, with keeping alive the memory of the exploits and accomplishments of our ancestors; with commemorating their service and sacrifice; with retelling their momentous odyssey in books and articles and speeches; and in inspiring new generations of Southerners (and Americans generally) to emulate their virtues. By the 1970s and 1980s many of the symbols and much of the history Southern folk had taken for granted over the years began to be questioned, disputed, and attacked. Indeed, Southern and Confederate culture, itself, came under a barrage of assaults on many fronts. Many in the so-called "civil rights" movements of the 1960s were not content to simply press for reasonable legal and constitutional changes; rather, some saw the resulting upheaval as an opportunity to demolish and eliminate just about *ALL* of Confederate culture and heritage — and to make some money in the process. Like the English bands that played "The World Turned Upside Down" at Yorktown in 1781, Southerners witnessed their world turned upside down and the denigration of almost anything and everything "Confederate."

Prior to 1990 the SCV had concentrated most of its efforts on the goal of commemorating Confederate veterans, their history and heritage, and in telling their story. But Stephen D. Lee's charge demanded that latter-day sons also, when required, defend the *PRINCIPLES* their forefathers advanced. What are those principles General Lee referred to? The late historian/author Professor M. E. Bradford, among others, summed them up: a belief that tradition should be our guide constitutionally and socially, a stout defense of the rights of the states, a strongly religious conception of civil society, a reliance on communities and families as basic to society and the social order, and opposition to egalitarianism politically and socially. All of our ancestors would have subscribed to these tenets, whether "old" Whig or Democrat, "fire-eater" or "conservative."

Increasingly, throughout the 1990s to the present, the SCV has been forced to defend the principles about which General Lee spoke and three hundred thousand Southern boys gave their lives to defend. Composed of lineal descendants of the veterans of 1861-1865, the SCV is the largest Southern heritage organization in the nation, and it occupies a unique position in the increasingly bitter battle for Southern and Confederate heritage and culture. The defense of that heritage has brought the SCV squarely into conflict with those, who not only want to eliminate Southern symbols, but who also wish to purge and destroy Southern culture itself, the Southern way of life. Those symbols will cease to have meaning if the culture and heritage they represent, the ideas they stand for, are no longer celebrated, believed, and felt. That is why the SCV has not only stoutheartedly opposed such things as the lowering of historic flags from official buildings and the elimination of "rebel" mascots, but has also assisted Southern citizens and students whose rights, culture and heritage have been attacked and imperiled.

Who is Morris Dees? Morris Seligman Dees was born in Alabama and received a law degree from the University of Alabama. One of his earliest associates was Millard Fuller, who would later found Habitat for Humanity. In 1960 Fuller and Dees formed the law partnership of Dees and Fuller in Montgomery. Their object, as Fuller expresses it in two autobiographical volumes, was "to get rich" and get rich quick. They did this through any number of enterprises: selling cookbooks, toothbrushes, tractor cushions—anything which would make money. (2) In his book *Love In the Mortar Joints*, Fuller states: "Morris Dees and I, from the first day of our partnership, shared one overriding purpose: to make a pile of money. We were not particular about how we did it; we just wanted to be independently rich. During the eight years we worked together we never wavered in that resolve." But Fuller grew disenchanted with that lifestyle: "But everything has a price," he recounts. "And I paid for our success in several ways. One price I paid was estrangement from the church." (3) In a few years Fuller left the partnership and dedicated his life to a new, more altruistic cause: Habitat for Humanity.

Dees, meanwhile, began raking in the bucks — and seeking to make friends in high places. While segregation was still the law of the land he had supported and worked in a campaign for Governor George Wallace, and his law firm was involved in defending a man charged with beating one of the Freedom Riders during the 1961 Montgomery "freedom" bus rides. The legal fee, states Fuller, "was paid by the Klan and the White Citizen's Council."(4)

But times were changing, and Morris Dees could read the signs. By 1971 Dees had been "reborn" as a "defender" of civil rights; in that year he, Julian Bond, and Joseph Levin founded the Southern Poverty Law Center to serve as a "civil rights law firm" and promote social justice. (Bond would resign from the SPLC when it became apparent his presence was deterring contributions by liberal Jewish donors).(5) In 1972 Dees served as a fundraiser for presidential candidate George McGovern and proved extremely adept at direct-mail solicitations; according to journalist John Edgerton in an article, "Poverty Palace: How the SPLC Got Rich Fighting the Klan," published in the liberal magazine *The Progressive*, Dees raised some $24 million for the McGovern campaign.(6) By 1975 Morris Dees had established himself (and the SPLC) as a leading light among "professional" civil rights advocates.

A major opportunity for national prominence came Morris Dees' way in 1975 with the infamous Joan Little case in Washington, North Carolina. The facts of the case were well reported at the time: Little, a black woman and convicted felon, was apparently approached by her white jailer for sexual favors, whereupon she stabbed and killed him with an ice pick. The case immediately was made a cause célèbre by left wing groups and the Communist Party and by a sympathetic press nationwide. Dees and the SPLC were involved in Little's defense, along with another high-profile "professional" civil rights attorney, Jerry Paul. Paul boasted the defense team had "orchestrated the press." As correspondent Mark Pinsky later wrote in the *Columbia Journalism Review*, "… the great untold (or unreported) story of the Joan Little trial, which I first learned from the members of the defense law firm and defense committee [italics mine], was the role of the Communist Party … controlling the entire (and considerable) political movement surrounding the case [….] Party members were visible and influential on the defense committee…."(7) Rallies in support of Little raised large sums of money, despite, states Pinsky, "persistent charges of large-scale [financial] mismanagement and misappropriation…."(8)

During the trial Dees revealed just how far he was ready to go to succeed. He attempted to bribe a witness — suborn perjury. He was arrested and removed from the court. While the felony charge was later dropped, presiding judge Hamilton Hobgood refused to re-admit Dees to the case, a refusal which was upheld on appeal when the U.S. Supreme Court refused to hear his appeal.(9)

The 1975 perjury arrest was not the last time Dees and the SPLC would be charged with bribing a witness to advance an agenda. In 1990

Dees and the SPLC sued well-known West Coast racialist Tom Metzger with the object of putting Metzger and his various enterprises out of business by destroying him financially. This famous case, "putting hate on trial" as it was called by the media, involved charges that Metzger inspired skinheads to fatally beat an Ethiopian immigrant. Greg Withrow and David Mazella were prosecution witnesses for Dees. Withrow also described in lurid detail how he himself was nailed to a cross on August 8, 1987. Because of his testimony, Withrow became something of a celebrity; he appeared on the Oprah Winfree program and was sponsored on an "anti-hate" tour by the Anti-Defamation League.(10) But in a report published on August 25, 2001, *The San Diego Union-Tribune* revealed Withrow had recanted his testimony and he was suing Dees, the SPLC, and the ADL for $32 million in damages. Withrow declared the story of the crucifixion was fabricated, and additionally Dees paid him $1,500 for perjured testimony in the trial; he added Dees also paid the other prosecution witness, David Mazella, as well.(11)

Charges of perjury are not the only legal problems Morris Dees has had. In 1979 Maureene Bass Dees, his ex-wife, sued him, alleging instances when Dees had committed incest with his stepdaughter and future daughter-in-law. At least once he was alleged to have engaged in homosexual conduct.(12)

In his two autobiographical volumes, *Love In the Mortar Joints* and *Bokotola*, Habitat for Humanity founder Millard Fuller offers a fascinating portrait of Morris Dees, a man on the make, a man whose goal was to make money, and lots of it, and to have friends in high places. Although the Southern Poverty Law Center was founded ostensibly as a "civil rights" organization to do such things as defend prisoners who faced the death penalty or sue on behalf of those suffering from discrimination, the Dees organization quickly became the richest and most powerful organization of its kind in the United States. According to investigative journalist Ken Silverstein in a major report published in *Harper's Magazine* (November, 2000), the SPLC counted (in 2000) assets of well more than $120 million.(13) Most of this is raised through direct mail solicitations, and very little of it is spent on behalf of the "poor, downtrodden, and oppressed." Most of the solicited millions remain in the hands of Dees and the SPLC. In 1998 the American Institute of Philanthropy, which evaluates the stewardship of charitable organizations, gave the SPLC an "F" rating in its administration of its funds.(14) A former associate, Millard Farmer, has stated: "He's the Jim and Tammy Faye Bakker of the civil rights movement, though I don't mean to malign Jim and Tammy Faye."(15)

Let's examine the methods of Dees and the SPLC.

From its beginning the SPLC created an easy target: the Ku Klux Klan. Never mind that the Klan, by the late 1970s and 1980s, was splintered into dozens of dwindling groups, down to less than 2,000 members nationwide, with almost no power or influence. As Ken Silverstein relates, "the news of a declining Klan does not make for inclining donations to Morris Dees and Co., which is why the SPLC honors nearly every nationally covered 'hate crime' with direct mail alarums full of nightmarish invocations of armed Klan paramilitary forces' and 'violent neo-Nazi extremists,' and why Dees does legal battle with almost exclusively with mediagenic villains...."(16) In his famous lawsuit against the United Klans of America in 1987, Dees won a judgment of $7 million on behalf of Beulah Mae Donald, whose son had been killed by individual Klansmen. The Klan's total assets amounted to one warehouse, the sale of which netted Donald damages of $51,875. But the SPLC in a direct mail campaign implied that it was forcing the Klan to pay Mrs. Donald the full amount. It used the Donald killing (including a lurid photograph of her dead son) to raise an additional $9 million. Mrs. Donald got nothing.(17)

In February 1994 two investigative reporters for *The Montgomery Advertiser,* Dan Morse and Greg Jaffe, published a revelatory series of articles on the SPLC, Morris Dees, and their fundraising tactics.(18) According to three former SPLC attorneys interviewed for the series, Dees selected the Klan as a target because he knew it would bring in tens of millions of dollars from conscience-ridden liberals across the nation. "The fundraising letters would make it seem to people who really didn't know the South as if the Klan was out of control ... And so he (Dees) could get Northerners who really didn't know much about the South to give him money," Deborah Ellis, former SPLC attorney, told *The Montgomery Advertiser* reporters. "The market is still wide open for the product, which is black pain and white guilt," the article quotes Gloria Browne, another former SPLC attorney, as saying.(19)

The Montgomery Advertiser's reporters found that because of his fundraising practices a number of Dees' associates left the SPLC in disgust. Former SPLC associate Courtney Mullin declared of Dees that he is "... not immoral, he's amoral ... I hesitate to say the words that I want to say because they sound so far out, but I really think the Center — in so far as Morris embodies the Center — is evil. They pretend to be on a side that has moral underpinnings (but) they do damage by their dishonesty .... I mean the little old lady from North Carolina sends her $5 thinking that she's going to help ... then it's just going to line the coffers of the Southern Poverty Law Center so they can have the most beautiful building in the world and have all this money in the bank. That's wrong."(20) In 1986 the SPLC's entire legal staff resigned in protest over Dees' refusal to address the issues of homelessness, voter registration, and affirmative action which they considered more important to poor minorities — but much less lucrative than appealing to largely white benefactors about the evils of the Klan.(21)

In fact, according to another story published in *The Birmingham News*, the SPLC had few minority employees on its staff and the ones working there were unhappy.(22) Over its nearly three decades of operation, the SPLC had hired only two black attorneys, both of whom had left disillusioned. Of the thirteen former black employees interviewed by *The Montgomery Advertiser*, twelve complained of racial problems while at the SPLC, problems which ranged from a paternalistic attitude to racial slurs.(23)

The SPLC spends twice as much (1999 figures) on fundraising as it does on legal services for civil rights abuse "victims."(24) In a random survey of regular donors who contributed to the SPLC, *The Montgomery Advertiser* found most had no idea the Center was so wealthy. Indeed, the American Institute of Philanthropy estimates the SPLC could operate normally for almost five years without raising one additional tax-exempt penny from well-meaning donors!(25) Despite its affluence, the Center files relatively few lawsuits against "hate" groups, and those are generally high profile, moneymaking ones. Yet the SPLC continues to solicit contributions "aggressively and effectively." Reporters Morse and Jaffe report that "three nationwide organizations who monitor charities have criticized the Law Center for misleading donors and spending too little on programs."(26)

The rash of alleged Southern black church burnings in 1996 gave Morris Dees and the SPLC another opportunity to use supposed "hate" for profit. At the time he claimed that the burnings were the work of a conspiracy of Southern "white extremists" [the Klan and others of like mind]. But subsequent investigation by a Federal commission found no conspiracy; in fact, most of the burnings had nothing to do with "white extremists" at all. *The Charlotte Observer* concluded Dees and the SPLC had "misinformed the media."(27) Reporter Andrea Stone in *USA Today* admitted "... some black civil rights leaders ... say Dees raises millions by exaggerating the threat of hate groups. For instance, in a recent report on arsons at black churches in the South, his ... newsletter included five 1990 fires in Kentucky. The article doesn't mention they were set by a black man."(28) No wonder another Dees associate, Stephen Bight of the Southern Center for Human Rights, said of Dees, "[he] is a fraud who has milked a lot of very wonderful well-intentioned people. If it's got headlines, Morris is there."(29)

Over the years Morris Dees and the SPLC have searched diligently for "hate groups" to expose and then use in fundraising schemes. Many of the targeted groups are not "hate groups" at all; some exist only on paper or only consist of a handfull of members. That hasn't stopped the SPLC. Soon after the infamous Oklahoma City bombing by Timothy McVeigh, the SPLC mailed out a solicitation linking McVeigh to "militia groups." In the best traditions of "yellow journalism" the SPLC screamed that the "militia movement" counted perhaps 40,000 members, mostly armed, and a majority linked to the Klan.(30) But subsequently Federal investigators found no connection between McVeigh and any militia group. Indeed, researcher Laird Wilcox estimated that members in such groups numbered only around 7,000, and most of them were not focused on race or violence, but on constitutional issues.(31) An FBI spokesman added his agency did not regard the militia movement as a danger.(32)

More recently the SPLC claimed Ohio had become a hotbed for rightwing "hate" groups. It listed forty such groups in the state, while a similar organization, the Center for New Community, declared seventy-three "hate" groups had set up shop in the Buckeye State. David Martin, an investigative reporter for the *Cleveland Scene*, checked those claims and found them woefully exaggerated and disingenuous. Instead of the "haven for hate" claimed by the SPLC, Martin found most of the cited groups were marginal, minuscule, and practically non-existent. One of the "groups" listed was a ninety-year-old sight-impaired man who had once published a newsletter.(33) Asked about the prevalence of such groups in the state, Ted Almay, superintendent of the Ohio Bureau of Criminal Identification and Investigation, replied: "I don't think there are 73 people in Ohio, let alone 73 groups" that fit that definition.(34) But don't ask the SPLC to tell the real story when a money-raising exaggeration will do.

One method the SPLC uses to spread its "anti-hate" message is its highly advertised "Teaching Tolerance" educational kit for schools and parent groups. Featuring a curriculum suitable for all levels in the classroom, "Teaching Tolerance" is touted as a $325 value "absolutely free to any school on request"— but for the taker, only "at cost"— that is, $30 a kit.(35) Instructional materials for teachers train them on how to completely remold — perhaps the word should be "brainwash"— their students by combating "hate" speech, various stereotypes, religious "bias," and so on. One element, titled appropriately "I Spy Sexism," encourages students to become "conditioned" to recognize "sexism, racism, classism, and homophobia" among their fellow classmates and denounce it and "do something." Another element encourages "creating a safe environment for gay and lesbian students." Traditional norms of behavior and traditional religion are attacked as intolerant and prejudiced. There is even a component titled "Writing for Change," that is aimed at fighting prejudice and discrimination by "deconstructing" the English language and the manner in which we write sentences — so as to avoid "hierarchy" and "avoid assumptions based on factors like age and race." Students are exhorted to explore "the impact of homophobia and heterosexism" in writing, while encouraged to become aware of "perceptions of diversity."(36) "Teaching Tolerance" is a supreme example of the SPLC raising hundreds of thousands of dollars from well-intentioned educators and parents while spreading cultural Marxism to thousands of America's schoolrooms.

For years the SPLC has offered propaganda and programs to train law enforcement to recognize and deal with "hate groups." Recently, the SPLC, in collaboration with Auburn University-Montgomery and the Federal Law Enforcement Training Center (FLETC) launched an online "hate-crime" training course. The course, "Introduction to Hate and Bias Crimes," offers law enforcement officials college credit and continuing education credits, as well as official FLETC recognition. For a mere $118 (with the SPLC providing scholarships of up to 50 perceent of the cost), qualified law enforcement personnel can enroll in the online semester course.(37) No doubt the officers will be "sensitized" appropriately through the ministrations of Dees and company.

The SPLC is a self-proclaimed defender of civil rights and "watchdog" against "hate" and "extremism," but what strikes many observers as curious is just about all of the group's enemies are on the political right wing. And, indeed, as the list of tried and true familiar targets — the Klan (now practically moribund), Aryan Nations (similarly almost non-existent), and various skinhead groups — becomes less and less credible, the SPLC has widened its reach and attempted to tie in conservative groups like the Council of Conservative Citizens and the

League of the South: these groups and others like them have become the "new" Klans, grist for the SPLC's direct-mail solicitations! Legitimate and mainstream questions such as immigration policy, English as our national language, gay rights, abortion, and "multiculturalism" now figure in SPLC Intelligence Reports as criteria for determining if someone or some group is "extreme" or "racist" or not.(38)

Ominously, the SPLC has also begun to aim its judicial venom at orthodox Christians. In a letter dated July 16, 2002, Dees outlined to a representative of the Americans United for Separation of Church and State a legal strategy to attack and defame Judge Roy Moore, the famous Alabama judge who placed a Ten Commandments monument in the halls of the Alabama State Supreme Court. In his comments Dees details a plan to portray Judge Moors as a "bigot" and a "lone religious nut in partnership with a fanatical church [Dr. D. James Kennedy and the Presbyterian Church in America!]. This is the story that will make this case so dirty that no appeals court will reverse [it]...."(39)

Interestingly enough, although numerous left-wing organizations promote class hatred and racial antagonism, such groups normally don't appear on the SPLC's web site as "hate" groups. The SPLC even endorses the work of some extreme left-wing organizations, terming them "human rights" groups. Researcher Laird Wilcox gives examples of two such radical left groups, the Center for Democratic Renewal of Atlanta and the Political Research Associates of Somerville, Massachusetts, both of which have had identifiable and long-time Marxist connections.(40)

Even more disturbing perhaps are some of the SPLC's legal tactics. The Center has long been notorious for suing (and bankrupting) an entire organization for the actions of a lone, individual member or members. Its lawsuits against Aryan Nations, the United Klans of America, and the Tom Metzger organization fall into that category. Such practices — termed legally "vicarious liability" — should cause serious alarm with civil libertarians, as Ken Silverstein recounts in *Harper's*. The SPLC is also notorious for spying and preparing dossiers on private citizens who are supposedly "linked" to "hate" groups and then sharing its "files" on these "hate-mongers" with law enforcement agencies and a receptive news media.(41) Favorite SPLC "spokesmen" such as publications editor Mark Potok show up repeatedly in print and on the air to offer "comment" on individuals and groups named on the SPLC's laundry list of "hate" organizations. In many cases, such comments are taken as gospel and there is little opportunity to rebut the criticism once uttered. Once the charge is made, it is difficult to explain or counter the (mis-) information.

The SPLC skillfully employs what can be termed "linkism." The tactic of "linkism" is simple: publish a list of individual members of one organization, indicate their personal memberships (even if long expired or only nominal) in other organizations, identify these other organizations as "hate" groups, and, voila, the first organization becomes, *ipso facto*, a "hate" organization as well. In other words, targeted individuals are guilty by association. How is this different from the worst excesses of McCarthyism?

Recently the SPLC has begun to direct these tactics against the Sons of Confederate Veterans. Certain prominent members of the organization have been targeted — placed between the crosshairs would better describe it. Dossiers have obviously been prepared, shaped accordingly with the "facts" carefully skewed to place the members in the worst possible light. Negative and unflattering "exposés" are next published in the SPLC's *Intelligence Report* and then "picked up" by an amenable (or willingly collaborative) press. In its Summer 2000 issue, the *Intelligence Report* published two major attack articles, both implying that the SCV was being taken over by what it termed "neo-Confederates": "A neo-Confederate movement, increasingly rife with white supremacists and racist ideology," it cries, "is growing across America."(42) Both the SCV and the United Daughters of the Confederacy (UDC) were being transformed into "white supremacist" groups in contradistinction to what the SPLC defines as their historic purpose of being "interested only in Civil War remembrance."(43) The SPLC apparently has not read General Stephen D. Lee's charge to the Sons, or perhaps it doesn't understand that the SCV defends the honor of its Confederate ancestors not just by "remembering them," but by advancing the constitutional principles and heritage they advanced one hundred and forty years ago. Apparently any attempt by the SCV or UDC to defend Confederate heritage, to defend the flying of the Battle Flag, to intervene on behalf of the rights of students' free speech, or to use the constitutionally guaranteed avenues of legal litigation to defend these rights is "racist" or "hate speech" in the eyes of the SPLC.

In the Spring 2002 issue of *Intelligence Report* the Center listed dozens of SCV officers whom it claimed belonged to what were "listed by the SPLC as hate groups."(44) Then, during the Summer of 2002 the SPLC's Mark Potok appeared on *CBS Evening News*, right before the SCV's national convention in Memphis, Tennessee, to offer negative comments on the "direction" of the SCV. Shortly thereafter, attack articles showed up in the pages of a leftwing weekly in North Carolina, *The Independent*, and then in the pages of the more established *News and Observer* (Raleigh, NC) — on each occasion to slander and denigrate SCV members and the organization as a whole.(45) The tactics of guilt by association and "linkism" were clearly in evidence. The SCV had now become a primary target of Morris Dees and the SPLC.

Unlike the SPLC's negative characterization, the Sons of Confederate Veterans is *NOT* an "extremist" or "racist" group. For more than one hundred years it has honored both the memory and the ideals of the Confederate soldier. But historical memory is *NOT* the SCV's only role; the SCV is NOT simply a "civil war roundtable" or "history club." The SCV, it is true, supports numerous educational and scholarship programs for students, is deeply involved in historic preservation activities, and supports historical awareness programs across the nation. But SCV members also love and will defend their precious patrimony, for their heritage is a rich and noble one which has been handed down to them from the hardy pioneers who settled at Jamestown, Port Royal, Bath Town, Savannah, New Orleans and St. Mary's, or who came down the Great Wagon Road to the fertile Carolina Piedmont.

On the Confederate States' national seal is the figure of a mounted President George Washington. Like their forbears of 1860-1861, the descendants of those reluctant warriors see themselves in a direct line from Washington, Madison, Jefferson, and so many others, defending the same principles and the same inherited cultural legacy. They want only to live those same principles and pass that heritage on to their children. They reject the vicious attacks of the SPLC and similar groups. And they ask fair-minded fellow citizens, news media and law enforcement officials examine the facts and review the abundant information about the primary source of those attacks: Morris Dees and his Southern Poverty Law Center.

NOTES:

(1) See the articles "Rebels with a Cause," *Intelligence Report* (Summer 2000); "The Neo-Confederates," *Intelligence Report* (Summer 2000); and "A House Divided," *Intelligence Report* (Spring 2000). *Intelligence Report* is the quarterly journal of the SPLC, and increasingly it has taken aim at the SCV.

(2) Millard Fuller. *Bokotola* (Chicago: Association Press/Follett Publishing Company, 1977), 3-4.

(3) Fuller. *Love in the Mortar Joints* (Chicago: Association Press/Follett Publishing Company, 1980), 41-42.
(4) Ibid., 47.
(5) John Edgerton, "Poverty Palace: How the Southern Poverty Law Center Got Rich Fighting the Klan," *The Progressive* (July 1988), 14-16.
(6) Ibid., 16.
(7) Mark Pinsky, "Reflections on Joan Little," *Columbia Journalism Review* (March/April 1976), 30-31.
(8) Ibid., 31.
(9) *Burlington Times News* (Burlington, NC), July 30, 1975. See also Edgerton, 16.
(10) Kelly Thornton, "Skinhead Reveals Betrayal of Movement Was All a Ploy," *San Diego Union-Tribune* (San Diego, CA.), August 25, 2001. The Anti-Defamation League places the Confederate Battle Flag (and the Celtic Cross) on its list of racist "hate" symbols. See "Hate On Display: A Visual Database of Extremist Symbols, Logos and Tattoos," at www.adl.org/hate_symbols/racist_confederate_flag.asp.
(11) Ibid. See also "Suing Hate Groups: What the Law Center Has Accomplished," *The Montgomery Advertiser* (Montgomery, AL.), February 15, 1994, and Southern Events, 7, 1.I.
(12) The appeals case is cited as Alabama Court of Civil Appeals CIV 2114 (1979), and can be found on the web at: www.zianet.com/wblase/endtimes/dees1.htm.
(13) Ken Silverstein, "The Church of Morris Dees: How the Southern Poverty Profits from Intolerance," *Harper's Magazine* (November 2000), 56.
(14) See American Institute of Philanthropy, *AIP Charity Rating Guide and Watchdog Report* (Spring 1998) and subsequent issues.
(15) Cited by Ken Silverstein, 54.
(16) Ibid.
(17) See the detailed article on this case, Dan Morse, "Center Made Millions Selling the Donald Case," *The Montgomery Advertiser* (Montgomery, AL.), February 15, 1994.
(18) See Dan Morse and Greg Jaffe, "Rising Fortunes: Morris Dees and the Southern Poverty Law Center," *The Montgomery Advertiser*, February 13-15 1994. The series ran over a period of three days, beginning with a Sunday front page spread. Among the various stories in the series are Morse and Jaffe, "Charity of Riches," on February 13; Morse and Jaffe, "Critics Question $52 Million Reserve, Tactics of Wealthiest Civil Right Group," February 13; Jaffe, "Number of Charities Soars,

Overwhelming Regulators," February 13; "Center Refuses Access to Financial, Board Records," February 13; Morse, "Opportunist or Crusader?", February 14; Morse, "Morris Dees Trades Cookbook for Law Book," February 14; Morse and Jaffe, "Dees Angers Civil Rights Leaders," February 14; Morse, "Salesman Dees Prone to 'Lapse into Hyperbole,' Some Say," February 14; Morse, "Critics: Center Fighting Shadows," February 15; Morse, "Center Made Millions Selling the Donald Case," February 15; Morse, "Center's Klanwatch Tracks Rainbow of Hate Crimes," February 15; Morse and Jaffe, "Klan Focus Triggers Legal Staff Defections," February 15; and "Suing Hate Groups: What the Center has Accomplished," February 15.

(19) Morse and Jaffe, "Charity of Riches," *The Montgomery Advertiser*, February 13, 1994.

(20) Morse, "Opportunist or Crusader," *The Montgomery Advertiser*, February 14, 1994. Mullin continues: "He fools so many people; he seems so committed. But he's so dishonest…I never saw any examples of him doing something because he had a moral belief. He was simply doing things to see what he could get of them." (Morse, "Opportunist or Crusader," *The Montgomery Advertiser*, February 14.)

(21) Silverstein, 56. A full discussion of the resignations and disputes with Dees' direction can be found in Morse and Jaffe, "Klan Focus Triggers Legal Staff Defections," *The Montgomery Advertiser*, February 14, 1994.

(22) *The Birmingham News* (Birmingham, AL.), February 17, 1994.

(23) Morse and Jaffe, "Charity of Riches," *The Montgomery Advertiser*, February 13, 1994.

(24) Silverstein, 56.

(25) Silverstein, 56, and Morse and Jaffe, "Charity of Riches," *The Montgomery Advertiser*, February 13, 1994.

(26) Morse and Jaffe, "Charity of Riches," *The Montgomery Advertiser*, February 13, 1994.

(27) *The Charlotte Observer* (Charlotte, NC), October 10, 1996.

(28) Andrea Stone, "Morris Dees: At the Center of the Racial Storm," *USA Today*, August 3, 1996, A-7.

(29) Ibid.

(30) Dick Foster, "10 Militias at Home in Colorado," *Rocky Mountain News* (Denver, CO.), September 6, 1995.

(31) Laird Wilcox. "The Watchdogs: A Close Look at the Anti-Racist 'Watchdog' Groups" (Olathe, KS: Editorial Research Service), 53.

(32) David Bresnahan, "FBI Spy 'Fronts,'" 1999 WorldNetDaily, statement by Greg Rampton, FBI special agent in charge of the Denver office.
(33) David Martin, "White Power Outage," *Cleveland Scene* (Cleveland, OH), March 7, 2002.
(34) Cited in Martin, "White Power Outage."
(35) Silverstein, 55. See also the "Teaching Tolerance" web link on the SPLC web page.
(36) See "Writing for Change" link at www.tolerance.org/teach/expand/wfc/wfc_sctn1_4html.
(37) See the article "Center Launches Online Hate-Crime Training" in the Winter 2001 issue of the *Intelligence Report*; also see the link www.splcenter.org/intelligence project/ip-hatetraining.html.
(38) See the recent issues of the *Intelligence Report*, previously cited, and the "Teaching Tolerance" web link for a list of all the new sins that now figure as verboten.
(39) Quoted in "Southern Poverty Law Center Strategy to Destroy Judge Roy Moore," Press Release, September 24, 2002, by the Christian Coalition of Alabama (John W. Giles, press spokesman).
(40) Wilcox, 59-82.
(41) Silverstein, 56.
(42) See "Rebels with a Cause" and "The Neo-Confederates" in the *Intelligence Report* (Summer 2000).
(43) See the segments on the SCV and UDC in "The Neo-Confederates," *Intelligence Report* (Summer 2000).
(44) See "Hate in the Ranks," *Intelligence Report* (Spring 2002), which lists approximately forty SCV members who are cited as belonging to "hate" groups by the SPLC.
(45) The *CBS Evening News* segment, "Eye on America," was aired on July 26, 2002. See Jon Elliston, "Dueling Rebs," *The Independent* (Durham, NC), August 21-27, 2002, 12-13, and various letters of response ("Back Talk," *The Independent*, August 28-September 3, 2002, and "Back Talk," *The Independent*, September 4-10, 2002). See Dan Gearino, "A Thin Gray Line, *The News and Observer* (Raleigh, NC), Sunday Journal, 1D-4D, and letter to the editor responses to the article in *The News and Observer*, August 28 and September 1, 2002.

(*Southern Mercury* magazine, July-August, 2003; vol. I, no. 1)

The Southern Poverty Law Center Expands its Tentacles…and is Still the "Merchant of Hate"
☙ *Chapter 8* ❧

I turn again to a subject which has been of interest to me now for fifteen years. As a good friend suggested, it was perhaps the one topic — and a long investigative essay I published on that topic in 2003 — which thrust me "over the Rubicon," politically, so to speak.

In the July/August issue that year of the (now defunct) *Southern Mercury* magazine, I had published "Merchants of Hate: Morris Dees, the Southern Poverty Law Center, and the Attack on Southern Heritage," a long and heavily-documented investigation of Morris Dees and his "anti-hate watchdog" organization, the Southern Poverty Law Center, headquartered in Montgomery, Alabama. In that researched study I used only sources from what I would call the "mainstream." Most especially I avoided references which might be construed as "right wing" or in any way ideological. Thus, major investigative articles in such journals as *Harper's* and *The Progressive*, as well as a multi-part series that appeared in *The Montgomery Advertiser* (Alabama) newspaper, formed the basis for my report. My study was then picked up and republished widely, showing up on the Georgia Heritage Council web site, in the pages of the traditionalist Catholic magazine *Culture Wars* (2008), and elsewhere. Copies were distributed widely (the late Sam Francis had 100,000 copies printed and sent out). I know for a fact Dees' operations were hurt by it.

But, when I write that I "passed over the Rubicon," I had little idea what kind of reaction my essay would provoke from the SPLC and various "hate-monitoring" groups on the far left of the American political spectrum. I was, in 2003, still somewhat naïve about the depth and ferocity of those forces advancing the progressivist agenda and narrative in the United States, and their unwillingness to abide any challenge or dissent.

Within a short time Dees' group, in response to my essay, had run a hatchet piece, titled "40 to Watch," listing forty designated major "hate-mongers" in the United States who were — to paraphrase his scribblers —"moving on up" in the recrudescence of "right wing hate" in America. I was on that list, and thus, I found myself (with a photo!) on a list with various American Nazis, skinheads, thugs and anarchists! Curiously, a representative of a group denominated "Skinheads of America" published a protest of my inclusion on the list: I had done nothing, committed no acts of "hate," they declared, to be "up there with them"!

That was bad enough, but what happened then was even more bizarre and surprising to me — after all, my previous activities in political matters had been mostly limited to working for Republican candidates, including chairing Pat Buchanan's 1992 presidential campaign in North Carolina. But I had also been associated with the traditionalist Catholic Society of St. Pius X, and had allowed my name to show up on advisory boards of the old *Southern Partisan* magazine, as well as a now-defunct journal which published controversial revisionist views about World War I and II. I had written for *Southern Partisan*, but most of my pieces were — I thought — innocuous enough (e.g., about Western actor Randolph Scott, an interview with historian Eugene Genovese, historical pieces on Nathaniel Macon and Robert Lewis Dabney, reviews of fiction by Russell Kirk, etc.). And on the world wars, revisionism, anti-semitism, and such questions, I had never published anything, nor participated in any way in the workings of that journal.

It did not matter. Now, every time I attempted to publish anything in a "conservative" outlet or when my name came up for a professional position, the "40 to Watch" SPLC hatchet job surfaced as well, like a dark, unwanted albatross. Even the local newspaper, The *News & Observer*, got into the act with a short article (I refused to talk with them). And most recently, in 2016 it was a "conservative"[!] publication, *The Daily Caller*, in a short piece on a "Scholars for Trump" group in which I was involved, which trotted out the same old SPLC attacks. [I suspect that had more to do with the fact I am pro-Confederate, and *The Daily Caller* is part and parcel of the Neoconservative establishment that increasingly hates Confederate heritage.]

I've grown used to the leftist assaults and hyperbole. And I can say truthfully that I have lost not one real friend because of it.

But in recent months, particularly with the election of Donald Trump as president, the wild mudslinging, promoted half-truths, vicious character assassinations, and personal defamation by the SPLC have greatly expanded. Today it is not just Southern heritage groups and the Sons of Confederate Veterans, right wing Catholics, historical revisionists, and those mixed-in, more unsavory types that are in the cross hairs of the SPLC. The organization — always and foremost a giant "money mill" for coaxing the last few dollars out of the pockets of leftist widow ladies in Boston or San Francisco in the name of "fighting hate"— now has set its sights on "establishment" conservatives as well: *National Review,* Alliance Defending Freedom, any group which opposes open borders immigration or same sex marriage, and President Trump, himself. And that has brought a response — critical pieces in such paragons of the establishment as the *Wall Street Journal.*

One must wonder where those conservative establishment figures were years ago when folks like me were being mercilessly slandered?

Those newly-aggrieved establishmentarians spin their own reasoning: For them the SPLC, "formerly did a good job of monitoring hate groups like the Klan and Aryan Nations, but has now has 'lost its way,' and strayed from its 'original mission,'" of fighting "hate." Such an explanation, such a tepid defense, would be laughable if it were not uttered so seriously and worriedly by such *National Review* hacks as David French.

Like the fevered and unhinged assaults of the Deep State, now more hysterical and more visible and vocal than ever, the SPLC is only following suit. As the Mainstream Media has treated us to accusations of Donald Trump and his followers' anti-semitism, Hitlerism, racism, sexism, and worse, the SPLC must keep pace. And so, dozens and dozens of "new" instances of right wing "hate" are hatched, calculated and spewed forth monthly, in an ever-expanding gambit which includes everything and anyone who even half-heartedly or only nominally opposes the cultural Marxist agenda. Criticize Black Lives Matter, even mildly, and you are a "racist;" oppose same sex marriage, and you are a "homophobe;" demur on women sharing men's bathrooms, and you are a "sexist;" advocate restrictions on illegal immigration or praise Western Christian heritage, and you are a "white nationalist." These, then, are the contemporary crimes, not just for the cultural Left but also for the SPLC. And even the weak and "respectful" questioning by establishment conservatives gets them thrust into the same roasting pot with those of us who have been there for years.

It couldn't happen to a more deserving bunch of guys!

(My Corner by Boyd Cathey, July 6, 2018, at: http://boydcatheyreviewofbooks.blogspot.com/2018/07/july-6-2018-my-corner-by-boyd-cathey.html)

Robert Lewis Dabney
and the Conservative Rout
↠ *Chapter 9* ↞

Back in 2008, the various Republican candidates for president unanimously stated their staunch opposition to same sex marriage. It was a given, or so it seemed. Indeed, even Barack Obama expressed his opposition in the run up to that general election, although one wondered at the time if such a stance were just a pose — apparently it was, as he quickly shed such opposition as it became politically expedient and his base seemed to demand it.

On abortion the GOP adopted a pro-life plank more than thirty-five years ago, while the Democratic Party began a not-so-slow transition to "choice" in the 1970s.

Over the past several years there has been a not inconsiderable movement among Republican and so-called "conservative" elites to soften, if not alter, their opposition to both abortion (e.g., most recently Scott Brown in New Hampshire's US senate race) and same sex marriage. It is no secret that a number of prominent neoconservatives have now "come out" in favor of same sex marriage.

As I wrote on September 5, 2014 at *The Unz Review*, "in recent years we have witnessed a growing parade of Republicans and so-called 'conservative' leaders announce their support for same sex marriage: both Laura and Barbara Bush, Dick Cheney, Condoleeza Rice, Donald Rumsfeld, John Bolton, Jonah Goldberg, Senator Rob Portman, just to mention a few. And in 2013, George W. Bush declared 'that straight people should not cast the first stone when it comes to judging gay couples'. [Timothy Stanley, *Citizen Hollywood*, 2014, p. 225]" And I seem to remember both Barbara and George H. W. were honored guests at a lesbian wedding in Maine....

Now, hold that thought for just moment. Just recently the German Ethics Council, the official national commission set up by the German Bundestag to address moral and ethical issues in the German federation announced the legal prohibition preventing incest and sexual relations between siblings should be legislatively removed. As one news source reported it: "The 26 member German advisory council on ethics, which was created to advise the German government, voted earlier this week (by a two-to-one margin) to move towards the decriminalization of incest between consenting adults in Germany in response

The Land We Love

to a case in which a brother and sister in Saxony had four children together." The article does go on to say the majority Christian Democratic/Christian Social Party will no doubt reject this proposal. Christian Democratic spokesman Elisabeth Winkelmeier-Becker offered this response, "The abolition of the offense of incest between siblings would be the wrong signal."

"The wrong signal?" Indeed! And this tepid response represents the "opposition" of the German "conservatives."

One more strand of straw in the wind: *New York Magazine* recently published (September 7, 2014) a profile of transgender millionaire tycoon Martin Rothblatt in which the emphasis was that transgender equality and liberation was the next major civil rights issue in the US. Indeed, Rothblatt has published a manifesto applying the narrative of racial segregation and oppression to his own desire to become a lesbian, titled *The Apartheid of Sex*. And Rothblatt is not alone. In its May 29, 2014, issue *TIME* magazine ran a major piece by Katy Steinmetz heralding "The Transgender Tipping Point" as "America's next civil rights frontier."

Lest we think such chatter or events in faraway Germany have little chance of generating eventual legislation and social change here, just recall our grandparents' general rejection of divorce. The social and moral stigma once associated with it has virtually disappeared, both in European and American society, save for the seemingly forlorn opposition by traditional Catholics (and it's increasingly under attack among Catholics).

I attribute this conservative retreat and surrender to a fundamental belief in egalitarianism which prevails not only in the thinking of the Left but also on the dominant and now mainstream Neoconservative Right. Establishment Left and Mainstream Right may differ on means and specific programs and proposals, but in the end, despite the weak protestations of a John Boehner, Jonah Goldberg, or Charles Krauthammer, positing "egalitarianism" as the fundamental American principle "includes, implicitly, the eventual and logical normalization and acceptance of across-the-board sexual and gender equality."

Of course, this "*trahison des clercs*" and conservative self-redefinition is nothing new, certainly if the Lincolnian revolution and reinterpretation of the Declaration of Independence and the American Founding is accepted as dogma. In the 1950s Russell Kirk and a few others attempted to partially recover an older Constitutional (and Christian) tradition, and for a twenty year period Mel Bradford engaged in a scholarly debate with Harry Jaffa over Lincoln and the meaning of the Declaration. Most recently Colgate Professor Barry Shain, in his important work, *The Declaration of Independence in Historical Context*, convincingly demonstrates that document was never intended as an ideological and egalitarian road map for the new nation. But despite such cautionary evidence, the triumph of Neoconservatism as the intellectual brain trust for Republicans and the almost Stalinist whiting-out of any other kind of conservative/traditionalist view, has certainly had its effects.

Well more than a century ago, it was debate over women's suffrage which dominated much of the discussion concerning social issues. One of its foremost opponents was the great Southern writer and philosopher — and former chaplain to "Stonewall" Jackson — Robert Lewis Dabney. Elected a member of the Royal Philosophical Society and internationally known at the time for his writings, Dabney even in the 1890s enjoyed the reputation as perhaps the most intransigent opponent of the "idea of progress." But not only did he criticize progressivists, he also harshly critiqued "the failure of conservatism" to oppose egalitarian advances and conservatism's egalitarian misinterpretation of America's Founding.

Without re-starting the debate over suffrage, Dabney has much to say to our generation's conservatives. In words, both prescient and which might have been authored later by Russell Kirk, Dabney describes the conservative collapse:

"This is a party which never conserves anything. Its history has been that it demurs to each aggression of the progressive party, and aims to save its credit by a respectable amount of growling, but always acquiesces at last in the innovation. What was the resisted novelty of yesterday is today one of the accepted principles of conservatism; it is now conservative only in affecting to resist the next innovation, which will to-morrow be forced upon its timidity, and will be succeeded by some third revolution, to be denounced and then adopted in its turn. American conservatism is merely the shadow that follows Radicalism as it moves forward towards perdition. It remains behind it, but never retards it, and always advances near its leader. This pretended salt hath utterly lost its savor: wherewith shall it be salted? Its impotency is not hard, indeed, to explain. It is worthless because it is the conservatism of expediency only, and not of sturdy principle. It intends to risk nothing serious, for the sake of the truth, and has no idea of being guilty of the folly of martyrdom. It always—when

The Land We Love

about to enter a protest — very blandly informs the wild beast whose path it essays to stop, that its "bark is worse than its bite," and that it only means to save its manners by enacting its decent role of resistance. The only practical purpose which it now subserves in American politics is to give enough exercise to Radicalism to keep it "in wind," and to prevent its becoming pursy and lazy from having nothing to whip. No doubt, after a few years, when women's suffrage shall have become an accomplished fact, conservatism will tacitly admit it into its creed, and thenceforward plume itself upon its wise firmness in opposing with similar weapons the extreme of baby suffrage; and when that too shall have been won, it will be heard declaring that the integrity of the American Constitution requires at least the refusal of suffrage to asses. There it will assume, with great dignity, its final position." [from his essay,"Womens' Rights Women," published later in *Discussions* (1890-1897), C. R. Vaughan, edit., pp. 491-493]

Have we not reached that tipping point when all that basically remains for us is to valiantly refuse "civil rights" for asses?

(Communities Digital News, September 29, 2014, at: www.commdiginews.com/politics-2/forseen-and-predicted-the-conservative-rout-on-social-issues-26877/)

The Historical Folly of "Nothing but Race"
⇾ *Chapter 10* ⇽

At the base of most of the ongoing political debates currently raging in the United Sates there are always, it seems, deeper questions, more philosophical and more historical contexts that need to be examined — what I would call "legacy issues."

Oftentimes assumptions are made or are disseminated by many self-proclaimed defenders of our traditions — by those "conservative apologists"— that bear little relationship to historical reality, and, in fact, fatally weaken or blur our understanding of it.

Many of these assumptions relate specifically to the conscious creation by the present (neo) conservative movement of a utilizable past which both justifies their present practice and fends off criticism from the hard Left that somehow, because they claim to be "conservative" and presumably defenders of the Constitution and inherited traditions of the country, they partake in forms of "racism," as well as sexism, homophobia, and white supremacy.

Much of this is motivated by a politics of fear that, I would suggest, comes from the fact the modern conservative movement, dominated now intellectually as it is by those whose philosophical and fundamental origins are over on the Marxist and Trotskyite left, has never freed itself from the Progressivist historical narrative about racism (=bad) and egalitarianism (=good), and the inevitable "movement of history" (which is always to the Left). It is as if it possesses a guilty conscience and its spokesmen are constantly afraid of being "labeled" racist or some other term of opprobrium.

Thus, even though these so-called "conservatives" presume to offer opposition to the "further Left" narrative on various economic and political issues, they are equally possessed by what my friend Dr. Paul Gottfried terms, rightly, a "politics of guilt," a social sin which they must continually and defensively expiate. And thus, the rather constant, at times frantic, self-justification and strenuous efforts by (neo) conservatives to distinguish themselves from any form or type of perceived "racism." And, concurrently, their efforts to paint the modern-day Democratic Party with the brush of the odious "historically racist" Democratic Party, and to emphasize the fact that fifty years ago "it was the — mostly Southern — segregationist Democrats who opposed the Voting Rights and Civil Rights Bills." Then follows a long litany of, again, mostly Southern Democratic political leaders and statesmen — including Senators Harry Byrd (and Robert Byrd), Richard Russell, and Sam Ervin — which is trotted out to "prove" the Democratic Party just a couple of generations ago was the "racist" party, the party that coddled segregationists ... and, yes, that "racist demagogue George Wallace!" Thank goodness, they then add, "we don't have that legacy!" (Think here, most notably, of the efforts of Dinesh D'Souza, Jonah Goldberg, or Sean Hannity.)

The underlying assumption here is that it has been the Democrats who incarnate historically the evils of racism, sexism, homophobia, and white supremacy — and in some ways, still do — while the clean-as-the-driven-snow Republicans (and [neo] conservatives) have championed equality, opposed racism, supported the Civil rights legislation of the 1950s and 1960s ... and, by the way, Martin Luther King Jr, was actually one of them, a dyed-in-the-wool "conservative!"

This narrative in many respects is fraudulent, does serious damage to the understanding of our history, and can be reduced to a form of rather crass political legerdemain, anchored as it is in an acceptance of the Progressivist historical vision. It enables Republican political gurus such as Karl Rove to embrace the neo-Reconstructionist and Marxist posturing of viciously anti-Southern historian Eric Foner, or Sean Hannity to tie in West Virginia's late US Senator Robert Byrd — who had many years before been a member of the Ku Klux Klan — to Hillary Clinton, or connect Arkansas's Senator J. William Fulbright to Bill Clinton.

It fails to comprehend dramatic historical change and the evolution of political parties. For much of this nation's history it was, indeed, the Democratic Party which was most representative of a traditional, Jeffersonian "conservatism." The Republican Party, founded in the 1850s, not only lacked that essential connection to and understanding of America's Founding, but in its war-time president, Abraham Lincoln, and succeeding GOP presidents in the second half of the 19th century, incarnated a vision of the American republic that, I would argue, was in many respects contrary to the vision of the Founders. An examination of Lincoln's views — on statecraft and the powers of the presidency, on the relationship of the various states to the Federal executive, on his faith in unchained financial capitalism, and, indeed, on his view of the Constitution, itself, offer ample confirmation of this.

Obviously, political parties and political thinking don't remain static. And, especially in the 1930s and beyond, the Democratic Party underwent a transformation. We should not forget when Franklin Roosevelt ran for president in 1932, his platform was actually, in many ways, more conservative than that of Republican President Herbert Hoover. Only after he entered office did he radically change his praxis.

At first, traditional states' rights conservatives (e.g., leaders like the Virginia Byrds, and North Carolina's Josiah Bailey and Sam Ervin) and the more leftwing New Dealers co-existed within "the Democracy," if uneasily, up through the 1950s. As numerous historians have detailed, the civil rights legislation of the 1960s certainly figured in what would become "the Southern strategy" of inviting disaffected white Southern voters — part of Nixon's "silent majority"— into the Republican Party.

Yet it would be a major mistake to see "race" as the only causative factor in this process. Indeed, although racial issues certainly existed, larger questions of social, economic and cultural dislocation, the break-up of community, and, above all, the legitimate, well-grounded fear of the loss of local and individual liberties as the Federal government assumed more power and more direct authority over how individuals and families ran their own lives, figured, if not so visibly, even more significantly.

I recall a friend of my father, a well-established farmer and one-time state legislator (the late Democratic State Senator Julian Allsbrook of Halifax County) telling me back in 1968, "I can deal with black folks voting — I will get their votes; but I cannot tolerate in any way the Federal government assuming direct control over practically every aspect of our social and political lives, and making us the new slaves!" I think the good senator's views reflected quite well those of his fellow Tar Heels.

Making "race" and "racial issues" the only points of discussion — the only determinants for action and reaction — in our history, something that both the Left and the pseudo-conservative Neocons do, leaves out too much that is essential to understanding our complex past.

This first became apparent to me when as a young Jefferson Fellow grad student at the University of Virginia I did research for my MA on the North Carolina Constitutional Convention of 1835 (and conventions in other Southern states). Given the recent (1831) Nat Turner slave rebellion in Virginia, I expected to find a concentration on slavery and the need to defend at all cost "the peculiar institution." But, rather, I discovered free blacks with property freeholds had voted in North Carolina prior to that year (and since the Revolution), and during the lengthy convention debates most of the state's prominent conservatives — both Democrats and Whigs — defended the suffrage of propertied free blacks. Such notables as state Chief Justice William Gaston, Judge Joseph Daniel, and Secretary of the Navy John Branch under President Jackson, all opposed the change. For these leaders, the issue was not so much about race as it was about class and whether a male elector had the property qualification — and thus the stability, and social and economic status within the community — to exercise the franchise.

There were, of course, a few voices who in their interventions mentioned the Turner rebellion, but remarkably, those views were not overpowering and did not reflect the "white fear" I had been taught by some of my professors to find. In not one recorded peroration did I detect anything approaching the kind of severe racial animus we are supposed to discover in the minds and voices of our antebellum ancestors. Even though the convention finally very narrowly voted to eliminate free black suffrage, it is revealing that even at that date, fifteen years after the Missouri Compromise, it was, in a sense, class, social position, and property that still dominated much of the thinking of the dominant political leadership of North Carolina, not race.

Since then, in reading about secession and about slavery as the "cause" of the War Between the States, about the "strange career of Jim Crow," about the history of the nation's two major political parties, and then the essentially ideological uses to which the fractured and tendentious template of race — and slavery —has been put, it is apparent such an approach is fraught with problems. Historians such as Thomas DiLorenzo, Clyde Wilson, Charles Adams, David Gordon, and others have highlighted how the ideological use of such "devil terms" as "race" and "racism" has resulted in a warped view of our past.

Underlying the current "conservative" movement's anxiety — the fear that Republicans and Neocons have — about being labeled "racists," then, is the acceptance of the debatable historical "fact" that America is all about race and that nothing else really matters, that severe economic factors, dramatic social and cultural changes, all flow from that single determining issue.

No; give me any day the wisdom, intelligence, devotion to the Constitution — and delightful Southern humor — of a true conservative Democrat, "Senator Sam" Ervin, over the Progressivism and globalist fanaticism of a Republican Lindsey Graham and Jeff Flake, or Neocon Bill Kristol.

That latter narrative I am not prepared, philosophically or historically, to accept.

(Abbeville Institute, September 20, 2017, at: www.abbevilleinstitute.org/blog/the-historical-folly-of-nothing-but-race/)

Secession and Catalonia: What Is a Nation?
⇾ Chapter 11 ⇽

In recent months, especially with the accession to the presidency of Donald Trump, there has been renewed talk, serious talk, ironic talk, about secession — particularly, from zealously Leftist anti-Trump militants in California and along the Pacific Rim areas of the United States. Advocates of what is called "Cal-exit" make their case that California, specifically, is not like other states and regions of the United States. Its population is increasingly non-Anglo and Hispanic — its politics, at least along the littoral areas, is dominated largely by far left-wingers — and its culture is more influenced by Silicon Valley, Hollywood, Mexico and various leftist totems. It voted by a heavy majority for Hillary.

Yet, far inland areas, mountainous regions of the state, populated by descendants of the rugged gold seekers, the Forty-Niners of 1848-1849, remain conservative. So, the question of secession of California from the Federal union might also need to be addressed on an intra-state level as well: should some strongly conservative districts be permitted to secede from California, itself, if the state should leave the union? What unity would they have with a new "Democratic Socialist Republic of California?"

It becomes complicated. If the question of secession — and not just secession of, as in the case of California, but of any entity — really be examined, then wide variations in culture, history, ethnicity, economics and politics should be considered, taken into consideration.

While secession can be a viable and satisfactory solution to insoluble national problems, it is not always in every case advisable. There may be good reasons for a region, or a state, or a province to depart from a larger entity. I would argue strongly the painful decision by the Southern states of the United States to secede from the American union in 1860-1861 was largely justified on historical, cultural and economic reasons, not to mention the politics involved.

Actually, the departures of those eleven states (or, actually, thirteen if you count the illegally thwarted departures of Kentucky and Missouri) came in two waves: the first began with South Carolina and continued with the exit of several Deep South states. Lincoln's call in April 1861 for troops to suppress South Carolina shocked the constitutional sensibilities of additional states in the Upper South, several of which had resisted the initial impulse to join the secession. And by early summer the Confederate States of America was a functioning nation, albeit a country facing invasion from its powerful former co-citizens.

But, I can think of instances when secession — that is, the break-up of larger nations or empires — is not only inadvisable, but positively injurious not only to the whole, but also to the respective seceding parts. The dissolution of the old Austria-Hungarian Empire in 1918, for instance, was not only a tragic mistake geopolitically, but made little sense economically, ethnically or historically. What was produced by the Treaties of Saint-Germain and Trianon was a succession of angrily dissatisfied, uber-nationalist states and displaced ethnic minorities imprisoned in new, arbitrary and irrational geographical expressions, waiting for the next powder keg to explode.

Interestingly, it was the heir to the wizened old Kaiser, Franz Josef, the Archduke Franz Ferdinand, who advocated additional decentralization of the old empire, with a third, Slavic kingdom, to join Austria and Hungary in a tripartite monarchy. That he and his wife, Sophie, were cruelly assassinated in Sarajevo in July 1914 by a Serbian nationalist, not only put into motion the coming of the First World War, but stymied what might have been a revitalized, regionalist future for the creaky old Habsburg Empire.

The castration of the ancient Russian homeland more recently is another case of good (American) intentions gone awry: the creation of new artificial states such as Byelorussia and Kazakhstan was not only historically and politically wrongheaded, but economically ill-advised. President Vladimir Putin's statement — rightly understood — that the break-up of the Soviet Union was one of the greatest disasters of the 20th century was intended in this sense (and not, as some Russophobic Neoconservative attempt to construe it, as a lament for Communism!).

Talking to a friend recently, I expressed some serious skepticism about the recent plebiscite in Catalonia on the question of secession from Spain. My friend, knowing of my longstanding defense of secession historically when it concerns the South, was surprised. I attempted in a very brief discussion to explain why I demurred in the Catalan case, but the conversation was cut short.

What I would suggest is the simple slogan that secession is always good policy is not really defensible, historically, culturally, economically, ethnically, or politically.

In the case of Catalonia, my arguments against secession are multiple, and range from the very practical and statistical, to the historical and cultural.

Let's start with the historical and cultural. Basically, the medieval County of Barcelona was united personally under the crown of Aragon in the mid-12th century. The *de facto* dynastic union of Aragon and Catalonia (the King of Aragon ruled as Count of Barcelona) became a *de jure* one, a legal one, in 1258. Thus, for eight centuries the region has been united with what essentially were Spanish crown lands. While the Catalan language, which while distinct from Spanish, is also similar to it, remained the *lingua franca* of rural areas, Castilian Spanish began to be spoken in more urban areas. But like the other kingdoms and principalities which came together to create Spain, Catalonia retained many of its customs, and regional and historic rights, within the new Spanish monarchy.

Historically, Spain was a composite, a dynastic federation and union of the ancient kingdoms of Castile and Leon, Aragon, Valencia, and then, the Kingdom of Navarra and the Basque territories in the north of the country, plus the formerly Muslim Kingdom of Granada in the South. Indeed, even at the time of the great monarch, Philip II — supposedly, according to Anglophile and Protestant propagandists of the 16th century, that all-powerful authoritarian monarch of the early modern era — Spain was known as "las Espanas," that is, "the Spains," to indicate that King Philip was not actually the absolute king of a unitary, centralized royal state, but rather the monarch over a collection of fiercely regionalist states, each with its own traditions, history and parliaments (or "cortes"), but all together composing a country. Philip was dependent on them for financing his government. Each of those regions, those ancient components, of Spain had legal codes ("recopilaciones de leyes") which guided jurisprudence; those historic and regional rights were called "fueros," which we would render in English to mean "states' rights." Eventually portions of those statutes and legislated customs were cobbled together in a common law for the entire country. Nevertheless, the historic regions jealously guarded their respective traditions, languages, customs and fueros, and continued to do so throughout the remainder of Habsburg Spain into the early 19th century.

Not only because of the dynastic question, but precisely over those fueros much of Spain underwent a series of bloody civil wars in the 19th century. And what many foreigners find ironic and incomprehensible is it was the so-called royalist "absolutistas," the defenders of the ancient regime and the old monarchy, the traditionalists who took the name "Carlists" after the dispossessed rightful heir to the throne, Don Carlos V ("de jure" king of "las Espanas") in 1833, who actually defended the historic regionalism and subsidiarity of the old regime. For them it was a powerful king who ruled from Madrid, but who was also limited in his powers by the historic, unbridgeable rights of the "kingdoms" that made up the country, which guaranteed more essential and more local liberties to the citizens. Like the martyred King Charles I of England, who declared at his illegal trial that he was more the defender of the "rights of the good people of England" than the rump parliamentarians, the traditional monarchs in Spain, with the legacy of the patchwork of historic states and their sacralized customs and legal "recopilaciones," offered far more self-government, far more "liberties" than any centralizing liberal state could or ever would.

During those several civil wars in the 19th century, Catalonia stood, by and large, with the traditionalist defenders of the ancient regime, the Carlists. It was the Carlists who defended the fueros and who advocated the return of a strong king who actually had power, but whose powers were also circumscribed by the historic regions and traditions of the country. It was the Carlists — and some of their most perceptive political philosophers (e.g., Jaime Balmes, Francisco Navarro Villoslada, Juan Vazquez de Mella) — who understood 19th century liberalism, despite its slogan of "liberty and equality," would actually do away with and suppress those old regionalist statutes and protections, those intermediate institutions in society, that secured more liberties for the citizens.

Only 40 percent of the eligible voters in Catalonia participated in the recent plebiscite on possible independence; of those around 90 percent voted "Si." But that means approximately around 30 percent of the electorate truly favors independence. And those political groups who most zealously support such a move are on the Left politically. They see the region, which is the most economically successful area of Spain and the most "Europeanized," as able to get a better deal economically within the European Union. They welcome globalism and a unitary European government with themselves also at the helm sharing power.

Of course, it is always good to hit the bloated central government in Madrid in the eye, but at what price?

The present-day proponents of independence do not represent the ancient and best traditions and historic legacy of Catalonia. Their advocacy of Catalan independence is not a comfortable fit with the long history of that region. The nationalism they advance owes far more to the liberal statism of the 19th century than to the Catalan heritage of local and regional self-rule. Catalonia is not a nation-waiting-to-be-born; its association as one of the integral and historic, largely autonomous regions within Spain is its tradition. Catalonia can best find its destiny in reasserting its role as a largely self-governing region — but within the historic federation of the Spanish kingdom.

(*The Unz Review*, October 10, 2017, at: www.unz.com/article/secession-and-catalonia-what-is-a-nation/)

PART II

DEFENDING OUR SYMBOLS AND OUR MONUMENTS

The eleven essays in this section include the following items: "A Letter from North Carolina," "Was Lee a Traitor?," "New Orleans: A People without A Past Have No Future," "Taking Down Our Monuments is Part of the Marxist Campaign to Transform America," "Defending the Monuments: The North Carolina Case," "Our Monuments: A Battle for Western Civilization and the South," "'Silent Sam' and the Disaster Known as Public Education," "Thoughts on Charlottesville and What It Means for Us," "Charlottesville – One Year Later," "Celebrating Lee Day, While Thousands of Women Go Marching Off to Hell," and "Those Leftist Crazies Want to Kill You If You Have a Confederate License Plate."

In these essays I take aim at the attacks on the symbols of Southern and Confederate heritage, on the assaults on the very public visibility of our past and its continuance in our memory and thinking. There is, it goes without saying, a multilevel and unrelenting effort nationally to remove, to take down, even destroy those monuments erected more than a century ago to commemorate and memorialize those veterans of 1861-1865, who were then passing quickly from the scene, just as their one-time opponents were north of the Mason-Dixon Line. Monuments, flags, and markers, we are told, must be taken down; textbooks, film and entertainment must be cleansed; and our culture must be remade: in short, nearly 160 years of history as symbolized by these visible reminders must be completely erased and reinterpreted. And that reinterpretation, born of a strain of radicalized thought termed "cultural Marxism" is both zealous and fanatically dedicated to its objectives.

The essays "Our Monuments: A Battle for Western Civilization and the South" and " 'Silent Sam' and the Disaster Known as Public Education" bring up to date the previous essay, "Defending the Monuments: The North Carolina Case," regarding the critical issue of Confederate symbols on public property in North Carolina, their legal status, the physical attacks launched on them, and prospects for their future. The item "Charlottesville – One Year Later" updates the earlier piece on the riots in Mr. Jefferson's city, "Thoughts on Charlottesville and What It Means for Us."

The following items examine specific instances and examples of these attacks.

A Letter from North Carolina
↷ Chapter 12 ↶

As residents here in the Tar Heel State know, the boards of several of the state's public universities have in recent weeks engaged in a high-profile campaign to change the names of historic and iconic buildings and landmarks on various campuses. First, the board of trustees of East Carolina University in Greenville decided to remove the name of Governor Charles B. Aycock (1901-1905) from an historic residence hall on that campus. His crime? He ran for governor on a segregationist, "Red Shirt" platform, even though he did more for black education than any governor in this state's history. Additional negative measures regarding Aycock are being seriously contemplated at UNC-Greensboro and Duke.

Most recently the board of trustees of the University of North Carolina at Chapel Hill has voted to change the name of Saunders Hall on that campus to "Carolina Hall." A small, noisy group of activists had pushed for something even more radical, say, naming the building after a "Civil Rights" leader. But the trustees, those profiles in courage, finally announced what they called a "compromise."

Colonel William Saunders, you see, was a reputed leader of the post-War Between the States Ku Klux Klan in the Tar Heel State (1869). I say "reputed," because the evidence asserted by early 20th century historian, J. D. deRoulhac Hamilton, is not conclusive, as Dr. H. G. Jones, former State Archivist of North Carolina, implies in an article in the NCpedia. Even if he were a member, the Klan in North Carolina quickly dissolved. (I seem to recall the late Senator Robert Byrd and Justice Hugo Black had been Klan members.) After that Saunders became one of the state's leading and most respected educators, compiling and editing the mammoth "Colonial Records" project which is still used by scholars for research into North Carolina history. And he served commendably as a trustee of the university and a champion of public education for all Tar Heels.

Of course, it should surprise no one these trustee boards are now dominated by Republicans, appointed by our self-styled "business Republican" governor, Pat McCrory, former mayor of Charlotte and the archetypal Chamber of Commerce, country club executive, who sees everything, including our history and our culture, through a prism of the almighty dollar ... and who, when confronted by the Cultural

Marxist "mouse that roars" here in the Tar Heel State, jumps back in abject fear and cries: "Jump? Just tell me how high!!"

Just a couple of years ago my old employer, the North Carolina Department of Cultural Resources, through its Historic Sites Division and with the support of all of his professional historians, approved the hanging of an historic Confederate Battle Flag in the hallowed old House of Representatives chamber (1840) as part of the War Between the States Sesquicentennial. McCrory, after receiving an ominous threat from the ubiquitous leader of the state NAACP, the Reverend William Barber, ordered — over the head of his own appointee and DCR cabinet secretary who had previously approved the display— that the flag be removed. And this came despite the fact placing the flag in the House chamber was based on the exact historical record and contemporary photographs, plus the approval of the on-staff historians (none of them ideological conservatives), who understood this was a recreation of an historical event, an attempt to replicate a specific moment in North Carolina's past, and not an incitement to any kind of racialism!

That did not matter to McCrory, who acted with alacrity — within just three or four hours — to have the flag removed and consigned behind closed doors in a museum.

And now the Republican-dominated board of trustees for UNC at Chapel Hill has, it seems, taken its marching orders from the McCrory-style Republicans. Bowing to a small, vocal group of Cultural Marxists, both professors and students, they have decided to remove the hateful "Saunders Hall" name and replace it with "Carolina Hall," which, in their broad-church approach they hope will please just about everyone! So much for these Chamber of Commerce Republicans.

All of which brings up a number of questions about historical memory, the uses (and abuses) of history, and the ongoing effort by Cultural Marxists to erase those portions of our history which do not please them and do not suit their ideological template. This kind of rewriting and erasure of history is reminiscent of, and, by leagues, worse than what occurred in the old Soviet Union; it represents a kind of symbolic totalitarianism which seeks to obliterate any symbol that indicates a different historical narrative than the one they are propagating.

Interestingly, this approach is enthusiastically bought into by many of those who supposedly claim to defend our heritage and traditions. After all, the national GOP political guru and George W. Bush advisor, Karl Rove, touts the Cultural Marxist South-hating writer, Eric Foner, as one of his favorite historians (recall that the late Professor Eugene Genovese wrote a scathing essay attacking Foner — a defender of Stalinism — asking "what did you know and when did you know it?" about Stalin's purges and genocidal campaigns). And the Neoconservative establishment has now canonized Martin Luther King and Abraham Lincoln as America's two untouchable secular saints, while condemning Robert E. Lee, John C. Calhoun, and Thomas Jefferson to the outer reaches of non-personhood.

The Neoconservative establishment, whether ensconced in their talking perches at Fox News, on the editorial pages of *The Wall Street Journal*, or in the articles of *National Review* or *The Weekly Standard*, partake of the same foundational principles and zealotry of the cultural left, across the board egalitarianism, liberal democracy, and a fanatical zeal for the global destruction of traditional societies. Their intellectual and spiritual godfather is the internationalist Marxist, Leon Trotsky, via his descendants, Norman Podhoretz and Irving Kristol, and their progeny who dominate Fox News (e.g., Charles Krauthammer, Jonah Goldberg, and Irving's son, Bill).

They despise the Old South and anything that smacks of an older constitutionalism and traditional conception of society. They join the fanatical Cultural Marxists, in fact, in the attempt to "cleanse and purify" society and our history of any uncomfortable artifact which reminds us of who we were as a people, of our essential founding. Certainly, at times they take a different route and express opposition to the hard left on a few issues (e.g. Obamacare), but in the end, they cave and go along. And they must do so, as their essential principles can lead them no place else.

This, then, is what is actually behind the name changing by those pusillanimous trustees, appointed by supposed "conservative Republicans" elected by North Carolina voters. Until Tar Heels come to understand this, and react forcefully against it, things will continue to worsen, and what is left of our history and our traditions will continue to disappear ... and once gone, most likely never to be recovered.

(Abbeville Institute, June 18, 2015, at: www.abbevilleinstitute.org/blog/a-letter-from-north-carolina/)

Was Lee A "Traitor?"
⇨ *Chapter 13* ⇦

Were Robert E. Lee and the Confederates "traitors" who violated their oaths to the Constitution and attempted to destroy the American nation? Or, were they defenders of that Constitution and of Western Christian civilization?

Over the past 158 years those questions have been posed and answers offered countless times. For more than a century since Appomattox the majority opinion among writers and historians was that Lee and the Confederate leadership were noble figures of a "lost cause," but sincerely mistaken about what they were fighting for. They were admirable and valorous, even to be emulated, if in the end the "righteous cause" of "national unity" was destined to triumph.

In May 2017 New Orleans removed its Robert E. Lee Monument, one of four the city decided to take down. As well, Charlottesville, Virginia, currently finds itself in the midst of a rancorous debate over its Lee statue. All over the South and the nation moves are afoot to take down monuments, remove flags, hide any symbols that in any way honor or remind the present generation favorably of the Confederacy and the "lost cause."

There has been much written about what the removals mean. How should we see these attempts to radically erase, uproot and alter portions of our history?

It goes without saying that each generation interprets the past — its past — to enhance, justify and confirm its view of itself. Certainly, the politically correct, cultural Marxist Left, which spearheads the effort to "cleanse" our society of Confederate symbolism, has erected its own set of symbols, totems, and myths to legitimize its present activities and its extreme revolutionary zeal. Thus, in the place of Lee, Jefferson Davis, and Stonewall Jackson, we witness the rising cults of Nat Turner, Harriet Jacobs, "the Secret Six" abolitionists, and the rehabilitation and virtual canonization of the bloodthirsty fanatic, John "Pottawatomie" Brown. In the America of 2017 we have a whole new set of martyrs and saints, whose message is carefully massaged and congealed, and then presented as models for us and for our children. And there can be no dissent from this new imposed vision.

The historical profession, almost to a man has joined in, with the likes of Stalinist historian, Eric Foner, now heralded as the nation's "leading historian on slavery and the War." Everything revolves around slavery and racism as the sole causes of the War, and an almost inexpungeable stain each generation must strive to overcome. Put very simply, it was historic white oppression that had to be defeated and destroyed as part of the advancing historical process, a process which is posited as inevitable and irreversible. It is represented as the latest conquest of the "Idea of Progress." And that campaign, that ideological narrative for the Left, continues with the present efforts to banish symbols honoring anything to do with the Confederacy and its leaders, even if morally irreproachable individuals like Robert E. Lee are included in the cross hairs.

Hollywood, once sixty years ago eager to honor the heroes and paladins of the Lost Cause, now paints anything Confederate as inherently evil, perhaps rivaling the Nazis in unredeemable brutality. How many times in recent months have we heard crudely educated college students from vaunted Ivy League schools, weaned on Hollywood "blockbusters" like *Abraham Lincoln: Vampire Hunter* and indoctrinated by cultural Marxist professors, parrot such slogans? Is their foul-mouthed sloganeering any different, really, from the high class academic sloganeering of Foner and others of his ilk?

What distinguishes the cultural Marxist historians' narrative from earlier views is not just its social omnipresence, but its rigid dogmatism that brooks no disagreement, no opposing views. Certainly, sixty or seventy years ago there were superb historians who looked at the War Between the States differently. We only have to mention a few: Charles Sydnor, Francis Butler Simkins, William A. Dunning, Avery Craven, Charles Ramsdell, and so on. Today they still are read, but only to illustrate how an earlier generation of historians "misread" history, or, worse, attempted to cover up the "sin of slavery" and "white oppression." Even arguably the greatest recent historian of the South, the late Eugene Genovese, comes in for his share of opprobrium and disdain from the culturally Marxist-dominated historical establishment for his profound and sympathetic probing of the thinking of antebellum Southern whites (e.g., *The Mind of the Master Class*).

But even back then, even if we suggest many writers treated the South and the Confederacy with a degree of understanding, even sympathy, there did not exist the kind of extreme scholarly totalitarianism we find in the academy and in publishing today. A Charles Beard could frame the American Founding in strongly economic terms, while others disagreed in scholarly tomes. The conflict of 1861-1865 was seen as both "repressible" and "irrepressible" (to use the title of a study by Arthur Cole, the term used first by William Seward). But there was no rigid "historical iron curtain" which dictated how historians thought and what they wrote.

And that difference distinguishes the earlier age from our own: for we are victims of a fanatical ideological zeal that increasingly knows few limits. Emerging out of this fanaticism is a type of religious commitment and conviction that dispenses with any opposing narrative as "fascist" or "racist" or "homophobic," and discards any inconvenient fact as "meaningless," if standing in the way of the inevitable political and cultural objectives. Nothing must stand in the way of Progress.

In fact, that onrushing "Progress" has no end, no finality, and cannot really end, for it is the revolutionary process, itself, that becomes the meaning and actual lived goal for its adherents. Theirs is a Revolution that, like a mortal illness, must continue and ceaselessly unwind, increasingly more unhinged and more unsubtle, as it goes along. But the objective of that Perfect Society where all racism, sexism, homophobia, and misogyny are banished, where complete equality of status and income are obtained, where the "chains of established religion" and traditions are broken, that apocalyptic paradise on earth will not be and cannot be achieved.

Every Revolutionary movement, every "ism," posits a final, perfected society. Whether early pre-Reformation zealots like the Cathares or Lollards, various millenarian sects, the Illuminati followers of Adam Weishaupt, or the socialists, anarchists, and Communists of more recent times, a future Utopian vision is held up as the final goal, the final stage in mankind's torturous path to earthly happiness and perfection. But that chimerical objective is always an illusion, and usually a bloody one, strewn with the corpses of thousands, even millions of victims, who stood in the way of its realization.

And with that latest revolutionary impulse comes the destruction of traditions, beliefs, and customs which have given society its actual foundation, its memory, those age-tested and handed-down ways of life which anneal and clothe society and protect it from decay and disintegration.

It is no exaggeration to see the attacks on the Lee statues and Southern symbols as part and parcel of this current assault, which aims not just at those more prominent artifacts of the Confederacy, but also takes aim at the very presence of Western and Christian civilization, itself. For, in fact, none of it can stand if the cultural Marxist narrative of irreversible and onrushing Progress, as they understand it, succeeds. It all must go, be removed, taken down, revised, re-interpreted.

The present campaign to remove Confederate symbols, then, should be viewed in this light. And it must be stoutly opposed with that full understanding.

(Abbeville Institute, June 18, 2018, at: www.abbevilleinstitute.org/blog/was-lee-a-traitor/?mc_cid=aad16763b6&mc_eid=8639a6a6ea)

New Orleans: A People without A Past Have No Future
⇢ Chapter 14 ⇠

Early this morning [April 24, 2017] the local television station WRAL, Raleigh, NC, broadcast news that the first of "four Confederate monuments in New Orleans ... honoring white supremacy" will come down today. The fate of these monuments has been debated now for a number of years, with the majority black city government wanting to expunge these reminders of New Orleans' history, while various heritage and preservation organizations have fought to keep them in place.

The one that comes down today is the "Liberty Monument," an obelisk erected in 1891 to commemorate the overthrow of Reconstruction. Proponents argued it is a symbol of "white supremacy" and racism, while defenders declared, although it may be offensive to some, it also an integral part of the city's history and, thus, should be kept where it is as a part of that history.

But it is the remaining three monuments which raise the most vociferous ire of traditionalists and those concerned about preserving the historical record: the city plans to take down statues to Generals Robert E. Lee and P. G. T. Beauregard, and President Jefferson Davis. Unlike the Liberty Monument, which symbolizes the political redemption of the city from Reconstruction, the Lee, Beauregard and Davis monuments commemorate exemplary individuals who ended up defending a lost cause. Through honoring them, the city fathers had honored the soldiers and the extreme sacrifices and hardships endured during a brutal war 155 years ago. But, as we know, history often does not treat well the champions of a lost cause; the victors usually write the histories and establish the narrative.

The effort to take down these symbols reflects a frenzied desire to, in effect, efface portions of our history, to revise the past, if it no longer comports with the ideological Marxist vision that is currently fashionable and politically-correct. Certainly, one can argue each generation engages in a bit of revising; that is part and parcel of what human beings do, to enhance their history and their genealogy, while downplaying events and individuals which may not fit smoothly into the current narrative.

Those who argue that the New Orleans monuments should come down suggest what is needed is a re-interpretation and a revised view of history, and that such monuments only serve to remind us of past "sins" of racism and white oppression, slavery, and rebellion.

Yet, a deeper issue demands consideration. What does such zealous "purification," such "censorship," such abrupt dislocation, do to our understanding of who we are as a people? What happens when we radically suppress, rearrange, and expel integral portions of our past? Does not such extreme surgery leave us bereft of a fuller understanding of our historical experience?

The great late nineteenth century Spanish philosopher, Marcelino Menendez y Pelayo, once said of Spain, that it was the shining champion, buckler, and defender of Christendom: "this is your heritage, you have no other," he cautioned. Cannot this same metaphor be applied to the South? Can there be, truly, a real South without not only monuments commemorating noble men like Robert E. Lee, but also an understanding that men like Lee and Davis and Beauregard occupy a pivotal role in our history, and that their vision and their lives were exemplary and admirable witnesses in the difficult historical era in which they lived? Must everything be compressed and reinterpreted by a sharply defined, ideological historicist litmus test?

Where, indeed, does such a process of homogenization and re-writing stop? George Washington, Thomas Jefferson, and other Founders of this nation were slave holders; must their monuments be taken down and their names suppressed, too? Must their legacies be radically revised, and their essential roles in the creation of this nation be ideologically perverted? The triumphant cultural Marxist school of historical writing, the Eric Foners of the historical establishment, would have it so, and in so doing, they turn history into fanatical ideology. Hollywood and the dominant popular culture follow along like yelping pups, parroting in offensive and over-the-top exaggeration the new dogmatism which reigns nearly supreme.

One cannot transgress the new totalitarian dogmatism. Not only our media, our entertainment, and our educational establishment, but even some of our friends who should know better, participate in this insane brainwashing acceptance which warps our understanding of our past.

Our objective, then, must be to redeem our history, recover the past, paint it in all its colors; but keep all our monuments and all our artifacts up and visible, recognizing that not everyone will see them in the same light. Yet, even those symbols some may find objectionable tell a story and open a window on our past. And to comprehend who we are, we neglect such a full vision at our great peril. A people without a past, that is, a real and discernible history, is a people with no real future.

(Abbeville Institute, April 25, 2017, at: www.abbevilleinstitute.org/blog/new-orleans-a-people-without-a-past-have-no-future/)

Taking Down Our Monuments is Part of the Marxist Campaign to Transform America
↦ Chapter 15 ↤

The present feverish campaign to remove Confederate monuments and other symbols which offend certain loud groups in our society began in earnest back in 2015, after the murder of several black parishioners in a church in Charleston, South Carolina. But that movement dates back much longer. Its real origins go back to the 1960s and early 1970s, and the triumph of a form of what has been called "cultural Marxism" in our universities and colleges, and a resultant and progressive transformation of views of American history in our popular culture.

Recall that even into the late 1950s and certainly up until the "Civil War Centennial" (1960-1965) not only in our popular culture, but in most of the history taught in our schools and colleges, the South, and in particular, the Confederacy, were viewed with some respect, if not sympathy. If slavery was condemned — and not just in the Northern states, but also by the South — still, in particular, the veterans of the tragic Confederate military odyssey, were portrayed by Hollywood in such films as *The Raid* (Van Heflin), *Rocky Mountain* (Errol Flynn) or *Jesse James* (Henry Fonda, Randolph Scott), as noble and heroic figures doing their duty. And who can forget such popular television programs as *The Rebel* (1959-1961, with Nick Adams) or *The Gray Ghost* (1957-1958, with Tod Andrews) with their romantic portrayals of those soldiers fighting for the "lost cause?"

And Southern culture and society, itself, was seen with considerably more nuance and appreciation than today's rigid and universal damnation. Again, Hollywood produced such superb cinematic visions as John Ford's *The Sun Shines Bright* and Disney's *Song of the South,* and countless others.

In the academy, classic histories by Avery Craven, William Dunning, Charles W. Ramsdell, Charles Sydnor, Francis Butler Simkins, and others were prominently used and taught in colleges. And the monumental ten-volume, *A History of the South* (published by the LSU Press) seemed to offer the final word on discussions of the Southern past. Yet, by the mid-1960s newer historians — Kenneth Stampp, Stanley Elkins, and others, influenced by a more Leftist ideology and more concentrated on the role of race — soon dominated the writing of

Southern and American history. It was their students and succeeding generations of historians who made no excuse for their blatant Marxism, and whose views eventually permeated not only the academia, but also our popular and political culture.

The dominant narrative for these ideological academics was that "race" and "racism" had been and continued to be the central issues which affected, influenced, and determined the rest of American history. And, thus, the logic went, since the Old South, most prominently the Confederacy, defended slavery and was then, by definition, "racist," the symbols and monuments that memorialized it in any positive way represented "racism" and a "racist" past which needed not only to be re-interpreted, but "cleansed."

But the assault on the Confederate past and on its visible artifacts and reminders, its flags, its monuments, it symbols, is, as we clearly now see, only the tip of the iceberg. For those who wish to remove our monuments honoring General Lee or Jefferson Davis, have made it manifest that Lee, Jackson, and Beauregard are only the first step in a much larger and all-consuming campaign to thoroughly "purify" and radically transform American society.

A few weeks ago one small frenzied group in Durham, North Carolina, the Workers' World Party, organized a violent demonstration and the destruction of the Confederate veterans' monument in that university city. Like other such groups — the "antifa" organizations, Black Lives Matter, and similar organizations — Workers' World supporters call for: the abolition of capitalism, disarming of the police and ICE agents, the fight for Marxist revolution, and the defense of "Black Lives Matter." All symbols and reminders of "white supremacy" and of "racism" must be eradicated and destroyed. And those symbols are not limited to the Southern Confederacy, but encompass nearly all of this country's Founders, most of its 19th century presidents and political leaders, its earliest discoverers and colonizers, and, in fact, its basic historic culture.

What is remarkable is the extent to which such avowedly extremist and Communist organizations now seem to dictate and shape the larger discussion and debate over monuments and symbols. It is as if the Democratic Party, the near entirety of the media, and vast swathes of the GOP frantically accept the narrative of "racism" as the central and dominant issue in American history, from which all else, all events, all history, flow. And, as such, this domination represents the general triumph of cultural Marxism in establishing both the standard terms of acceptable debate and the required outlook, against which no dissent is permitted.

Given this situation, it is extremely difficult for me to have any sympathy whatsoever for WRAL-TV's main newscaster, David Crabtree, in Raleigh, North Carolina, who continues *ad nauseum* to blubber about the "hurt" and the "hatred" that monuments to Lee or to the "Women of the Confederacy" (on the North Carolina State Capitol grounds) inflict on poor black youth living in the Tar Heel State's capital city in 2017. Like other "religiously-oriented" personages who have accepted the cultural Marxist narrative, Crabtree clothes his views in a language of supposed Christian love and charity, and a desire for "social justice." But in fact, he has swallowed whole hog the Marxist vision of society and *de facto* turned his back on historic, traditional Christian belief and on our historical and cultural legacy. He has become, perhaps unwittingly, one of those "public dogs" wagged by the revolutionary Marxist "tail," who uses his public persona and widely-heard voice to advance its longer range program of destruction, deformation, and complete transformation of what is left of the American nation.

Such pawns of the Revolution are useful idiots, but useful only to a certain point, after which they are usually discarded as having fulfilled their purposes, but not permitted to "cross over Jordan into the Promised Land." Like the Mensheviks and Social Democrats in Russia in 1918, they will be eliminated or liquidated after the Revolution moves on to it next stage.

Crabtree and others like him may fret about the "pain" a statue to Lee may give, but his logic leads ineluctably to much more than just the purging of Confederate images: it leads to the denuding of American history and the end of anything resembling the America created 241 years ago — it leads to the fearsome silencing of those who oppose that transformation — and it may well lead to the scaffold, as all such fanatical revolutions usually end in pools of blood.

Frankly, those facilitators of revolution always seem to get finally what they deserve — a bullet to the back of the head, as they wonder, simple-mindedly and incredulously, why their "social justice" concerns weren't implemented by their one-time allies amongst the hard core extremists.

For the rest of us it is to do our best to defend our patrimony, to demonstrate — like the articles of the Nicene Creed where denying one precept undermines and implicitly denies the others — that to destroy Confederate symbols opens the door wide to the destruction of all our symbols and the radical Marxist redefinition of the American nation, itself.

It appears an almost insuperable task, but it is our duty before the shadow of our ancestors and before the verdict of history.

(Abbeville Institute, October 6, 2017, at: www.abbevilleinstitute.org/blog/the-marxist-campaign-to-transform-america/)

Defending the Monuments: The North Carolina Case
⇾ *Chapter 16* ⇽

After the Charleston shooting in 2015, all across the old Confederacy memorials, monuments, flags and other symbols of the South's Confederate history came under renewed and severe assault. It seemed the last vestiges of that heritage might be swept away in a paroxysm of politically-driven outrage and media-hyped efforts to purge the landscape of those symbols.

In many ways North Carolina became ground zero for these efforts. But the Tar Heel State also witnessed a pushback from defenders of the state's heritage who organized successfully and were able, for the moment at least, to fend off the worst of those attacks. Most significantly, working with a conservative and Republican General Assembly, the state's Sons of Confederate Veterans division, was able to secure passage of one of the nation's strongest Monuments Protection Laws [NC General Statute 100-2.1].

Passed almost unnoticed and with minimal opposition in 2015, that legislation has proven to be a major road block for the social justice warriors intent on a cultural and historical "cleansing" of the Old North State. Indeed, the frustration of many of the more exalted and self-proclaimed Marxists has resulted in direct action such as the violent destruction of the Durham, NC, monument to Confederate veterans by gangs associated with the Communist Workers World Party. [See, "8 now face charges in toppling of Confederate statue in Durham, www.newsobserver.com/news/local/counties/durham-county/article167689007.html"]

The razor-thin election of Democrat Roy Cooper as North Carolina's governor in 2016 brought new impetus to efforts to "do something" about the hundreds of monuments honoring North Carolina's some 125,000 Confederate veterans and their sacrifices. The Cooper administration selected as its primary target perhaps the most prominent and visible of all such monuments in the state, three iconic monuments on Capitol Square surrounding the state's historic 1840 State Capitol: the Henry Wyatt Monument, the Monument to North Carolina Women of the Confederacy, and the giant Confederate Monument facing Hillsborough Street.

But how to get around — to get past — the 2015 Monuments Protection Law?

Although offering strong protection for all of North Carolina's historic monuments, markers and symbols on public property, the Monuments Protection Law did permit certain, very specific and limited exemptions for road construction, for repair, and because of public safety. It was those exemptions to which Governor Cooper and his team looked.

Given authority to receive and review such proposed exemptions is the North Carolina Historical Commission, which has purview in such cases [cf. North Carolina G.S. 100-2.1; G.S. 143B-63-65; and G.S. 121-12]. And it was to the Commission at its meeting on September 22, 2017, Cooper's administration made its proposal to take down the three monuments on Capitol Square and relocate them to the Bentonville Battlefield, near rural Newton Grove. The governor made his proposal based in an interpretation of the 2015 law, specifically section G.S. 100-2.1 (C) (3), which permits exceptions to the law if, "An object of remembrance for which a building inspector or similar official has determined poses a threat to public safety because of an unsafe or dangerous condition."

At its September 2017 meeting the Commission deferred all action; instead, it named a select committee of its members to examine the law and history, and to collect comments and opinions of academics and the public, and to report back at a full meeting in April 2018. A public hearing was held on March 21, 2018, at which monument supporters greatly predominated. And more than 7,000 comments were collected by the end of March when the comment period was closed.

The North Carolina Division of the SCV contracted with a prominent constitutional attorney to prepare its case defending the location of the monuments under state law, and many others weighed in with strong arguments.

The following is a prepared statement I submitted (slightly edited) to both the members of the North Carolina Historical Commission and its select committee:

Despite all the debate over the meaning and history of the monuments, the primary consideration here is a legal one. If Governor Roy Cooper's proposal to remove the three targeted monuments from Capitol (Union) Square cannot be legally entertained under the Monuments Protection Act of 2015 [G.S. 100-2.1], then all subsequent debate and discussion, while certainly important and significant in defining meaning and history, will remain secondary to the specific question before the Commission, and the Commission will be incapable of acting on the proposal.

Let's take a closer look at the law. It was enacted with very specific provisions incorporated into its sections affecting all of North Carolina's existent historic "objects of remembrance," monuments, works of art, and memorials situated on public property, protecting them from hastily and rashly considered or politically motivated action. The language and intent of the legislative authors actually recalls the originally proposed Monuments Protection Bill of more than a decade ago, proposed by the late Senator Hamilton Horton of Winston-Salem. Let us also recall that the 2015 legislation was passed unanimously by the North Carolina Senate.

With particular reference to the role of the North Carolina Historical Commission detailed in Section 100.2.1 (a), while the General Assembly specified the Commission must give its approval prior to any removal, relocation or alteration of any monument, the Commission is also strictly limited in its possible action, as the law states, "except as otherwise provided in subsection (b) of this section."

That subsection (b) clearly states: A monument on public property may only be relocated, either permanently or temporarily, if either of the following two conditions apply:

(1) For the preservation of the monument (in the sense that natural or physical decay, or other natural effects are causing it damage);

(2) When public construction projects, highways, etc. would impact it in its present location.

But, if either of these two reasons are invoked, then the following rules must apply:

***An object of remembrance that is temporarily relocated shall be returned to its original location within 90 days of completion of the project that required its temporary removal;

***An object of remembrance that is permanently relocated shall be relocated to a site of similar prominence, honor, visibility, availability, and access that are within the boundaries of the jurisdiction from which it was relocated;

*** And, an object of remembrance may not be relocated to a museum, cemetery, or mausoleum unless it was originally placed at such a location.

The Land We Love

The three exceptions to this section are contained in subsection (c):

*Concerning highway historical markers;

*Relating to private monuments placed on public property where there is a legal, written agreement governing potential removal or relocation;

*And in regard to a monument where a building inspector/equivalent official has determined that the monument has become a public safety hazard (through natural physical effects).

Let me summarize. Except for, (1) preservation or needed repair to monuments on Capitol Square, or (2) because of road and/or building construction which would affect them detrimentally, or (3) due to certification that a monument represents a clear public safety hazard because of its intrinsic physical condition, the North Carolina Historical Commission is not empowered legally to approve or initiate any action in regard to monuments under G.S. 100.2.1. Moreover, if permanent relocation is proposed, the new location must be "of similar prominence, honor, visibility, availability, and access that are within the boundaries of the jurisdiction from which it was relocated."

Governor Cooper's proposal for removal and relocation is submitted under this third exception, suggesting the monuments represent a clear public safety hazard. Yet, his proposal directly contradicts the considered legal view of the very legislators of the General Assembly who enacted the 2015 law. In interpreting a law it is the intent and meaning invested by the legislators which must be considered the benchmark and standard for interpretation. This is a long-standing constitutional jurisprudential practice, confirmed and sanctified by our judicial system.

In the specific case of Governor Cooper's proposal, both President Pro-Tem of the North Carolina Senate, Senator Phil Berger, and Speaker of the House, Representative Tim Moore (with the concurrence of two dozen additional House of Representatives legislators), that is, those who enacted the law, have publicly stated in the strongest terms, more than once, the governor's proposal does not fulfill the conditions nor does it fulfill the intent laid down in the third exception (Cf., Senator Phil Berger's full statement, "Berger Calls on Cooper to Withdraw Unlawful Request to State Historical Commission," published on September 21, 2017, and Speaker Tim Moore, on September 22, 2017, as quoted by WRAL-TV, "Legislative leaders warn Cooper, commission on statue removal").

The key wording of the law in exception three includes "public safety hazard." That is, a monument has become a physical hazard to the public; it does not mean that members of the public, for instance, demonstrators, have become a "hazard to the monument." This later case is a situation of potential vandalism, and not a natural "public safety hazard" envisaged or covered by the law.

Additionally, the proposed relocation of the monuments to the Bentonville Battlefield cannot in any way satisfy the requirement that the new location be of equal prominence and visibility as the North Carolina State Capitol. Although a State Historic Site, Bentonville is off the beaten track and lacks the much greater visibility, access, and prominence of the North Carolina State Capitol. During the biennium, 2012-2014, the State Capitol building was visited by 191,730 visitors, while Bentonville was visited by 91,665, less than half the number for the Capitol (*Biennial Report, 2012-2014*. The North Carolina Office of Archives and History. Raleigh: North Carolina Department of Cultural Resources, 2015, p. 95). But the number for the State Capitol does not factor in the hundreds of thousands of citizens who walk through the grounds of the Capitol each year and thus are able to view the monuments on the grounds.

Senator Berger's summary words on this point to the governor (September 21, 2017) are definitive and must be considered as such: "The North Carolina Historical Commission does not even have the authority to grant your request, and it would likely lose in court if and when North Carolinians sued over the removal of the monuments …The North Carolina Historical Commission cannot legally grant your request."

Additionally, there is confirmation of this legal opinion from the attorneys of the University of North Carolina at Chapel Hill, who, when importuned to submit a similar proposal to the North Carolina Historical Commission for the removal of the "Silent Sam" monument at the University under the third exception of a "public safety hazard," rejected the request. To quote from a report and legal opinion cited in *The News & Observer* ("UNC trustee leaders defend Folt for not removing Silent Sam Confederate statue," August 25, 2017, www.newsobserver.com/news/local/education/article169386747.html): "Through advice from its legal counsel and that of the UNC system, university leaders reached the conclusion that they do not have the authority to take down the monument." I should also point out this opinion is shared by even those who wish the monuments removed. *The Greensboro News-Record*, no defender of the monuments, in a prominent editorial ("Monuments hold a protected place," January 18, 2018, www.greensboro.com/opinion/n_and_r_editorials/our-opinion-monuments-hold-a-protected-place/article_945e4c15-0733-5e10-a916-62c9492e-c8b8.html), admitted Senator Berger's legal interpretation, as lawgiver, and the intent of the law, make it practically impossible to remove the monuments using the reasoning of the governor.

Given this essential and fundamental information, the governor's proposal to remove the three monuments which memorialize the experiences of as many as 125,000 North Carolinians in the brutal conflict of 1861-1865 does not satisfy the conditions clearly set down in law.

A second consideration, and one that I expect will draw much more comment, concerns the erection and meaning of the monuments. There are numerous references collected on the *ncpedia* and by *docsouth* web sites, offering details surrounding the erection of those monuments. That debate, like all debate regarding our national and state iconography, will in all likelihood continue to rage. But, and I say this with more than thirty years of detailed research and investigation into those symbols erected by our ancestors, there is one overriding fact which should be understood: over the past history of our state, the facts haven't changed; but the interpretations have.

One hundred years ago prominent "establishment" historians such as Charles Beard and Avery Craven, and North Carolina's own R. D. W. Connor (the nation's first National Archivist) could variously envisage the 1861-1865 war as essentially about economics or perhaps constitutional principles, fought by good and sincere men on both sides. In recent years, opinion has reflected the views generally of those leftist historians such as Eric Foner, that the war was specifically and uniquely about slavery and racism. But the essential facts haven't changed, even if much of historical opinion has.

In examining in detail the contemporary accounts presented for why those monuments were erected, including newspaper accounts, speeches and memoirs, the overwhelming sentiment expressed by such organizations as the Ladies' Memorial Association (later the United Daughters of the Confederacy) and the United Confederate Veterans is one to honor the veterans, many of whom were dying off during that exact period. I would suggest this has been a consistent practice in American history — South and North, usually forty or fifty years after the conclusion of a major conflict: erecting monuments and other symbols to honor its wizened veterans, most in their 80s or 90s. It occurred after World War II and more recently after the Vietnam conflict (e.g., the Vietnam Monument on Capitol Square).

The accusation has been made that those who erected the monuments did so to celebrate racism and its triumph legally, specifically in the form of Jim Crow legislation. However, certain researchers have also pointed out the suggested congruence and symmetry between the enactment of Jim Crow legislation and the erection of monuments to the Confederate dead are misplaced and historically questionable, as researcher Michael Armstrong, in an investigative essay for The Abbeville Institute, published on October 11, 2017, has detailed. ("Why Were Confederate Monuments Built?" www.abbevilleinstitute.org/blog/why-were-confederate-monuments-built/)

The example which is uniformly cited to prove a racist origin is a racially-hateful remark made by Julian Carr at the unveiling of the "Silent Sam" monument at UNC-Chapel Hill. Yet, Carr's comments, which are discordant with the rest of his 3,200 word speech, are contextually out of place. While they do represent a racially-charged aside, they stand out as real exceptions to the meaning invested by the organizers and supporters of that monument, a meaning that is quite clearly to honor veterans and their sacrifices, and not to celebrate slavery or the evils of racism.

The issues surrounding the erection of the monuments and the individuals and groups responsible, and the views and attitudes of those persons, I would suggest, should also be seen in historical context. Even among some of those not identified as staunch defenders of Confederate heritage, there is a recognition that removal and/or relocation of symbols of our past presents considerable and serious dangers for a full understanding of our history. In reference here, I would cite three thoughtful essays by noted and prominent writers, each highly respected across this state and nationally.

The first is by Professor Peter Coclanis, the Albert R. Newsome Distinguished Professor of History at UNC-Chapel Hill ("Julian Carr did wrong, but also a good deal right," www.newsobserver.com/opinion/op-ed/article175617056.html). Dr. Coclanis and journalist Rob Christensen ("The complex origins of Confederate monuments," www.newsobserver.com/news/politics-government/politics-columns-blogs/

rob-christensen/article174818011.html), take a much more nuanced and careful view of the historical period and of the life and work of Julian Carr, pictured these days as a bigoted, reactionary racist, but who, in fact, was much more complex, a "progressive" individual much devoted to the improvement of the lives of all North Carolinians. And the third item is by Pulitzer Prize-winning Tar Heel Edwin Yoder ("A misguided name-changing cult among UNC schools," www.newsobserver.com/opinion/op-ed/article23131068.html), in reference to the renaming of Saunders Hall at UNC-Chapel Hill, once again stressing the contextual complexity and the error of judging past history with a single reductionist and presentist historical viewpoint as the only measure.

Let me add to this consideration the opinion of Professor Alfred Brophy, the Reef C. Ivey II Professor of Law, University of North Carolina-Chapel Hill, who in a long, heavily-documented essay, specifically on the renaming of the William Simkins dormitory at the University of Texas ("The Law and Morality of Building Renaming," http://blurblawg.typepad.com/files/lmbr.pdf), despite sharing a belief that Confederate monuments may project a hurtful imagery and symbolism to portions of our population, believes the existence of such symbols in positions of prominence may be of greater value than their relocation or removal:

'To continue the analogy to regime changes and monuments that attempt to establish a controversial interpretation of history, one might think of Confederate monuments. When they were placed in the late nineteenth and early twentieth century, one purpose — in addition to honoring family members — may have been to establish a pro-Confederate history. They put that version of history in conspicuous places. But I wonder if politics — 150 years after the Civil War began — has so changed that the monuments are not so much about organizing political space. Maybe the monuments have themselves become a testimony to history and part of the historical landscape rather than a positive effort to remake how we think about history.... That particular exercise in forgetting points out the reason why I have come full circle, back to my youthful opposition to renaming. As I see the calculus now, removal of a name threatens our memory of the past."

And he adds an example closer to home, in respect to a dormitory named for Justice Thomas Ruffin on the UNC campus. Ruffin defended slavery from the state's highest judicial bench, yet Professor Brophy, weighing the pain and hurt occasioned by his decisions, also believes:

"I think we should keep his name on the dormitory on the University of North Carolina campus because it is part of our history and because we should remember that there was a time when his ideas were triumphant ... I hope that those who ask for changes will also investigate whether the cause of promotion of knowledge of our past is best accomplished by removal of a name or whether removal facilitates, instead, the process of forgetting."

Let me suggest, in conclusion, the real reason for this proposal has nothing to do with finding a better or more appropriate place for the targeted monuments. Rather, it involves politics and a particular ideological interpretation of the factual record these monuments — their presence — equals a defense of slavery, and, in fact, racism. If this is the standard that is now adopted for memorials, then nearly every monument on Capitol Square must, logically, be removed, including the monuments to Presidents Washington, Jackson, Polk, and Johnson, and to the North Carolina governors, all of whom could be considered racists or defenders of racism. Even the Vietnam Veterans monument has become a target, as there are those who see American involvement in Vietnam as an example of "racism."

Our question, then, must be: where would such a process inevitably end? Already plaques honoring George Washington (e.g., Christ Church, Alexandria, Virginia) have been removed, and efforts are underway to banish Christopher Columbus and Father Junipero Serra (in California) and rename our military institutions which bear the names of Confederate generals. And Presidents Jefferson and Jackson have also begun to suffer erasure and exile. The list seems to increase almost daily.

Certainly, it is understandable given the torturous history of race relations in this nation that some of our citizens may feel offended by those symbols. Yet, for millions of Tar Heel citizens — an overwhelming majority in every poll taken on this issue — those monuments are memorials to real ancestors, flesh and blood men and women who suffered and died, and not icons celebrating slavery or racism. (For the polls, see: Elon University, Meredith College, and Marist College.)

The Monuments Protection Law was enacted precisely to prevent such rash action as is being proposed — action which would denude us of a full understanding and representation of our history. We may not like what we see, we may find parts of our past hurtful, even offensive; each of us may find this or that event or person not to our liking. Yet, would it not be much better to take a broader view, and incorporate those memorials and symbols into our instruction and the education we provide to our citizens?

That is the true and wise spirit of North Carolina and the spirit that, I would suggest, mirrors the overwhelming sentiment of the citizens of this state, as well as enacted law.

The decision of the North Carolina Historical Commission and whatever legal (or legislative) action that may follow will have enormous consequences not just for the Tar Heel State but for monument and heritage defense all across the South.

(Abbeville Institute, May 30, 2018, at: www.abbevilleinstitute.org/blog/defending-the-monuments/?mc_cid=0b3e24a491&mc_eid=8639a6a6ea)

Our Monuments: A Battle for Western Civilization and the South
✦ Chapter 17 ✦

The days of August 20-22, 2018, were tumultuous in the Tar Heel State. First, on Monday night, August 20, approximately 200 to 250 raucous demonstrators gathered in a mob on the campus of the University of North Carolina-Chapel Hill and proceeded to tear down the century-old statue, "Silent Sam," a monument memorializing the more than 250 university students who fought and died during the War Between the States. University police, whose primary goal is to protect university property from vandals and destruction, stood down and did nothing to protect the monument, apparently acting on orders from university administrators. (www.newsobserver.com/news/local/education/article217035815.html). It was a flagrant challenge to state law and an offensive attack on the traditions of the citizens of the state.

National news media covered the assault on "Silent Sam." In fact, observers throughout the South, also confronted by unhinged demands that they take down or relocate Confederate monuments, watched these events unfold with great interest: North Carolina had become ground zero in the ongoing war against our heritage, a multifaceted and seemingly unstoppable "cultural war" against not just Confederate symbols, but also against all the symbols of our Western Christian civilization.

All across the nation — and not just in the states below the Mason-Dixon Line — there has been an insistent effort to take down, remove, and, at times, destroy those monuments that represent our history and heritage. Certainly, it has been the statues honoring Robert E. Lee, P. G. T. Beauregard, Jefferson Davis, and Confederate veterans who have been highlighted most specifically as targets by this movement and featured in the Mainstream Media. Indeed, very likely a majority of American citizens not that familiar with this advancing campaign probably believe it is only those Confederate symbols which are the object of this frenzied attack, and that once those monuments are disposed of, further demands for "cultural cleansing" can be blunted and contained, or will just go away.

In many ways, this temporizing approach appears to be the view of much of the establishment "conservative movement," and as well, of many leaders of the Republican Party.

It is an approach which leads to cultural suicide.

An excellent example of this pusillanimous position came in an article by John Hood, chairman of the board of the conservative John Locke Foundation, in Raleigh, North Carolina [www.johnlocke.org/person/john-hood/] a couple of days before the toppling of Silent Sam. In his essay on the status of the three Confederate monuments now standing on Capitol Square in Raleigh, Hood demonstrates obvious discomfort at having to defend symbols admittedly of his own Tar Heel heritage, bemoaning [*Winston-Salem Journal*, August 18, 2018]: "Why not erect more monuments and public art to commemorate a broader range of individuals, movements, and events? That's a noble enterprise which could unify North Carolinians across the political spectrum…. There has to be a better way." [www.journalnow.com/opinion/columnists/john-hood-monument-protests-marred-by-illegality/article_eba5fd41-52ae-5447-90e8-36769d462a01.html]

Hood was a vigorous and very vocal Never Trumper whose positions on most issues mirror standard establishment Republican boilerplate. And like them he answers accusations of racism, bigotry, and white supremacy from the Farther Left, as a dog answers the dog whistle of his owner … and like how most Neoconservatives respond in fearful fright to their Farther Left critics.

What actually bothers him are not the ideologically-motivated attacks on the monuments as symbols of Southern heritage and history, but, as he makes clear, the physical attacks on them. And to prove his *bona fides* to the Farther Left, he adds his own exculpatory *mea culpas* for his state's and region's "history of hate," and points proudly to his own record of reparations (of the financial kind) for slavery, racism, and white supremacy:

Although my love of state history is broad and deep, it does not extend to the Confederacy itself, the founding principles of which I view with contempt. Not only do I celebrate the abolition of slavery, the destruction of Jim Crow, and the expansion of freedom, but I also believe these events deserve far more official commemoration than North Carolina has yet erected…. I admire the planned North Carolina Freedom Park, for example. To be constructed in Raleigh on land between the General Assembly complex and the Executive Mansion, the park would "celebrate the enduring contributions of African Americans in North Carolina who struggled to gain freedom and enjoy full citizenship." Similarly, the Z. Smith Reynolds Foundation has just announced its Inclusive Public Arts

Initiative, which will fund up to 10 new projects across the state with grants of up to $50,000 each. The intent is to "share stories of diversity, equality, inclusion and equity as they relate to the people and places of North Carolina, especially those whose stories have not been or are often untold," the Foundation stated..... Indeed, the grant maker for which I serve as president, the John William Pope Foundation, helped pay for a mural painted several years ago at North Carolina Central University's law school.

Hood, like the other epigones of the establishment "conservative movement" — the "Big Con" as Dr. Jack Kerwick terms them — is unwilling to engage in the intellectual battle required because, essentially, he agrees with the Farther Left historically and philosophically, and he is willing to temporize: just don't damage the monuments physically, and, somehow we can all do a "Rodney King" and get along — "There has to be a better way."

Two days after the toppling of Silent Sam, on August 22, came a meeting of the North Carolina Historical Commission. The Commission met to take action on a proposal by Governor Roy Cooper (D) to move the three iconic Confederate monuments (i.e., the Henry Wyatt Monument, the Monument to North Carolina Women of the Confederacy, and the Confederate Veterans' Monument) on Capitol Square in Raleigh, North Carolina, to the Bentonville Battlefield. The Commission had appointed a subcommittee at its meeting of September 22, 2017, to research the legality and advisability of such an action. The governor made his proposal purportedly based on his interpretation of the North Carolina Monuments Protection Law of 2015. But after due examination the subcommittee reported they could find no way around the conditions set down in the Monuments law, they were, thus, unable to approve the governor's proposal. The final vote of the full Historical Commission was 9-2, against relocation, with two members demanding the Commission simply ignore state law.

But what the Commissioners also did was attempt to placate the Farther Left by strongly condemning racism, white supremacy, and the principles which, they declared, motivated the Confederacy — recommending signage be erected near the existent Confederate monuments to put them into historical "context." And that the state executive should proceed with proposing additional monuments to celebrate the state's "diversity and minorities."

It is thus obvious the "John Hood syndrome" — and the historical and ideological narrative which sends the political and cultural establishment into paroxysms of fear, not wishing to be labeled a "racist," "white supremacist," or "fascist" — played a primary role in their considerations. Although the law prevented them from relocating the monuments, with alacrity and haste they proposed a way around those reminders of North Carolina's heritage, and it will be fascinating to witness how this latest stage in our culture war develops.

And who are those who have largely inspired and organized this multifaceted campaign of cultural destruction, and who have injected fear and fright into the hearts of not just the leadership of the Democratic Party, but increasingly have neutered real opposition from "conservatives" such as John Hood? Who are they — the proverbial tails who wag the establishment dog?

There are two groups who have played primary and critical roles in this ongoing effort and in the destruction of the Confederate veterans' memorial in Durham back in August 2017, and, more recently, in the tearing down of the "Silent Sam" monument on the grounds of the University of North Carolina:

(1) The Democratic Socialists of America, who have been deeply involved in the demonstrations, petition initiatives, and other actions aimed at removing the "Silent Sam" monument from the Chapel Hill campus. They have given their full support for student Maya Little and her vandalism of the monument back on May 7, 2018 (See their Web site, accessed at: www.dsanc.org/news/2018/5/7/we-stand-with-maya-little) and for subsequent demonstrations.

(2) The Communist Workers World Party, whose members led the mob and participated in the destruction of the Confederate veterans' monuments both in Durham and at UNC. They provide many of the semi-professional demonstrators who have been complicit in the lawlessness which occurred both in August 2017 in Durham and, then, one year later in August 2108. (www.newsobserver.com/news/local/education/article217035815.html). They advocate "mass struggle" and "revolutionary solutions," including: "Abolish Capitalism — Disarm the Police & ICE Agents — Fight for Socialist Revolution — Defend Black Lives Matter." The Workers World activists have turned Durham into a national center of revolutionary Communist ferment. (A detailed description of their activities may be found on their Web site, accessed at: www.workers.org/).

These radical groups have spearheaded the efforts and mob actions, and they hold both the state Democratic Party and many Republicans in subinfeudated bondage to their rhetoric and demands. They set a linguistic narrative and policy template which have captured not just major portions of our politics, but are fawned over by the near totality of our media and are taught as unchallenged truth by our educational system and in our colleges. To dissent is to risk an organized and violent demonstration, demands for censorship, and, at a minimum, the smearing of one's reputation by the press.

Unlike John Hood and those like him, these groups and individuals fully know what they are doing and what the results would be should they succeed. They respond only to our unbending, intelligent, and fierce opposition.

The compromising approach which attempts to placate the Farther Left — which is that of Neoconservatives generally in the cultural war we find ourselves in — puts me in mind of a quote I first heard used by my mentor Russell Kirk; it is from Hilaire Belloc's *This and That and the Other* (1912) (p. 282):

"[T]he Barbarian is discoverable everywhere in this that he cannot make; that he can befog or destroy, but that he cannot sustain; and of every Barbarian in the decline or peril of every civilization exactly that has been true. We sit by and watch the Barbarian, we tolerate him; in the long stretches of peace we are not afraid. We are tickled by his irreverence, his comic inversion of our old certitudes and our fixed creeds refreshes us: we laugh. But as we laugh we are watched by large and awful faces from beyond: and on these faces there is no smile."

Is this not the very essence of modern Neoconservatism's — and of John Hood's — craven compliance in what is, in fact, an ignominious retreat, an insouciant giving way to the enemies of our civilization — And a position which leads exactly to, and actually encourages, what happened on the campus of the University of North Carolina, Monday, August 20, the very physical violence John Hood says he wishes to avoid?

The standard template employed by those self-denominated "social justice warriors" is that the monuments to the Confederate dead represent "racism," "a defense of slavery," and "white supremacy." Yet, as is apparent from reports from across the nation (and from Canada and Western Europe; see, for instance: hwww.cbc.ca/news/canada/toronto/ontario-wants-john-a-macdonald-statue-1.4783329), Confederate monuments are only a first step. After them — indeed, now concurrently with the attacks on them — come assaults on symbols memorializing Christopher Columbus, Franciscan Fr. Junipero Serra (who founded so many of the early Spanish missions in California), Andrew Jackson, Woodrow Wilson, George Washington, the politically-incorrect names of cities, towns, streets, and even colleges — any visible marker of our Western Christian civilization. The list is enlarged almost daily.

What John Hood and his Neoconservative associates do not understand … or, refuse to understand … is their praxis leads to the imminent and very real peril Belloc wrote about in 1912, and to the triumphant return of the "rough beast" determined to destroy and replace Western Christian civilization that poet William Butler Yeats foresaw at the cataclysmic end of the World War I in his poem *The Second Coming* (1919): that "rough beast" held at bay for twenty centuries "vexed to nightmare by a rocking cradle" in Bethlehem, who now "slouches" as the Demon Serpent of the Old Testament to be (re)born.

The John Hoods of this world wish to have it both ways: they are unwilling to antagonize the dominant and vociferous voices on the Farther Left, while they give the illusory appearance of opposition to the Barbarians.

Such allies in the civilizational war in which we find ourselves are no allies at all: like the chicken in the middle of the road, they will be ground under by the cultural Marxist "semi" that comes hurtling down the highway.

Back in 1951 English-Cornish poet Jack Clemo (1916-1994) foresaw the age in which we now find ourselves:

"The darkness comes as you foretold.
You hear the fretful moan,
The alien winds that rave
As bitterly the grey truth breaks
On disillusioned Church and frantic world.
You see what form the judgment takes,
What harvest faithless generations reap:
The folds half empty, no clean pasture for the sheep;
Soil sterile where the liberal waters swirled
Which now have hardened into mud
Of festering ethic, fruitless hands grown chill

With their starved, pallid blood;
And the sky freezing still." [from Jack Clemo, *The Broad Winter*]

And the poet's answer, as must be our answer:

"When I saw this I chose to dwell
With torturing symbols of the Citadel."

We must stand for — we must dwell within — our Citadel, our inheritance and culture, our very identity and being as a people representing 2,000 years of Western Christian heritage, or we shall disappear into the abyss of history.

If it had not been for those staunch and uncompromising defenders of our heritage and history — mainly North Carolina Sons of Confederate Veterans, who were unwilling to give way in 2015 — the North Carolina Monuments Protection Law would never have been enacted. And without that unalterable resistance, that willingness to hold high the principles and honor of our Confederate ancestors, the results of the August 22 meeting would have been entirely different.

This war — this time — is not a time for compromise or for leaving the battlefield. The battles have just begun. Either our enemies win, or we do. The options are that simple ... and that stark. Our civilization and culture are at stake.

John Hood, take note.

(Originally published by Abbeville Institute, August 23, 2018, and revised; accessed at: www.abbevilleinstitute.org/blog/a-battle-for-western-civilization-and-the-south/)

"Silent Sam" and the Disaster Known as Public Education
⇾ Chapter 18 ⇽

In the wake of the August 20, 2018, toppling of the "Silent Sam" monument on the campus of the University of North Carolina at Chapel Hill to students who volunteered to become Confederate soldiers in 1861-1865, our television sets were filled with videos of scraggly, rough-bearded and unkempt Millenial men, and obese and definitely unattractive women, screaming profanities and shouting imprecations about racism, white supremacy, and the dangers of "fascism"— that is, demonstrating for "peace and justice."

But behind those fierce images lurks a deeper, even scarier truth.

Many in the mob of August 20th — and who came back on Saturday August 25th — were non-students, itinerant professional militants of various Marxist, Antifa, and Black Lives movements. But many also were students at that institution. And students who have absorbed supposedly the finest public education that money (and mommy and daddy) can buy at one of the most prestigious universities in the South.

There was, for example, student Margarita Sitterson, the granddaughter of former Chancellor of the university, J. Carlyle Sitterson, who boasted of her presence in the lawlessness of August 20th and her active participation in tearing down the monument:

"So basically what happened was there was four banners on each side — well actually one banner on each side, and they were all connected by sticks, and people wrapped rope around the sticks and we pulled back and forth and back and forth until it fell down." [Peter Abrosca, "Granddaughter of Former UNC Chancellor Admits to Tearing Down Confederate Statue, 'Silent Sam,'" Big League Politics, August 20, 2018, at: https://bigleaguepolitics.com/watch-granddaughter-of-former-unc-chancellor-admits-to-tearing-down-silent-sam-statue/

Sitterson added: "My grandfather — he went here for college, then he became a professor, then he became a dean [inaudible], then he became chancellor." Sitterson said "she was ashamed and that she carried guilt because she is white, and white people owned slaves."

Notice the narrative: it is an absorbed instructional template and standard that is employed in nearly all university courses about our history, our literature, our politics, and in most other courses taught to our children; it dominates almost totally the curricula of our universities and colleges, just as the University of Alabama Crimson Tide has dominated college football. It posits two measures by which all human history and experience, all human knowledge and expression, are evaluated and, then, (re)interpreted: racial oppression by the white race of black and brown people, and sexual oppression by men of women.

Thus, re-interpreting our history and culture to discover sometimes deeply embedded examples of "racism" and "white supremacy," and of "male exploitation" and "oppression of women," has become the central characteristic of our college curricula, the marker and measure by which all academic disciplines now are analyzed and taught.

Analyze a Shakespeare play … say *Richard III* or *The Merchant of Venice*; then look for the abasement and "enslavement" of women, or a hidden "racist" reference or overtone — obviously, since Shakespeare was male and white. Or consider operas by Mozart (*Abduction from the Seraglio*) or Rossini (*L'Italiana in Algeri*), with their "overt racist hostility to Muslims and women," such now in Europe these works are either no longer presented or are banned outright, or their lyrics and action rewritten. And, closer to our time, think of the attempts to ban *The Adventures of Tom Sawyer, Gone With the Wind*, and the Uncle Remus stories of Joel Chandler Harris.

And when these works are discussed in our universities, or portrayed publicly, increasingly it is done with reinterpretations, studied warnings about the implicit racism and misogyny that modern scholarship has discovered in them. Indeed, the very language and traditional expression used to analyze the history and the classic products, the art, and culture of our civilization, have been radically altered, with a whole new, made-up linguistics now employed which effectively cuts us off from the past, while furthering the goals of revolution.

Obviously, students like Margarita Sitterson — the descendant of a famed UNC educator — and thousands more like her, sitting in classes at the mercy of cultural Marxist ideologue professors who do little more than inculcate the theories of "critical race theory" and the "feminization of history"— have already, in most cases, suffered years of poor education and early indoctrination in our public high schools, that is, been "softened up" for this process before entering college.

These are the same students who, while able to describe in excruciating detail what they have been fed about the "racism" and "white oppression" supposedly existent in the United States circa 2018, and the onerous "exploitation of women," cannot read basic texts or pass basic exams in math, or in English, or in history.

In late 2016 Dr. Walter Williams, the black educator, wrote "a very large percentage of all incoming freshmen have no business being admitted to college." On the major College Board test, "Only 32 percent of white students scored at or above proficient in math, and just seven percent of black students did. Forty-six percent of white test takers scored proficient in reading, and 17 percent of blacks did. The ACT, another test used for admission to college, produced similar results. *The Journal of Blacks in Higher Education* reports, in an article titled "A Major Crisis in College Readiness for Black Students," 34 percent of whites who took the ACT were deemed college-ready in all four areas — English, mathematics, reading and science. For blacks, it was only six percent." [Dr. Walter E. Williams, "Cruelty to Black Students," CNS News, September 20, 2016, at: www.cnsnews.com/commentary/walter-e-williams/cruelty-black-students]

As Professor Williams indicates, it is black students, most of whom are unprepared for college life, who suffered most by being boosted by affirmative action and entitlements. But the results for white high school graduates are equally appalling.

And these form the pool of students whose parents fork over anywhere from $20,000 to $50,000 a year to our universities to educate them.

For broader confirmation, consider a parallel choice: a career in the United States military. Under President Trump and his signing of a new defense bill, the armed services are instructed to recruit new enlistees — the US Army alone, about 17,500 new recruits every year.

But there is a problem: in addition to the fact that many potential candidates are obese, as Army Chief of Staff Mark Milley states: "...one in four cannot meet minimal educational standards (a high school diploma or GED equivalent), and one in 10 have a criminal history. In plain terms, about 71 percent of 18-to-24-year-olds (the military's target pool of potential recruits) are disqualified from the minute they enter a recruiting station: that's 24 million out of 34 million Americans... fully 30 percent of those who have the requisite high school diploma or GED equivalent fail to pass the Armed Forces Qualification Test (the AFQT), which is used to determine math and reading skills...." [Mark Perry, "The Recruitment Problem the Military Doesn't Want to Talk About," *The American Conservative*, August 15, 2018, at: www.theamericanconservative.com/articles/the-recruitment-problem-the-military-doesnt-want-to-talk-about/]

It is any wonder that a rowdy mob, drenched in cultural Marxist dross which passes for education — a mob turned into raving lunatics by teachers and college professors who are little more than fanatical ideological agents of continuing revolution — now seeks to destroy Confederate symbols and soon to obliterate anything reminding them or us of twenty centuries Western Christian, and yes, white and largely male, culture?

The administrators at the University of North Carolina at Chapel Hill, like the administrators at most colleges throughout the land, have yet to comprehend this; indeed, many sympathize with the lunatics. They must understand we are in a multilevel cultural war, and on the outcome of this war depends the very existence of our culture and our identity as a civilization.

Too many political and civic leaders continue to bury their heads in the sand, look the other way, or hope the "problem" will just go away. But it won't, for it is like a rapidly-spreading cancer which must be excised and removed … else it kill the host body.

(My Corner, August 26, 2018, accessed at: http://boydcatheyreviewofbooks.blogspot.com/2018/08/august-26-2018-my-corner-by-boyd-cathey.html) A revised version of this essay has been published by *Chronicles* magazine, November 2018, titled "From 'Silent Sam' to Screaming Selfies," pp. 27-28.

Thoughts on Charlottesville and What It Means for Us
↣ *Chapter 19* ↢

Saturday night, August 12, 2017, the media was filled to overflowing with nothing but lurid and hysterical accounts of the "violence" and the "massacre" by so-called "white nationalists" (alternately identified as "white supremacists" or "white racists") inflicted on poor, innocent "counter demonstrators" in Charlottesville who were "protesting hate and bigotry." That's the narrative that showed up, including wall-to-wall coverage on Fox, overpowering everything else, and spewed forth as if handed down from Mount Olympus by assorted "wise" Republican senators, including most notably Marco Rubio, Orrin Hatch, and John McCain, whose biggest complaint was that Donald Trump somehow did not specify that the violence was exclusively caused by something that is termed the "Alt-right."

Nary a word about the ultimate and real responsibility of the American Left for a continuing history of violence, nary a word about the responsibility of the so-called "resist Trump" organizations and their actions, nary a word about the uncontrolled rampaging of the Black Lives Matter movement (e.g., Ferguson, Baltimore, etc.), nary a word about the stepped up and planned confrontations by the "antifa" (self-titled "antifascists") militants. That is, not one word about the history of virulent street action, fire bombing, trashing of private property, and, yes, attempts to kill anyone (e.g., Representative Steve Scalise) to the perceived right of, say, John McCain, anyone who might in any way say a good word about Donald Trump, or defend older American traditions and beliefs.

Continually, the networks portray what happened Saturday as simply the manifestation of extremism and bigotry from the Right. And practically the only voice that got even remotely close to a rational perspective came from, quite ironically, a black professor, Carol Swain at Vanderbilt University, who distinguished between the very legitimate desires, aspirations and fears of America's under-attack white majority and the misapprehension that somehow those desires equal inevitably "white racism" or "white supremacy." As Swain indicated, what has happened during the past few decades is a palpable marginalization of millions of hard working Americans, mostly white and mostly Christian, who have been sidelined and left behind by the advancing progressivist revolution (these last words are mine). They are not naturally "racists" or even "white supremacists," but rather they seek to guarantee their own survival, and the survival of their families, their communities, and their culture. They have seen the standards, beliefs, traditions, morality and customs they inherited and have cherished — they have seen them attacked, ridiculed, and, in many cases, banned, even criminalized.

The so-called "Alt-right" march and their demonstration in Charlottesville, then, must be seen as something of a predictable boiling over of that legitimate and simmering sentiment. Protesting the attempt to take down the historic Robert E. Lee statue was not, in this sense, the underlying reason for the Alt-right protest. Rather, it served as a much broader, if much angrier and extreme, reminder of what is and has been occurring in our society, a symbol of the continuing destruction of this nation and its history by those who zealously possess and attempt to impose a world view, a template, which is the antithesis of those beliefs and faith millions of us have inherited and which we hold dear and believe.

The attacks by nearly the entirety of the media — including notably Fox — on the "Alt-right" demonstrators as "white racists" and "white supremacists," then, is not only misguided scattershot, but it partakes in the dominant and ideologically leftist Deep State establishment narrative which posits as absolute truth that "hate," "bigotry," "racism," *ad nauseum*, only come from what they identity as the "far" or "extreme" right, or more recently, "Alt-right." And those terms are all-inclusive for anyone who dissents even in the slightest from the ongoing progressivist Revolution.

Thus, when the president condemned violence from "both sides," it was as if Mount Vesuvius had erupted and had poured down its ash and lava all over Pompei! The Mainstream Media went literally berserk in outrage and demanded that he specify by name the "right" and "rightist violence." And in jumped with both feet the obsequiously sickening Marco Rubio and Karl Rove, obedient to the standard Deep State mindset, urging the president to condemn "white nationalism" and "white supremacy."

And so it went throughout that afternoon and evening … until I finally couldn't take it any longer, and switched over to watch John Wayne in John Ford's 1950 film masterpiece, *Rio Grande*. (It is always a gracious reward at the end to hear the Yankee band strike up *Dixie* as the Union troops pass in review!)

Certainly, the Alt-right demonstrators in Charlottesville included some extreme elements. Certainly, some would advocate a form of "supremacy," or rather a return to a time when white people had more authority in this nation. And, yes, they were very angry — angry after watching the dozens of violent manifestations by those revolutionaries of the Left, those "resisters" and "antifa" Marxists and Anarchists, those rampaging Black Lives Matter zealots for whom any law enforcement action against any black person is, *ipso facto*, "racist" and "police brutality," legitimizing their burning out of whole neighborhoods in Baltimore and Ferguson. And, yes, driving a car murderously into the assembled counter-demonstrators, however much provocation there may have been, was unjustified and counter-productive and very probably criminal.

All of this was predictable and even perhaps inevitable, given what has happened in the country. Indeed, is it not a product of the over-the-top rhetoric, the apocalyptic imagery and the violent reaction from the forces and minions of the Deep State managerial establishment to last year's election and any attempt to reverse their jealously-guarded domination over us all?

Recently, Peter Brimelow, editor of VDare.com wrote a piece on his web site, entitled "there will be blood." And the implication was and is this: for far too long, we middle Americans, we "deplorables," oppressed and suppressed by an increasingly revolutionary, radically multiculturalist, culturally Marxist, suffocating overlay which drains out our historic being and essence as a people, have more or less obediently acceded to the Revolution and its infectious cancer. Beginning last November, but actually before, that passivity was interrupted, and millions of citizens, understanding, if intuitively, that their lives and their country were slipping away from their control, stood up and cried: "No further!"

And the dominant forces in our culture have responded furiously. At first those of us who wished to defend our traditions and our historic Western Christian culture sought to meet their assault traditionally, within the accustomed methods and pathways of our republic. But it was they — the forces of the increasingly hysterical Deep State and their storm trooper antifa street fighters, Black Lives Matter and its fatuous race hustlers like William Barber, the radicalized and demented university students, and not just them, but the near totality of the Democrat Party and most establishment Republicans, all fatally infected by a Revolutionary progressivist venom — they who first unleashed the violence in words *AND* in deeds.

Ironically, it is Robert E. Lee who defiantly stands for what was and is admirable and right about America. And his lesson is being lost through all that is currently occurring. A man who despised slavery and freed the slaves in his charge (that had belonged to his father-in-law George Washington Parke Custis) in 1862, a man descended from the Founders of our old Republic and who fully understood what the Founders intended, a man who loved the Union but loved liberty more, a man of a truly Christian and gentle disposition — Lee stands out in our history as one of our greatest figures, respected and deeply admired by such diverse leaders as Winston Churchill and Dwight D. Eisenhower. Yet, he also comprehended what the tyranny of an over-reaching Federal government might mean. And he made a momentous decision to stand with his state *AND* for the American Constitution. In a real sense, he stood 155 years ago against the incipient progressivist Revolution, and despite overwhelming odds, he almost succeeded in leading the Confederate nation to victory against that revolution.

Rather than recur then to some grab-bag terminology the media calls the "Alt-right" — which has yet to be accurately defined and described, other than becoming a "devil" term for the minions of the Deep State — those of us, those deplorables, those who awakened from a silent slumber last November, those of us who wish only to reclaim the right of our people, our culture, our civilization to survive and continue unmolested — we should look to the model of that *"chevalier sans peur,"* that noble Virginian, Robert E. Lee, who tried to preserve the American confederation, but also understood there are times when one must, regretfully and painfully, take bolder steps to save that which is admirable and laudable in our history and our culture.

This, then, should be the watchword of our faith. We have been aggrieved and assaulted; we must respond according to the appropriate levels, not more, not less. We must be wiser and more intelligent than our enemies in the Deep State, for they possess most of the major weapons. Yet, with determination and the necessary prudence, and the wisdom and lessons of our ancestors, and above all, with Faith, we can succeed.

We defend our historic culture and our faith; we do so morally and ethically; but we do not stand down, nor do we shy away from the conflict.

(*The Unz Review*, August 15, 2017, at: www.unz.com/article/thoughts-on-charlottesville-and-what-it-means-for-us/)

Charlottesville — One Year Later
✧ Chapter 20 ✦

August 11-12, 2018, marked the one year anniversary of the events —the riot — which occurred in Charlottesville, Virginia, back in 2017. And government-funded PBS weighed in few days earlier (August 6) with a special primetime edition of its television program *Frontline*. The feature, "Documenting Hate: Charlottesville," is a tendentious cinematic attempt at shaping the historical narrative by the Leftist-funded, pro-Marxist group ProPublica. It portrays what happened in Mr. Jefferson's city as a "violent riot and massacre by Nazis and violent Alt-Right fascists."

ProPublica, which pretends to be a center for "investigative journalism," has in some ways taken over from the increasingly discredited Southern Poverty Law Center (SPLC), as a self-proclaimed vehicle for "shining the light of publicity" (and launching personal attacks) on what it terms nefarious "right wing extremists." Of course, a closer look at this tax exempt, non-profit research organization reveals it is funded by some of the biggest "hitters" — the most affluent billionaires — on the far Left of the Democratic Party.

Here is what the Wikipedia says about ProPublica:

ProPublica was the brainchild of billionaires and Democratic donors Herbert and Marion Sandler, former chief executives of the Golden West Financial Corporation, who have committed $10 million a year to the project. The Sandlers hired Paul Steiger former managing editor of the Wall Street Journal, *to create and run the organization as editor-in-chief.*

Notice what this paragraph says: Major Leftist Democratic donors — Wall Street billionaires — create this new "anti-hate" group, and then, hire the former managing editor of the — yes, supposedly "right wing" — *Wall Street Journal* (owned by Rupert Murdoch, who also owns Fox).

Connect the dots — connect the dots between the globalist Left-wing capitalists on Wall Street, the globalist capitalist *Wall Street Journal*, and the Democratic Left.

ProPublica's "Documenting Hate" uses as background President Trump's "moral failure" over Charlottesville: he refused to blame only the Right — those Nazis — for the violence. ... But stated there was enough culpability to go round on both sides. (Remember it was such high-profile minions of the "conservative movement inc." like Ben

The Land We Love

Shapiro, Glenn Back, and Jonah Goldberg, all of whom had been Never Trumpers, who joined the Left and led the charge to condemn the president and imply that he was a "racist" for his "failure.")

Indeed, Black Lives Matter and Antifa — who did not have a march/rally permit, while the Unite the Right demonstrators did — gathered specifically to challenge and engage in combat with the Rightists and, in effect, caused the riot.

Never mind; ProPublica's narrative said not one word about that Leftist violence. From viewing their *Frontline* exposition you would only think it was just that dangerous and armed group of Nazis, who, we are also told, have infiltrated all facets of American life (including the military) who initiated and committed mayhem. And, of course, behind it all stood and stands the political figure who has legitimated the "climate of hate" — Donald J. Trump.

A larger question remains, and not just about the fate of the monument to Robert E. Lee in Charlottesville, but about all the symbols of our history all across the Southland. It is a question all Southerners who value and treasure their rich patrimony and inheritance should ask themselves: as the radical cultural Marxists engage in a concerted campaign — with the connivance of the news media (including Fox) and much of what passes for the establishment "conservative movement" — to wipe the horizon clear of all monuments to our history, our heritage, and our heroes: where are the thousands of Southern-born folks who should be turning out and demanding that those extremists leave our monuments and symbols alone?

At home watching the latest episode of *America's Got Talent* or Steve Harvey? Out mowing the grass and drinking a cool one?

In other words, arranging the deck chairs on the RMS *Titanic* while the cultural Marxist iceberg does its work?

In other words: where are our fellow citizens when the local gang of professional Marxists, Black Lives Matter militants, and Antifa hooligans — with tacit okays from leaders of both political parties, and with the nodding approval of the press — organize a loud, semi-violent demonstration against those monuments which, they say, are "symbols of racism" and "white supremacy," and threaten to destroy them (just like they did in Durham, NC)?

Where are our fellow citizens when the local liberal and spineless Republican office-holders, afraid of being labeled "racists," hold quickly-planned "public input sessions" to decide the fate of those symbols?

Where are our fellow citizens when the few heritage defense organizations who do exist hold public events, such as Lee Day, Confederate Flag Day, or Confederate Memorial Day observances? Sitting on their duffs while those elements who wish to extinguish not just our heritage, but us as well, continue on their cancerous and destructive rampage to transform our institutions and culture?

Back in 2007, as chairman of North Carolina's annual Confederate Flag Day (sponsored by the Sons of Confederate Veterans), I brought down nationally-known traditionalist conservative author, Dr. Paul Gottfried, to address our event. His speech was both a salute to Tar Heels who assembled to honor their heritage and a clarion call to Southerners to defend their heritage, and his presentation was reprinted later in the *Confederate Veteran* magazine.

In a more recent essay he asks the same question I ask of my fellow citizens now, and not only of my fellow Southerners: where are you? Here is part of what he writes ("Southern Cultural Cleansing: A Northern Perspective," June 26, 2018, at: www.reckonin.com/paul-gottfried/southern-cultural-cleansing-a-northern-perspective):

As a Northerner, I am appalled by the very limited opposition to this government-sponsored vandalism that has come from Southern whites, many of whose ancestors were involved in the struggle for Southern independence. When I watched the events in Charlottesville unfold last year, I kept asking myself why millions of Southerners had not descended on the Confederate war monument located in the city center to protest its removal, before those with a different agenda took advantage of the protest for their own use. In a commentary, I contrasted the generally weak Southern response to the ongoing extirpation and blackening of their ancestral history to the way Italians in New York City responded to the efforts of the local Taliban to pull down statues of Columbus. The question I addressed is why Italian Americans cared more about Columbus, an Italian who sailed to the New World under a Spanish flag five hundred years ago, than Southerners cared about honoring the memory of a great American hero who was one of their own.

What complicates this matter for me is the vicious attack on the Southern past is part of something that goes well beyond the states who formed the onetime Confederacy. It is the opening round of what is likely to become a violent struggle for a total Cultural Marxist transformation of this country. Those who engage in politics as usual have tried to dislodge this concern from our minds. But the reconstruction continues to take place, and the defacing and ripping down of Confederate monuments is symptomatic of something much bigger and more ominous. For those who haven't noticed: our media and educational institutions are inciting this transformation; and our established conservative movement is doing zilch to prevent it from happening.

As our vicious and unhinged enemies attempt to liquidate our past where are those thousands of sons and daughters of the South (and their allies from other parts of the nation) willing to stand up and say to the culture crazies: "Halt! No further: leave our symbols alone — go back to your filthy hovels — better yet, be true to your convictions and take the next boat to North Korea (about which your web sites wax admiringly). I'm sure the Fearless Leader Kim can find a use for your brains-dulled-by-drugs, unwashed selves!"

(MY CORNER, August 9, 2011, at: http://boydcatheyreviewofbooks.blogspot.com/2018/08/august-9-2018-my-corner-by-boydcathey.html, and republished, August 11, 2018, slightly edited, at: https://www.reckonin.com/boyd-cathey/charlottesville-one-year-later)

Celebrating Lee Day, While Thousands of Women Go Marching Off to Hell

⇾ *Chapter 21* ⇽

I was in Raleigh, North Carolina, back on January 20, 2018, to join more than 350 North Carolinians gathered in the old House of Representative chamber of the historic 1840 State Capitol to celebrate North Carolina's 29th annual celebration of Robert E. Lee Day. It was an impressive ceremony which reminded the attendees of the precious historical legacy and cultural inheritance we have received and is so gravely endangered these days. I came away encouraged: there were men, women, and children, various members of the military and surviving veterans of World War II, Korea, Vietnam and Desert Storm, with their families, all joined in memory of veterans — not just Confederate soldiers but all veterans — who went before us, those who selflessly defended their homes, their land, and their faith, so that we might enjoy and experience those gifts … and pass them on to our children.

When I walked the short distance from a crowded parking lot to the State Capitol, I noticed my car was surrounded by dozens of other cars emblazoned with bumper stickers with such messages as: "Dump Trump, Keep Your Hands Off My Vagina," "Abortion Free and Legal," "Open Immigration NOW!," "Lesbians Unite to Smash the Right," "Resist!" — those are just the ones I noticed. And I wondered if, when I returned, my little Kia (with a Confederate license plate) would be scarred or damaged by those latter-day liberated amazons. As I walked up the sidewalk to the Capitol I noticed hundreds of women — most of whom I would have certainly avoided had I met them at a social gathering — headed for a rally, an event concurrent with our event, just a few blocks away on what is called the Bicentennial Plaza, a much larger event for certain, but in no way comparable in quality or merit.

It was the Raleigh extension of the "Women's Resist" movement, a grab bag manifestation of a whole motley crew of what is best described as an expression of "feminist, anti-racist, anti-sexist, Marxist and anti-Trump sentiment," which was held on the one year anniversary of the inauguration of Donald Trump as president of the United States.

Despite a mammoth Pro-Life Rally in Washington the day prior — perhaps as many as 200,000 participants and the president addressing them (the first president to do that) — it was the women's march that was practically the only thing the media could or wished to concentrate on, those hundreds of thousands of #Resist movement women (with some of their poor, bedraggled husbands and brainwashing-in-process young daughters and sons in tow), now supplemented by the supposedly-sexually-abused #MeToo militants, out in the streets demonstrating for a variety of feminist and civil rights causes.

If there was and is anything which should convince us of the absolutely deleterious and poisonous effects of modern public schooling and university education and the effects of our entertainment behemoth, it was to behold those women (and their menfolk) heading to their rally. Most carried signs, bearing expressions which, when not just foul-mouthed or profane, partook of what I would call "illiterate-speak." That is, sloganeering based on fiercely weaponized and half-baked nuggets of thought; those bits of ideas spread throughout our dominant culture, which for them are in fact unquestioned and which under normal circumstances would not bear up under any close analysis or scrutiny.

Those women live their lives based on Progressivist slogans, incorporating a deconstructed — or, rather, reconstructed — language of short catch-all phrases and terminologies, buttressed by pseudo-scientific gobbledegook: "racist," "sexist," "homophobe," "voting rights," "gender equality," "transgender rights," the list is interminable. Their explanations and definitions are usually circuitous, and generally all come back to a foundation in what they call "equality" and "liberation" from traditional — and thus "oppressive" — rules and moral (and natural) law, which they almost always misunderstand or simply ignore. In other words, those foundations which have created our civilization and given it life over the past more than twenty centuries are discarded, become mere impediments in the way of Progress that must be overthrown, or at least radically altered, transformed or reinterpreted.

One thing you can be sure of is that tomorrow we shall see another "right" invented for whatever new barbarity will be intuited to have been miraculously found in the "penumbra of the Constitution," and there will be some federal judge or judges out there who will confirm this is exactly what the Founders and Framers of the Republic truly intended, whether it be for some dehumanized "metrosexual" male who all of a sudden "declares" that he "feels" like a woman and demands he be allowed to use a lady's restroom, or for some husky female who decides that she should be a tackle on the Minnesota Vikings football team so she can run up against a player who weighs in at 320 pounds (and has three convictions for wife abuse).

Now it is transgender rights and gender fluidity, but tomorrow it will be incest and polygamy, no doubt. And there will be a series of "experts" and assembled PhDs in psychiatry and counseling brought in to testify such practices are indeed just fine and — shall we even use the word? — Normal.

Yes, that is most assuredly what James Madison, John Jay, Alexander Hamilton, and other fathers of this republic envisioned!

I have argued previously what we see presently in our society, and not just with the so-called "women's movement," is a form of collective madness, the existence of an artificial counter-reality; a condition in which certain broad strata of our population, ingesting decades and, yes, centuries of both intellectual and spiritual disinformation, have constructed around themselves a pseudo-reality to match their ideological indoctrination. Reality for them must match what they have been told and instructed to believe. So, instead of accepting the God-given reality and the natural order as created, instead of accepting their own creaturehood and an understanding of the flawed nature and limitations of humanity, itself, they construct a revolutionary counter-existence to explain things and events, what German philosophers might call "gestalt," as a way of justifying their beliefs and resulting actions.

And thus there is the need to diagnose and explain why the rest of us — those who reject their worldview — do not accept the new template and the new reality they propound. Whether it be the attempts of historic liberalism of the 19th century to define traditionalist, religious and royalist thinking as "reactionary," "anti-democratic," and "opposed to the inevitability of Progress," or more recent efforts in the old Soviet Union, when not exiling dissenters to the Gulag, to send those who opposed the new orthodoxy to mental and psychiatric hospitals for treatment and "re-education," — no matter what the example — those who advance the counter-reality (which in essence is a rebellion against God and His creation) seek to deauthorize and delegitimize their opponents.

Just recently a veritable gaggle of "expert" psychiatrists and non-medical pundits spent an inordinate amount of time on air, "diagnosing" Donald Trump as "mentally unfit" for office. Obviously his physical examination tests were skewed, obviously his doctor (who was also Obama's) was lying ... this is what we were told. Even as I caught a bit of NPR riding in my car to Raleigh (the program "What! What! Don't Tell Me") and later that night (Jimmy Fallon), the not funny attempts at humor, characterizing Trump as "mentally abnormal", were shot through with bitter scorn and hatred, a drippingly vile condescension exhibited not just toward the president, but at anyone who would not follow the new dogmatism and accept the new reality. (Remember FBI agent Peter Strzok's description of being able "to smell Trump supporters at Walmart?")

The Progressivist syllogism goes as follows:

Premise #1: What we in the media, academia and the dominant culture dictate and proclaim as true cannot be legitimately contested;

Premise #2: But Donald Trump and millions of those "deplorables" in the despised "fly-over country" (to quote the condescending pornographic novelist Philip Roth) deny and refuse to accept what we demand they accept;

Conclusion: Therefore, Donald Trump (and all those unwashed deplorables) are "mentally sick" and "unadjusted," requiring counseling and correction, and if that doesn't work, condemnation and exiling from the public square.

(And, let me point out, one doesn't have to agree with the president on every issue to fall victim of this new dogmatism — I certainly have my disagreements on some issues.)

And thus we see the broadly erupting epidemic, which becomes fiercer as the days pass, of suppression of "dissident" speech on college campuses in the name of protecting students from racism, sexism and homophobia; of firing or penalizing employees who question the Progressivist narratives on race and sex; the censoring of those on Facebook or Google who question the new totalitarian templates; the abject fear of any politician (Democrat or Republican) or any public personality of transgressing the steadily-moving-to-the-Left goal posts on race or sexual "liberation." To do so will result in overwhelming demands for a complete and groveling apology — and perhaps a handsome donation to the NAACP or Planned Parenthood, to help make up for the "sin" committed against the new dogmas.

I have termed the counter-reality that produces this palpable intellectual and spiritual totalitarianism as a form of lunacy, a kind of madness that inverts and attempts to pervert creation and nature itself, so as to match a synthetic and imposed, essentially anti-human, ideology. To protect itself from dissent and probing questions, it must continually be on the offensive, continually convulsed and convulsive like all fanaticisms, and always on guard that some "reactionary," in some place, will speak up and notice its intellectual vacuity and artificiality … and its horrid and genocidal effects.

Those women yesterday professed they were marching for "equality," for the expansion of something they called liberty. But they have no idea of what genuine liberty is or entails.

In his volume, *The Poet and the Lunatics* (1929), G. K. Chesterton's character Gale asks the question: "What exactly is liberty?" He responds, in part:

"First and foremost, surely, it is the power of a thing to be itself. In some ways the yellow bird was free in the cage...We are limited by our brains and bodies; and if we break out, we cease to be ourselves, and, perhaps, to be anything.

"The lunatic is he who loses his way and cannot return.... The man who opened the bird-cage loved freedom; possibly too much... But the man who broke the bowl merely because he thought it a prison for the fish, when it was their only possible house of life — that man was already outside the world of reason, raging with a desire to be outside of everything."

True liberty, and its exercise, requires it have an object and a terminus. In our European and Christian civilization, with its fundamental inheritances from the three great historic centers of learning and wisdom — Rome, Athens, and Jerusalem — that means we are entrusted with essential rights and liberties which are both inherited and defined by who we are as a people and by our relationship to our Creator and to those institutions who give us existence and life. This is our inheritance; we have no other. To attempt to overthrow or pervert it is to open the doors to self-destruction.

Those women I saw marching, and the millions of other Americans like them, are modern revolutionaries, and, to use Chesterton's parable, are lunatics, "already outside the world of reason," whose unrestrained rage to destroy is only matched by their profound inability to create anything of real and lasting value.

And thus that smaller crowd at Lee Day at the State Capitol, while overshadowed in numbers (and by media coverage), represented hope and recovery, and the blessed assurance that our battle goes on … and that numbers and fame, while significant and certainly important, are as nothing if we are on God's side.

(*The Remnant*, January 22, 2018, at: https://remnantnewspaper.com/web/index.php/fetzen-fliegen/item/3676-celebrating-lee-day-while-thousands-of-women-go-marching-off-to-hell)

Leftist Crazies Don't Want You to Exist
✧ Chapter 22 ✦

I try to collect all the business I must do in Raleigh into one day. One trip a week into North Carolina's increasingly cosmopolitanized and rapidly de-Southernized capital city is about all I can take these days: it's become too much like just about any other homogenized, faceless metropolis in any other part of the country. Most of Raleigh's historic and traditional Southern charm and character have been erased and overawed by transplants and interlopers from "up North" and elsewhere who feel their mission in life is to remake the Tar Heel State's capital into a copy of the decaying cities they left behind! Unlike Columbia, South Carolina, Raleigh wasn't burned by Sherman back in 1865, but the city fathers back then, I'm certain, would be appalled at what has happened since then to a once gracious Southern city. As the late superb Southern writer Tom Landess once said about modern-day Atlanta: "Where is Sherman when we really need him?"

When going into town I usually park in the public for-pay lot across the street from the North Carolina State Archives where I used to be gainfully employed. It's a short block to the historic North Carolina State Capitol (1840), where on May 20, 1861, North Carolina representatives voted unanimously to secede, and a short, usually pleasant walk to most any office or business downtown. Curiously, there are some, usually newer residents of the capital city (mostly transplants, I suspect) living either out near Cary and Apex or way up in the northern extremes of the city, past the outer beltline, who have never even been "downtown" (when I was working downtown I used to get queries from persons who wanted to come to the Archives, but had no idea at all how to get there).

Anyway, I was making one of my mostly weekly forays into what has become for me "the heart of darkness," and I parked my 2006 Kia Spectra in the public lot. The lot was nearly full of cars, and as I got out I viewed literally hundreds of mostly women, but a few men and children tagging along, all gaily vested in summertime outfits, many carrying placards and signs.

Almost immediately I was aware that these folks were protesters assembled in the capital city for some event, and from their signs — the ones I read — they were there to protest President Trump, his immigration policies, "police brutality," those "racist" Confederate monuments, "income inequality," and a multiple of other societal "wrongs," all of which I would say were on the Left, or better said, the Culturally Marxist Left.

One lady who walked by my car apparently noticed my state-issued Sons of Confederate Veterans license plate with its Battle Flag and the sticker I affixed to my car back in 2015: "Putin for President," which always gets a few views and second-takes!

I smiled at her — as I was always taught to do by my good Southern parents — and said: "How's it going?" The lady (she probably wouldn't have liked that word) responded: "I'm great." Then she added almost immediately: "Why that racist Confederate license plate and that Putin bumper sticker?"

Now, let me describe this female: she could have passed for anyone's favorite aunt. She had greying hair, large sun glasses, a smart-looking summer dress, and a large handbag. She could have been on her way to vacation Bible school for all I knew. She was white and from her demeanor appeared to be middle or upper middle class. At the beginning of our short *tete-a-tete* she had one of those frozen plastic smiles on her face that you see on various store clerks at the end of a long work day or perhaps on a car salesman if he thinks you might purchase a vehicle from him. But when she opened her mouth and spoke, it was with a distinctly clipped non-Southern accent. As my grandfather used to say, I knew "she won't from around here!"

I responded to her question politely, with a smile on my face: "The license plate is state-issued, and it means that I am a member of the North Carolina Sons of Confederate Veterans, which is a heritage group defending our state's traditions and history." And I added with a broader smile: "The Putin sticker is mainly there to provoke thought … and maybe conversation."

I could tell from the lady's expression she wasn't at all amused. "These are racist and fascist symbols!" She exclaimed, becoming agitated as she spoke.

"Not really," I responded. I tried to smile, but it was no use.

I changed the topic: "Are you here for a protest," I asked. She answered huffily: "Yes, I am with the North Carolina Peace Action Center. We believe in peace, in pacifism. I'm a member of the United Church of Christ, and we believe in international brotherhood and social justice, equality, and the dignity and rights of the individual." (I think that was what she said, but I am only summarizing her). "We are protesting fascism and racism, and demanding full equality and voting rights, and that our legislature take immediate action to stop upholding white privilege!"

At that point I understood this brief conversation was going nowhere and that nothing I could say, other than forced pleasantries, might make matters better. So, I just smiled, hoping to quickly end the conversation. But I couldn't help myself and had to say one last thing as I tried to get away: "Equality doesn't exist in this world. Respectfully, I would suggest that all those cultural Marxist slogans you're stating only end in much greater pain, hardship, and social disaster. Now, I must really go to my appointment. Nice to meet and talk with you."

I thought that would end it, but it did not. And before I could steal away, she uttered in a rising crescendo: "You must be a Trump supporter!" As I continued to move away from her, I nodded my head.

"Trump supporters are f — ing fascists! You neo-Confederates are racists!" She angrily shouted. And I thought if I didn't move on quickly she might slug me with her handbag.

There it was: from this respectable looking lady, who probably was around 60, certainly not impoverished (materially), most likely college or university-educated, a member (apparently active, as well) in an established mainline Protestant church — the "F-bomb," uttered at a stranger, someone she had just casually met getting out of his car on a hot summer day in Raleigh, North Carolina. She had never seen me before (unless — extremely doubtful — she had attended a Confederate flag event!), she didn't know my name — but she understood correctly that I was a "Trump supporter" in 2016, and obviously, with that Confederate license plate, well, then, I was the epitome, the symbol, of all that stood in the way of her goal of remaking America into a cultural Marxist utopia.

"Full equality?" And I was reminded of the "equality" pictured by various writers who had either experienced the Communist kind or who were wise enough to understand what it meant: George Orwell's depiction in his fanciful novel, *Animal Farm*, but even more aptly, perhaps in Arthur Koestler's dystopian novel *Darkness at Noon* (1940), a thinly-veiled account of Stalin and his great purges, or even more, by the late Spanish traditionalist, Rafael Gambra, in his marvelous volume, *El silencio de Dios* (1967), which desperately needs an English translation.

I don't think that protesting woman, despite her probable university training and membership in the UCC, would have fathomed anything those writers wrote, or understood anything they were saying.

And she would never understand what Southern heritage means and encompasses.

What I found perhaps most disturbing in this short encounter — and something not even the Stalinists of old were that guilty of — was the near complete decline linguistically, in language. How had things in our society degenerated so far that a perfect stranger would, after less than two minutes of conversation, decide to unleash the "f-bomb" on me? Has our national discourse declined this far?

And, in reflecting, the answer is a definite "yes," and all we need to do is make a cursory search online (or via the television) of just recent statements and imprecations uttered by the more noteworthy minions of the Left in American society. Just before I began writing this column, I was able to go online and find about fifteen instances in which the foulest four-letter words were spoken publicly, to national audiences, or to large groups of online recipients. Robert De Niro or Peter Fonda, anyone?

And, no, I do not accept the faux-argument that it was Donald Trump who began all this decline and abuse in the English language. This degradation was there in full force long before he ever became president — it was there in the dialogue sequences of almost every Hollywood block-buster since at least the 1980s. It was there on our college campuses, countenanced by the professoriate; it was there in our culture. It was there for years in the vicious attacks on Confederate heritage and our symbols. All Donald Trump did was tear off the scab which thinly disguised the gutter mindset of our supposed political, cultural and educational arbiters. His unanticipated and unexpected presence in the White House infuriated and maddened them — forcing them, as the fetid pus under those scabs, to come forth in all their oleaginous stench and foulness.

So, in this age of Donald Trump I should have expected that "peace demonstrator" I encountered — that self-proclaimed pacifist and "anti-racist" social justice warrior advocating for "equality" and "justice" — to act exactly as she did. Her vaunted and repeated deep concern and desire for equality and for dialogue does not include me, or the millions like me — or you. Only if we repent continuously for our past sins of racism, repent for the multiple sins of all our (white) ancestors, and for the white privilege we somehow enjoy (although I'll bet my meager retirement income is far less than that lady's financial resources!), then there might be a tiny glimmer of hope for us in that lady's view. And even then, with the goal of open borders and the long-range population replacement strategy of the Left, whatever I could say would assuredly mean little to her.

In the end, we are in an immense battle, a cultural war to the death, what Pat Buchanan wrote about and described back in 2002 with his volume *The Death of the West*, and in subsequent works — such as the brilliant Paul Gottfried has documented in his critical studies on the intellectual earthquake that has shaken Western European and American civilization to its foundations.

In the end, one side must win, and one side must lose. It is that simple.

And how that final conflict, that war to the death is fought is now an open question as never before, certainly since the assassination attempt on Representative Steve Scalise and the House Republicans or the attack by a Leftist crazy on the Family Research Council (after those professional "hate monitors" at the Southern Poverty Law Center had labeled it as a purveyor of "right wing hate").

As I have said — and written more than once — the one major advantage we have is we don't believe in gun control. Every neighbor I have out here in my lower middle class neighborhood in still-Southern Eastern Wake County is armed with shotguns and .44s or .38s, while our opponents scream "gun control." So, if and when their lunacy becomes too overpowering and they decide to march out this way looking for "fascists" and "Neo-Confederate racists" to hound and threaten, our target practice training will come in good use.

Let'em come!

(Abbeville Institute, July 7, 2018, at: www.abbevilleinstitute.org/blog/leftist-crazies-dont-want-you-to-exist/?mc_cid=1c56e79b16&mc_eid=8639a6a6ea)

PART III

WHAT THE NATIVITY SAYS TO SOUTHERNERS

Half way through this collection of essays it seems appropriate to stop for a moment and to reflect. The events of recent years — the attacks on the symbols of our heritage, our monuments, our banners, the history we impart to our children, what is taught in schools and portrayed in film and on television, would seem to indicate the defense of Confederate traditions and heritage is a thankless task which is becoming more difficult by the day. Yet, our trust is in something much greater than the latest decree by the United States Supreme Court or the latest law enacted by Congress. All the Hollywood movies, all the ideological instruction in our colleges and schools, all the political posturing by on-the-make, spineless politicians, will not, in the end, stand against He who created us.

Certainly, it seems, humanly-speaking, an insurmountable task, a Sisyphean task of continually butting heads against inevitability. Yet, our forefathers, whether on the blood-stained field of Gettysburg, or in the trenches around Petersburg, never lost their faith in Divine Providence, even after military defeat on the battlefield.

As President Jefferson Davis said years after the conclusion of the War for Southern Independence: "… the principle for which we contended is bound to reassert itself, though it may be at another time and in another form." He, like many of our forefathers, never lost hope, for they knew that eventually, either here on earth or beyond, justice and right would be administered, and that duty and fealty to principles and faith are far more important than momentary success.

The Vigil of the Nativity — Reflections on the Hope that Came to Us Two Millenia Ago
❖ Chapter 23 ❖

Today is the Vigil of the Nativity of Our Lord, a day filled with anticipation and scarcely concealed joy as we await the memorialization and recreation of that ineffable Event — unimaginable in human terms — that forever changed human history.

The sin of Adam — Original Sin — affected all mankind and left descendants marked, indelibly stained by that original fault. Adam's sin was a form of disobedience, but a disobedience so grave and monumental against God's Creation, that only the Coming of the Messiah, the Second Person of the Trinity of the Godhead, could repair it. And the Son of God would be Incarnate in a woman who would be pure and herself immaculate, untouched by the inheritance of sinfulness (by the merits of her Son). Only such a spotlessly pure womb would be fitting for the Incarnate God. And only the Incarnation into one of His creatures would serve the purpose of demonstrating that Our Blessed Saviour would come to us, not only as God, but also in the form of Man — this was fitting because it was to Mankind that He was sent.

For hundreds of years the People of Israel had awaited the coming of a Messiah to lead them, to liberate them and, if you will, to repair Adam's Fall. But this vision — whether expressed in the revolts of the Maccabees or in later violent episodes like the revolt of Simon bar Kokhba against the Romans (132 A.D.) — implied not just satisfaction for sinful ways, but increasingly the establishment of an earthly and insular kingdom for and of the Hebrews.

And although Our Lord and Saviour indeed came first to the Jews, and offered them His reparative Grace and Salvation, it was by no means to be limited to them. Indeed, His message was universal (as it had been to Abraham). And those Hebrews who accepted the Messiah — and those gentiles who also joined them — became the Church, the "New" Israel, receptor of God's Grace and holder of His Promises and carrier of His Light unto all the world.

While a majority of old Israel rejected Our Lord, demanding His Crucifixion before Pilate, those who followed Him and believed in Him entered the New Covenant, a New Testament. It is in this sense that the Christian church inherited the promises of Israel and the Old

Testament, and fulfilled those prophesies. And that fulfillment continues.

St. Paul in his Epistle to Titus [2:11-15] summarizes both the dazzling and miraculous wonder of Our Saviour's Grace amongst us and its inexhaustible power to transform us, as we await His final Coming in Glory: "The grace of God our Saviour hath appeared to all men, instructing us, that, denying ungodliness and worldly desires, we should live soberly and justly and godly in this world, looking for the blessed hope and coming of the glory of the great God and our Saviour Jesus Christ: Who gave Himself for us, that He might redeem us from all iniquity, and might cleanse to Himself a people acceptable, a pursuer of good works. These things speak and exhort: in Christ Jesus our Lord."

We — the Christian church, those chosen out of Grace who accept God's gifts — are in a journey to that final day when Our Lord will return. We have been given for that journey the armament of Our Lord's graces in the Sacraments and through His love, our Faith, and a Hope that whenever we are tempted to despair, pulls us back and redirects our vision.

Years ago when I was doing my doctoral work in Pamplona, Spain, I had several dear friends. One of them, by name Teofilo Andueza, although he and wife lived in the city, kept his family's ancestral home and farm up in the Pyrenees Mountains. On numerous Sundays we would travel out there; the women would busy themselves in the kitchen to prepare roasted lamb chops, pork shoulder, "patatas fritas," various "ensaladas mixtas," all sorts of desserts (flan and pastries), and, of course, there would be plenty of Rioja wine and cognac. After eating — which usually continued off and on for most of the day — we would sit and smoke some "puros" (Cuban cigars — well, I didn't worry about *THAT* aspect of Cuban Communism back then!).

I remember on one occasion Teofilo took me up to the crest of a nearby mountain; below we could see the city of Pamplona, as he related how in 1873 the city was occupied by "liberals" who supported the central and centralizing government in Madrid, but elsewhere in all of Navarra, in every rural village and small hamlet, the people had risen up as one under the military banner of "God – Country – States' Rights – and the Rightful King" (against the liberal king then installed in the nation's capital). In July 1936 Teofilo, his father, and his elderly grandfather (who as a teen had joined the 1873 Traditionalist rising) all volunteered to fight under that same banner, the standard of the Traditionalist Carlist Communion against the secularist and socialist

Spanish Republic (which is so loved by the establishment Neoconservatives these days).

Like his grandfather in 1873, Teofilo was barely sixteen when he enlisted in 1936. And while his grandfather was too old to see active, front line combat in the Spanish Civil War of 1936-1939 (serving in rear-guard duty), Teofilo saw combat in some of the fiercest battles against the Red Republic and marched in the Victory parade in Madrid in 1939.

But like my other Carlist Traditionalist friends — who were termed "Intransigentes" by more moderate (and compromising) partisans on the Right — Teofilo believed Francisco Franco had not carried through with the actual re-establishment of a Christian kingdom as promised — too many foreign influences, too many compromises, and, lastly, opening the door in 1953 to all the worst aspects of American commercialism and cultural decay. The national reawakening promised in 1939 had not taken place, its fruits dispersed, and in exchange, Spanish society had increasingly accepted the worst features of American culture and secularist thinking.

At the top of that mountain crest, as we looked down at Pamplona, Teofilo became emotional. "My grandfather fought against that liberal contagion one-hundred years ago," he exclaimed. "And in 1936 three generations of my family dropped everything and went to war against the communists and socialists, to a crusade for Christ the King — that He might reign in society, and for our historic rights." And then, he turned to me, took me firmly by the shoulder, and said: "And now, if it were just you and me — and we were on God's side — once again we would be victorious, for even if we are only two, nothing is impossible to men if they fight on God's side!"

Teofilo's words had and continue to have special meaning for this Southerner with deep roots in the American Southland, and with several great and great-great grandfathers who fought for the original vision of states' rights under the old Constitution created in Philadelphia in 1787. Like our great paladins who led the South during four cruel years of war, like Jackson and Lee, like General Bishop Polk and Bedford Forrest, despite the overwhelming odds and the seemingly final defeat militarily, my Spanish friend had never given up, had never lost the faith in the truth of his belief … and the final hope that God's good justice would eventually triumph.

I have remembered that incident constantly over the years, especially when things appear dark or despairing. For not only did Grace and Salvation and the Healing for sin come into the world in a humble Cradle in Bethlehem a little more than 2,000 years ago, but Hope came also. And it buoys us up, gives us balance and equilibrium, and acts as "Faith's Sentry" to protect our Faith from harm and the threat of despair and apostasy.

For Southerners who carry forward the light and faith of their ancestors and who treasure those traditions, these promises are critical and reassuring. For the Southerner, the right Cause is never a lost Cause. The past is never really "past," the past is always within us, it informs us and is our lifeblood, points us to the future, and anneals us in its grace.

In the year 312 A.D., facing an immense military challenge, the Emperor Constantine prayed to the Christian God, asking what he should do. As related in Eusebius' *Ecclesiastical History*, he had grave doubts about the traditional Roman gods. He prayed earnestly that the Christian God would "reveal to him who He is, and stretch forth His right hand to help him." His prayer changed the course of human history. The answer came in a vision of a cross emblazoned across the noonday sky, and upon it the inscription read: *"In hoc signo vinces"* — By this sign you shall be victorious. The emperor then ordered that his soldiers have the Christian cross emblazoned on their shields.

Victorious at the Battle of the Milvian Bridge, Constantine then issued orders that the Christian church was to be fully free in its mission and the exercise of its functions. Although he did not make Christianity the official religion of the empire, Constantine bestowed favors on it, built places of worship for Christians, and presided over the first general church council. He became the first emperor to embrace Christianity and was baptized on his death bed. In less than 300 years the faith of Christ born in humble surroundings in remote Judaea and persecuted mercilessly and ruthlessly, nourished by the blood of martyrs, now emerged from the catacombs, triumphant, a light unto the pagans, to continue its salvific mission.

Is this not the power of Faith supported by Hope? That even if we be in the catacombs, even if we see our civilization and culture coming apart at the seams, even if we see the Church subverted and false prophets in positions of immense authority preaching false doctrines — even in these circumstances, we hold *"fortes in Fide,"* firm in the faith, bolstered by Faith's Sentry.

So, then, as we approach the Holy Day of indescribable joy, we know with assurance that the ineffable Gift from God of salvation and forgiveness is ours, and that no one can take our Faith from us, buoyed, as it is, by the unbreakable assurance of Hope — which came to us that Christmas so long ago.

"Even if it were just you and me — and we were on God's side — once again we would be victorious, for even if we are only two, nothing is impossible to men if they fight on God's side!"

Saving Grace entered the world two millennia ago, and with it the Hope we possess. And there are broad smiles on our faces and joy in our hearts.

A Merry and Blessed Christmas. Take heart, the South will rise again!

(My Corner by Boyd Cathey, December 24, 2017, at: http://boydcatheyreviewofbooks.blogspot.com/2017/12/december-24-2017-my-corner-vigilof.html)

PART IV

EIGHT SOUTHERN HEROES
(and TWO DEMONS)

The nine following essays and one interview examine the thinking, achievements, and importance of several figures who affected Southern history and culture, from the late 18th century until the late 20th century. Eight of these individuals — Nathaniel Macon, James Johnston Pettigrew, Jefferson Davis, Robert Lewis Dabney, Mel Bradford, Eugene Genovese, Sam Ervin, and actor Randolph Scott — illustrated in their lives and careers what I would call a "Southern philosophy of society," and several played roles in shaping not just the thinking of Southerners, but also the South's political course.

North Carolinian Nathaniel Macon was one of the most significant political leaders in the United States during the first half of the nineteenth century. In a very real and palpable sense he was the critical link between the generation of Founding Fathers and the Framers of the Constitution and such eminent and influential Southern statesmen as John C. Calhoun. In his own lifetime he was called "the Father of the House [of Representatives]" and "the Father of States' Rights." In his thirty years in the United States Congress, first in the House and as its Speaker under President Thomas Jefferson, and then in the United States Senate during the crucial decades of the 1810s and 1820s, no man had more direct influence over the formation of a constitutionalist and "Southern philosophy" of statecraft, or, better said, in the reaffirmation of the beliefs and principles that inspired the early American nation than Macon. Jefferson, in his later years, called Macon "*Ultimus Romanorum*, the last of the Romans," a valiant reminder of what the American nation was supposed to hold as essential to its character. Revered by friend and foe alike, sought after for advice and admired by figures as diverse as Andrew Jackson and John Quincy Adams, Macon exemplified the virtues of simplicity and probity of character both in his public and private life. Understanding his states' rights, localist conservatism is necessary if we are to fathom subsequent Southern history.

In 1996, as Registrar of the North Carolina State Archives and having completed a massive report years earlier on Macon for the State

Archives, I was able to assist Stephen J. Barry in his dissertation on Macon for the State University of New York (SUNY)-Buffalo. After its completion Barry sent me a copy, an appendix to which contains a listing of approximately 900 letters written by and to Macon during his life: many of those missives I read during my research and later when I was at the University of Virginia. And I have often wished an edition of them might emerge. Perhaps in the future an enterprising scholar will attempt that task. For the moment I offer here an essay I wrote as the Foreword for a new edition of Congressman Weldon N. Edwards' *Memoir of Nathaniel Macon of North Carolina*, originally published in Raleigh, 1862, and republished by The Scuppernong Press (2014).

Confederate General James Johnston Pettigrew, from a distinguished North Carolina planter family, is justly famous for his command of one side of the Confederate flanks on the third day of Gettysburg, and then his tragic death in the retreat from that battle at Falling Waters, Maryland. Yet this incredible polyglot, this man of many talents, was a superb writer and elegant word smith, whose volume, *Notes on Spain and the Spaniards*, is not just a brilliant travelogue of his adventures in Spain and Europe in 1859, but a finely honed — at times deeply philosophical — view of his ideas about society and culture. Indeed, one can see implicit analogies in *Notes on Spain* between Pettigrew's profound understanding of Spanish culture and his own beloved South country. And through it all comes some of the most acute criticism of modern, liberal society, and an engaging defense, if indirectly, of the traditionalist South. Pettigrew's death cut short an unfulfilled career of an impressive writer who should be much better known.

The significance and role of Jefferson Davis is well known. His wartime activities, sometimes lauded by historians, other times criticized, remain the subject of debate. In the essay printed here the emphasis is on his post-war writings and activity and the greater-than-life symbol for Southerners he became long after the 1861-1865 conflict was over on the battlefield. Davis was a man — a statesman — of great faith whose positive reputation steadily grew after the war. In 1980 the Southern Agrarian writer, Robert Penn Warren, in his extended address, "Jefferson Davis Gets His Citizenship Back," captured some of the complexities of Davis' character. By then Warren had distanced himself from other Agrarians, but yet fathomed that "spirit of contradiction," that noble defiance of statism and advancing liberal democracy which seems so foreign to the modern world.

Robert Lewis Dabney, during his lifetime, was known largely as having been chaplain to General "Stonewall" Jackson, and for penning a popular postwar defense of the Confederacy. Yet, his later forays into controversy, over public education, women's suffrage, Wall Street capitalism, and what he saw as the degradation of the republican system, were incalculably of greater importance. Despite the fact Dabney does not enjoy the fame or renown of Davis or Macon, his influence, nevertheless, was felt by succeeding generations of Southern writers and authors, most notably the "Fugitive" writers and the Southern Regionalists. And, indeed, his critique of industrial capitalism and the less-savory results of industrialism, as well as his trenchant attacks on liberal democracy, signal him as one of the more perceptive writers of the postwar period, and not just in the South.

Melvin — "Mel" — E. Bradford stands out as perhaps the most brilliant and remarkable Southern writer of the late twentieth century. His early death in 1993 deprived the South of one of its most eloquent and erudite defenders. His decades-long debate with Professor Harry Jaffa over the true meaning of the "Declaration of Independence" and the vision of the Founders which motivated the original republican enterprise, culminated in his *magnum opus, Original Intentions: On the Making and Ratification of the American Constitution* (1993), a remarkable work which should be better known. His biographical studies of the Founders and hundreds of essays in defense of Southern tradition, not to mention his literary achievements, deserve a paramount place in the historiography of the South.

Eugene Genovese (1930-2012) was one of the pre-eminent historians of the old South. His many books and scholarly articles, always abundantly researched and elegantly written, were in many ways a defiant "*non possumus*" to the seemingly rampant conversion of the study of Southern history into an ideological weapon to employ against anyone who questioned, even meekly, the progressivist incline and authoritarian "group think" direction that seems to dominant the profession these days. A friend of Mel Bradford, Genovese credited Bradford, and before him the writings of Richard M. Weaver, with revealing for him the richness and virility of Southern conservative thinking. It represented a thoughtful, at times brilliant, exposition of the Founders' vision, and even more, a profoundly and sincerely religious view of life that annealed Southern society and culture. Genovese's conclusions, increasingly, did not endear him to his former confreres on the Marxist Left. The interview I conducted with "Gene," "A Partisan Conversation:

An Interview with Eugene Genovese," first appeared in *The Southern Partisan*, Fall 1985 (volume V, number 4).

Among these eight exemplars of Southern heritage and a Southern philosophy, there is one contemporary political figure, an individual whose significance and voice have yet to be evaluated for their real meaning: Senator Sam J. Ervin of North Carolina. "Senator Sam," as he was called later in life is known mainly as the chairman of the famous "Watergate Committee" which investigated the scandals that occurred during the second term of President Richard Nixon. In a certain bizarre twist of fate this brilliant constitutionalist, judge, and defender of the traditional South has been converted, insanely, into something of a folk hero of the fashionable Left due to Watergate. But that view is terribly jaundiced, largely missing the import of Ervin's thinking and his deeply held views on the American Constitution and his brilliant defense of constitutionalism in the face of the frenzied "civil rights" revolution of the 1960s. Senator Ervin, perhaps the most eloquent and learned of that disappeared breed of white-haired, silver-tongued Southern solons, left a remarkable record — warnings about what undue tinkering with the Constitution would produce, superb perorations on history and tradition, a wry wit punctuated with a homespun humor, and a manner of speaking that exuded Carolina graciousness. The American nation suffers from the lack of such statesmen.

At first it might seem odd I would include actor Randolph Scott in this distinguished group of political, military, and cultural leaders. Yet Scott, that archetypal Western icon, whose acting career in Hollywood oaters spanned thirty-four critical years in American and Southern history, 1928-1962, is the perfect symbol culturally of the spirit of the Southern gentlemen, a characterization he incarnated so often in his films. He hung up his spurs with that quintessentially elegiac celebration of the passing of the Old West, *Ride the High Country*, in 1962. For him — and for the traditionalist beliefs he represented throughout his life — it was a supremely noble salute to those annealing principles which were disappearing not only in America, but also, it would soon become apparent, in his beloved Southland.

When asked in 1962 why he would no longer make any more movies, his response was, in his usual laconic way: "the motion picture industry is in a steadily declining state, what with nudity and the like flagrantly displayed in films today." And that was in 1962! For Randy Scott fealty to a code of honor, loyalty to a cause, duty to one's country and its founding principles were paramount. Thus, his cultural imprint on the imaginations of millions of both youngsters and adults during the Great Depression, during World War II, and, lastly, in the 1950s, is incalculable.

The article I include was originally published in *The Southern Partisan* magazine shortly after Scott's death in March 1987. Somehow it managed to find its way into the hands of Scott's widow, Mrs. Patricia Stillman Scott, who contacted me, writing that I had understood her husband "as no one else had." Thus began a correspondence which continued to her death in 2004. During that period I made video copies for her of all the Scott films I had — during his lifetime she had not concerned herself with acquiring copies. We exchanged photographs of our pets (she was a cat person, I am a dog person), and she shared photographs of her bridge partners, including Mrs. Bob Hope, Mrs. Ray Milland, and others of the older, more conservative Hollywood crowd. And I gained a greater understanding of Randolph Scott, the man, the gentlemen, and the Southerner. What a privilege that was for me.

Finally, there are two "demons" who are examined in this segment: Abraham Lincoln and popular "conservative" historian and pundit, Victor Davis Hanson. Lincoln mania and the virtual canonization of Father Abraham continue, nearly unstoppable, in contemporary society. Yet, acute and profound commentators like Bradford, Charles Adams, Thomas DiLorenzo, Thomas Fleming, William Marvel, and Lerone Bennett have offered solid criticism of Lincoln's role in enabling the growth of the managerial state we observe around us today.

The other demon in this section is touted historian Victor Davis Hanson. Certainly, there are numerous others who literally hate the South, or at the least, disparage and disdain the South's Confederate heritage, identifying it with slavery and attacking it as "racist." But Hanson, the darling of the Neoconservative punditry and journalistic establishment that dominate the contemporary "conservative movement," stands out with a particular ruthlessness in his visceral hatred for anything Confederate and his continued assaults on the South for its failure to bend to the idea that America is based on the Idea of Equality ... an assumption which is historically and intellectually false.

Nathaniel Macon and the Origin of States' Rights Conservatism
⇝ *Chapter 24* ⇜

Back in 1975 the Warren County [N.C.] Historical Association initiated a comprehensive project to study the life and legacy of Nathaniel Macon. As a part of this project, both archaeological and architectural studies of his old Buck Spring plantation, near the Roanoke River, were commissioned. Working with the professional staff of the North Carolina Division of Archives and History, the Macon project had, it was proposed at the time, a longer range potential objective: a possible state historic site to honor North Carolina's most historically significant political leader, whose legacy and philosophy and character influenced not only generations of Tar Heels, but also a host of very illustrious Southerners, their thinking, and the very manner in which they lived their lives and viewed the society around them.

Working with architectural historians and experienced archaeologists, I was commissioned to prepare both a chain of title for the Buck Spring site, as well as a detailed written history of Macon and his life. All of this would be organized in a major report which might be used to justify the future creation of an important historic site, sadly never realized, giving credit finally to this giant of North Carolina and American history. At that time I was finishing up a doctorate in graduate school. A few years earlier Macon and his under appreciated significance to the history of this nation had figured in my MA thesis presented at the University of Virginia. I was amazed at the incredible importance "the Squire of Buck Spring" had in the new American nation, and, more interestingly, the influence he had on such later and much better known figures as John C. Calhoun and President John Tyler.

Yet, in 1975 Macon was basically unknown, and his role and importance in American history, so appreciated before the War Between the States, were largely ignored or glossed over.

Quite a bit of this contemporary ignorance must, I think, be attributed to Macon's philosophy. He was, indeed, to quote his contemporaries, "the father of states' rights" and the figure most critical in the actual development and survival of the states' rights philosophy that still, in some ways, percolates in American politics.

Above all, it was Macon's probity of character and his steadfast devotion to principle which won him general admiration from across the entire spectrum of antebellum political opinion. Leaders as diverse as Presidents John Quincy Adams and John Tyler expressed great admiration for Macon; many attempted to tie in their own views, even those ideas that seemed at odds with Macon's, to those of the Squire of Buck Spring. After leaving the U.S. House of Representatives in 1816 and being elevated to the United State Senate by the North Carolina General Assembly, Macon's influence only grew and became more pervasive, especially in the South.

It was his role during the debates over the Missouri Compromise which signaled the emergence of a genuine states' rights philosophy. But it was not just that hotly debated issue which occupied his attention. Questions regarding internal improvements, the establishment of a national bank, and the general role of the Federal government in questions hitherto considered the concern of states, also occupied him. For him all such issues, and increasingly the contentious issue of slavery, were a part of a larger question, of how the Constitution was to be interpreted.

As early as March 1818 he wrote to North Carolina congressman Bartlett Yancey as follows:

I must ask you to examine the Constitution of the United States ... and tell me, if Congress can establish banks, make roads and canals, whether they cannot free all the slaves in the United States?....We have abolition, colonization and peace societies — their intentions cannot be known; but the character and spirit of one may without injustice be considered that of all. It is a character and spirit of perseverance bordering on enthusiasm, and if the general government shall continue to stretch its powers, these societies will undoubtedly push it to try the question of emancipation....

With the debate over Missouri looming, Macon wrote to Yancey again, in April 1818:

If Congress can make canals they can with more propriety emancipate. Be not deceived, I speak soberly in the fear of God and the love of the Constitution. Let not the love of improvement or a thirst for glory blind that sober discretion and sound sense, with which the Lord has blest you. Paul was not more anxious or sincere concerning Timothy, than I am for you. Your error in this will injure if not destroy our beloved mother, North Carolina, and all the South country. Add not to the Constitution nor take therefrom. Be not led astray by grand notions or magnificent opinions. Remember that you belong to a meek State and just people, who want nothing but to enjoy the fruits of their labor honestly and to lay out their profits in their own way.

In early 1819 the actual debate in the Senate over the admission of Missouri to the union commenced, and, as Missouri was a territory where slavery existed, that contentious question became central to the debate. A resolution — a compromise — put forward by Senator Jesse Thomas of Illinois proposed admitting Maine as a "free" state and Missouri as a "slave" state but prohibiting slavery in the rest of the Louisiana Purchase north of latitude 36 degrees, 30 minutes.

Many Southern leaders, including the then Secretary of War John C. Calhoun, were prepared to go along initially with the compromise, but Macon, singularly, rose to oppose it. And it was in his famous Senate speech on the question that heralded the birth of a full-fledged "Southern philosophy." The speech deserves to be quoted at length:

All the states now have equal rights and are content. Deprive one of the least right which it now enjoys in common with the others and it will no longer be content…. All the new states have the same rights that the old have; why make Missouri an exception? Why depart in her case from the great American principle that the people can govern themselves? All the country west of the Mississippi was acquired by the same treaty, and on the same terms and the people in every part have the same rights….The [Thomas] amendment will operate unjustly to the people who have gone there from other states. They carried with them property [slaves] guaranteed by their states, by the Constitution and treaty; they purchased lands and settled on them without molestation; but now, unfortunately for them, it is discovered that they ought not to have been permitted to carry a single slave….Let the United States abandon this new scheme; let their magnanimity, and not their power, be felt by the people of Missouri. **The attempt to govern too much has produced every civil war that ever has been, and will, probably, every one that ever may be.** [bold print added]

And finishing with an amazingly prescient vision of the future, Macon continued:

Why depart from the good old way? Why leave the road of experience to take this new one, of which we have no experience? This way leads to universal emancipation, of which we have no experience…. A clause in the Declaration of Independence has been read, declaring "that all men are created equal." Follow that sentiment, and does it not lead to univer-

sal emancipation? If it will justify putting an end to slavery in Missouri, will it not justify it in the old states? Suppose the plan followed, and all the slaves turned loose, and the union to continue, is it certain that the present Constitution would last long?

The debate over the Missouri Compromise marked a significant turning point in American history and, eventually, in the diverging views of the leaders of both the South and the North. Although Macon had been engaged in a losing effort to block the compromise, his forthright and clear-sighted defense of strict constructionism and his beloved "South country" had singled him out as a prophet. Not many years after his remarkable intervention in the Missouri debates, a whole generation of Southern congressmen and political leaders would acknowledge him as the intellectual father of states' rights. In 1821 a chastened Thomas Jefferson, who had also foreseen how the crisis would affect the nation — Jefferson, who termed the stark reality made visible by the debates as "a fire bell in the night" — called Macon "the Depositor of old & sound principles," and wrote him: "God bless you & long continue your wholesome influence in public councils." In a letter Jefferson addressed to Macon on March 26, 1826, a few months before his death, the former president declared that Macon was "*Ultimus Romanorum*" — "the last of the Romans" — "whom I consider as the strictest of models of genuine republicanism."

Despite his staunch support for states' rights and "old republicanism," Macon was greatly esteemed by a wide variety of American political leaders. President John Quincy Adams, a man of almost diametrically opposite views, in his Memoirs described Macon as "… a stern republican … a man of stern parts and mean education, but of rigid integrity, and a blunt, though not offensive, deportment … one of the most influential members of the Senate. His integrity, his indefatigable attention to business, and his long experience give him a weight of character and consideration which few men of superior minds ever acquire." In 1828 it was widely rumored that Adams, despite differences with Macon, considered him as his potential vice-presidential choice.

In 1824, after the illness of leading states' rights presidential candidate, William H. Crawford, Governor George M. Troup of Georgia put forward Macon as a candidate for president: "I know of no person who would unite so extensively the public sentiment of the Southern country … as yourself." In 1825 Macon received twenty-four electoral votes for the vice-presidency. In 1826 and 1827 he was elected President *Pro-Tempore* of the United States Senate.

As he approached the end of his long career, recognition of his significant role in American history and political development came from some of the most significant voices of the time. From Calhoun, John Tyler, and Thomas Hart Benton came encomiums and words of admiration and the recognition that Macon had played a pivotal role in the history of the first sixty years of the American nation.

While many readers in our modern age may think Macon's most pointed comments deal with the institution of slavery, it was not defending the "peculiar institution" that was at the base of his philosophy. Indeed, his stringent commentary on the Federal bank and government support for internal improvements equally reflect a states' rights consistency and integrity. Slavery, because Macon recognized it as a particularly dangerous lynchpin for the American nation, certainly occupied a salient part of his commentary. But the greater issue for him was the growing power and control of the Federal government and the eventual destruction of the older Constitutional system erected by the Founders.

In 1835, in his last major public role, Macon was elected to preside over the North Carolina Constitutional Convention. While he made few interventions, he generally opposed changes to the state constitution. For him, "all changes in government were from better to worse."

In June 1837 Macon summoned his doctor and the undertaker and paid them in advance. He died on June 29 that year, at Buck Spring. In a simple ceremony on his plantation he was interred, attended by grieving slaves, with whom he had worked side-by-side in his fields. He instructed his executor and son-in-law, the Honorable Weldon N. Edwards, that no monument mark his grave, but that a pile of smooth stones be placed upon the site.

His epitaph he spoke eighteen years earlier, in Congress: "The attempt to govern too much has produced every civil war that ever has been, and will, probably, every one that ever may be." Macon understood and clearly foresaw the results of the destruction of liberties and the erosion of states' rights and the emergence of an all-encompassing Federal government.

The pile of stones at Buck Spring remains, as does the philosophy that Macon first enunciated, despite the accomplishment of the shattering prophecy he uttered. And, now, it is up to another generation to attempt to retrieve and recover the Founders' vision.

This essay serves as the Foreword to a 2014 reprinting of Congressman Weldon N. Edwards' *Memoir of Nathaniel Macon of North Carolina*, originally published in Raleigh, 1862, and now republished by The Scuppernong Press, Box 1724, Wake Forest, North Carolina 27588; copies may be obtained directly via the web site, www.scuppernongpress.com

(*The Unz Review*, November 23, 2014, at: www.unz.com/article/nathaniel-macon-and-the-origin-of-states-rights-conservatism/)

What Was Lost 152 Years Ago: James Johnston Pettigrew and His Notes on Spain and the Spaniards
↦ *Chapter 25* ↤

One-hundred and fifty-two years ago, April 9, 1865, was a Palm Sunday just as today, and in the central part of war-torn Virginia, a major turning point occurred in American history. General Robert E. Lee, that *"chevalier sans peur"* — that knight without fear — surrendered the tattered remnants of the proud Army of Northern Virginia to General Ulysses S. Grant, setting in motion the end phase of the War for Southern Independence.

That war was in reality not a "civil war," that is, it was not a war between two aggrieved parties within the American nation. Rather, it was a war between two ideas of government, and, in reality, two ideas of history and progress. For the North, which now controlled the Federal government, it was a war to suppress what was seen as a rebellion against constituted national authority. For the states of the Southern Confederacy, it was a defense of their inherited and inherent rights under the old Constitution of 1787, rights which had never been ceded to the Federal government. And, more, it became for them a Second War for Independence against an arbitrary and overreaching government that had gravely violated that Constitution.

Thus, at Appomattox were set into motion momentous events in the future of the reconstituted American nation. With the defeat of the South, the restraints on industrial, and, eventually, international capitalism were removed. The road to centralized government power was cleared. But even more significantly, there was a sea change in what we might call "the dominant American philosophy."

In the old antebellum Union the South had acted as a kind of counterweight to the North and a quickly developing progressivist vision of history. Certainly, there were notable Southerners who shared the growing economic and political liberalism of their fellow citizens north of the Mason-Dixon Line (e.g, DeBow's *Review*). Yet, increasingly in the late antebellum period, the most significant voices in the Southland echoed a kind of traditionalism somewhat reminiscent of the serious critiques being made in Europe of "the Idea of Progress" and of the deleterious effects of 19th century liberalism.

The historian Louis Hartz once commented in the antebellum South, particularly during the 1840s and 1850s, the South country experienced what he termed a "reactionary Enlightenment." The great novels of Sir Walter Scott dominated in Southern libraries; Chateaubriand and the works of the writers of Romanticism were devoured by the reading public (which was quite large). The Oxford "High Church" Movement (1840s and beyond) found many devotees and converts. Many scions of Southern families were sent to Europe for education.

Not just George Fitzhugh, but other notable writers such as George Frederick Holmes, James Henley Thornwell, and Robert Lewis Dabney (who wrote his most devastating criticism after the war of "the New South Creed"), questioned the progressivist narrative and defended the stasis of Southern society. For them "stasis" was not the same thing as "static" and "backward," but rather an understanding that an equilibrium in society, ordered under the unchanging rules of God's law and the laws of nature, was the surest way to meet, sift through, and verify the many challenges offered by the ideologies of the times. It was essentially a conservative vision.

These Southern writers did not oppose all progress, but, then, much of the "progress" they viewed around them was illusory and destructive not only of their society, but of their very existence as a people.

In 1860 one of the Confederacy's most talented generals, whose life was cut short in the retreat from Gettysburg, the Tar Heel James Johnston Pettigrew, authored his account of his sojourn in Europe (1859), *Notes on Spain and the Spaniards*. It is one of the most remarkable, if still largely unknown to the general public, books ever written by an American. [Note: There is a University of South Carolina Press reprint of the original; and Clyde Wilson's biography of Pettigrew, *Carolina Cavalier*, is an excellent introduction.]

Let's take a closer look at Pettigrew and his *Notes on Spain*.

Pettigrew came from a prominent North Carolina planter family. Like many young Southern men of his class, he traveled in Europe, but most importantly, to Spain. His vibrant and deeply thoughtful descriptions rival the most brilliant of philosophical "travelogues," and compare favorably with Hilaire Belloc's *The Path to Rome*. For Pettigrew, *Notes on Spain* became a vehicle for a not-so-veiled, favorable comparison of Spanish customs and culture with those of his own Southland, and even more importantly, a searing critique of the "philosophy of Progress" and the idea that "science" and "evolution" were the new salvation for mankind. His superb defense of orthodox revealed religion and his unparalleled put down of "scientism" remain, by any standard, impressive.

That volume contains many superb and poetic passages that deserve quoting. Upon entering the magnificent Seville Cathedral, for instance, Pettigrew observes that:

"... A faint gleam of light, struggling through the painted windows of the dome, fell upon the lofty crucifix, and seemed to point to the life of purity beyond. At such a time, one cannot but feel that there is an ethereal spirit within, a spark of the Divine essence, which would fain cast off its prison house of mortality and flee to the Eternal existence that gave it birth. This edifice is one of few creations of man that realizes expectation. Morning, noon, and night, none can enter without acknowledging that he stands on holy ground. The accessories, the trembling swell of the organs, the sweet odor of incense, the beautiful works of art, which elsewhere distract the attention, here combine in universality of grandeur to establish that harmony of the soul so conducive to devotion; and if the excellence of the architecture consist in the accomplishment of the rational purpose assigned, to this must the palm be awarded. Political economists may reason that such an expenditure in unproductive stone withdraws from the general circulation a sensible capital; the severe reformer may preach against the adoration of saints and images; but their remonstrance will fall pointless upon the heart. There are occasions when humanity rises above the earthly rules of logic; and acknowledges obedience only to those hidden laws which govern the divine portion of our nature, and whose sequence is beyond the reach of human intellect." [Notes, pp. 186-187]

Experiencing life in a Spanish village drew forth Pettigrew's views of patriotism and a defense of community. Certainly, thinking of his own native land, he muses:

"Local attachments are pronounced, by the modern school of social philosophers, to be relics of barbarism, ignorance and prejudice, forgetting that prejudices are given us by the all-wise Deity, as well as reasoning faculties, and equally for some beneficent purpose. The time may come when prejudices will disappear, when one's country will have no claim upon him than China or Hindostan, and the sufferings of the Bushmen will arouse as lively a feeling of sympathy as those of his fellow citizens. But this millennium has not yet reached Spain. Patriotism, an attachment to, a preference for one's own home, is still a virtue prolific of measureless good, and for its foundation rests upon enlightened prejudice." [Notes, p. 55]

Such language is reminiscent of that great English conservative, Edmund Burke.

At the Cathedral of Our Lady of Pilar, in Zaragoza, Pettigrew offers one of his most profound and philosophical passages. After an almost poetic recounting of his entry into the edifice and his dawning sense of awe and reverie, he offers a defense of revelation and traditional religion in words that bespeak what Russell Kirk termed moral imagination:

"Every revealed system [of religious belief] must rest for its foundation upon either reason or faith. The former decides upon evidence, scrutinized by the light of a critical intellect; the latter seeks its 'evidence of things unseen' only in the heart. How many of us have intelligence, learning or leisure to investigate the grounds of our belief in even the simplest article of faith? What immense erudition is requisite to decide whether the gospels containing a narrative of the Saviour's life be forgeries, revelations or mere histories? How often do sects split upon the mere literal rendering of a Greek sentence? And if the learned, who have devoted their whole lives to this alone, be so feeble, how shall we expect strength of wisdom from the mass of mankind, who have not the first element of critical science? We believe in the existence of a Saviour, and denounce as infidels and horrible monsters all who refuse assent to our faith. And why do we thus believe? Because we have been told so in our youth by persons of learning and probity, in whom we have confidence, and whose better judgment in this matter we substitute for our own.... Even for the earth we need something more than morality or its virtues.... Some of the pleasantest recollections of my life are these Spanish cathedrals, where the somber grandeur of the architecture and the devotion of the congregation harmonized in elevating me above the mere materiality of existence." [*Notes*, pp. 77-79]

Pettigrew, as did other contemporary Southern men of intellect, recognized there were stark differences between his beloved Southland and an increasingly industrialized North. He sums that belief up, once again in *Notes on Spain*, when leaving France and entering Spain, a land in which he visualized analogously his own Southern homeland:

"Adieu to a civilization which reduces men to machines, which sacrifices half that is stalwart and individual in humanity to the false glitter of centralization, and to the luxurious enjoyments of a manufacturing, money age!" [*Notes*, p. 51]

The late historian Eugene Genovese, in his magisterial treatise, *The Mind of the Master Class*, explores in detail the high level of intellectual thought — profoundly traditionalist and anti- (or perhaps pre-) capitalist — which existed in the Old South. The virtual absence of that prescriptive and traditionalist voice in the post-war period and beyond signaled a sharp direction change for the as-yet-young American nation, the results of which continue to be felt today. It was the triumphant epigones of liberalism and imperialism, of the "nouveaux riches" and the political class they spawned, who would take the reins of American government and dictate its tawdry culture.

If the benighted American nation, besotted by cultural decadence and political corruption and intrigue, is ever to recover, it could do no better than to revisit the insights of men like Pettigrew and Dabney, the constitutionalism of Calhoun, and the moral discussions of James Henley Thornwell.

(Abbeville Institute, April 11, 2017, at: www.abbevilleinstitute.org/blog/what-was-lost-150-years-ago/)

Remembering President Jefferson Davis
⇾ *Chapter 26* ⇽

Back in early June of this year an anniversary came and passed, almost unnoticed by most pundits and the media. June 3 was the two-hundred and sixth anniversary of the birth of Jefferson Davis. Born in Kentucky in 1808, actually not far from the birthplace of his future nemesis, Abraham Lincoln, Davis in another time might have risen to become in his own right a celebrated president of the United States. As it was, it was his thankless duty to captain the forlorn Confederacy through four years of tragic and bloody war which saw the end not only of the society and culture he loved, but, in effect, the practical end of the old constitutional republic originally set up by the Founders.

From a good family and with advantages that augured well for future prominence, Davis at an early age demonstrated both leadership potential and intelligence.

Like many other well-bred Southern boys of the period, he received a superb classical education. In 1815 Davis entered the Catholic school of Saint Thomas at St. Rose Priory, a school operated by the Dominican Order in Washington County, Kentucky. At the time, he was the only Protestant student (he was an Episcopalian) at the school. He would carry a strong affection for the Catholic Church throughout his life. His famous correspondence with Pope Pius IX, an inveterate foe of liberalism in any form and who was pro-Confederate, is famous, and indicates the pope recognized the Davis as a formal head of state. After the war, while Davis was a prisoner in Fortress Monroe, Virginia, the pope addressed to Davis a famous letter demonstrating his great sympathy for the Confederate president.

A West Point graduate, Davis distinguished himself in the Mexican-American War as a colonel of the Mississippi Rifles volunteer regiment, and as United States Secretary of War under President Franklin Pierce. Both before and after his time in the Pierce administration, he served as a U.S. Senator from Mississippi. As Senator, he argued against secession but believed each state had an unquestionable and constitutional right to secede from the voluntary Union of the Founders, just as they had seceded from England seeking political liberty. Davis resigned from the Senate in January 1861 after receiving word that his

State of Mississippi had voted to leave the Union. Davis explained his actions saying:

"[T]o me the sovereignty of the State was paramount to the sovereignty of the Union. And I held my seat in the Senate until Mississippi seceded and called upon me to follow and defend her. Then I sorrowfully resigned the position in which my State had placed me and in which I could no longer represent her, and accepted the new work. I was on my way to Montgomery when I received, much to my regret, the message that I had been elected provisional President of the Confederate States of America."

Davis was a patriotic American who tried to save the Founders' republic from Northern revolutionaries, and who reluctantly departed the Union with the old constitution intact to form a "more perfect Union." He contended he would rather be out of the Union with the Constitution than to be in the Union without the Constitution. The Southern States, he stated, seceded in order to save the Constitution of the Founders. Davis remarked in July 1864:

"I tried in all my power to avert this war. I saw it coming, and for 12 years, I worked night and day to prevent it, but I could not. The North was mad and blind; it would not let us govern ourselves, and so the war came, and now it must go on till the last man of this generation falls in his tracks, and his children seize the musket and fight our battle, unless you acknowledge our right to self-government. We are not fighting for slavery. We are fighting for Independence, and that, or extermination, we will have . . . Slavery never was an essential element. It was the only means of bringing other conflicting elements to an earlier culmination. It fired the musket which was already capped and loaded. There are essential differences between the North and the South that will, however this war may end, make them two nations."

Reminded during the war of the destruction of his Mississippi plantations by occupying Northern troops, he dismissed it as the cost of war, yet confessed that he pitied his poor Negroes who had been driven off by those troops and abandoned to misery or ruin. He resisted arming the slaves as they were not trained as soldiers, were needed to raise food for the armies in the field, and he would not use them as mercenaries and cannon-fodder as Lincoln had done to avoid conscripting unwilling white Northerners.

At the end of the War, when a fellow traveler remarked that the cause of the Confederates was lost, Davis replied: "It appears so. But the principle for which we contended is bound to reassert itself, though it may be at another time and in another form."

In 1881, Davis was critical of the Gilded Age corruption and political ignorance of the United States Constitution and remarked: "Of what value then are paper constitutions and oaths binding officers to their preservation, if there is not intelligence enough in the people to discern the violations; and virtue enough to resist the violators?"

President Davis was never indicted for treason. He demanded a fair trial in order to argue the constitutionality of the South's actions in 1860-1861. This was denied by his Jacobin tormentors, and the reason was revealed by Chief Justice of the U.S. Supreme Court, Salmon P. Chase, in 1867. Chase admitted that:

"If you bring these leaders to trial, it will condemn the North, for by the Constitution, secession is not a rebellion. His [Jefferson Davis] capture was a mistake. His trial will be a greater one. We cannot convict him of treason."

[as quoted by Herman S. Frey, in *Jefferson Davis*, 1977, pp. 69-72]

President Davis died on December 6, 1889. In 1893 his body was transported by funeral train to Richmond where he was interred at Hollywood Cemetery. At each stop thousands of mourners, white and black, paid respects. In Raleigh historic photographs show a mammoth procession down Fayetteville Street. My grandfather (on my mother's side), then a sixteen-year-old apprentice, stood along the street paying respects to Davis, and he would, sixty-five years later, recount that moving and indelible experience to me, his young grandson. Our history — our traditions — do not really die. Sometimes they just remain dormant, to be re-awakened by new generations who rediscover them and the supreme importance that they have played, and can continue to play, in our lives, if we let them.

Was it not the great poet, Robert Lee Frost, born of a pro-Confederate family, who stated in his poem, *The Black Cottage*:

For, dear me, why abandon a belief
Merely because it ceases to be true.
Cling to it long enough, and not a doubt
It will turn true again, for so it goes.
 Most of the change we think we see in life
Is due to truths being in and out of favor.

Let us listen to the poet — and recall the life and service of the noble Jefferson Davis.

[With thanks to my friend, Bernhard Thuersam, Executive Director of the Cape Fear Historical Institute of Wilmington, NC, for his contribution to this essay]

(Communities Digital News, June 16, 2014, at: www.commdiginews.com/history-and-holidays/remembering-president-jefferson-davis-19633/)

Robert Lewis Dabney and His Attack on Progressivism
↣ *Chapter 27* ↢

Introduction

Most Americans who know anything of Robert Lewis Dabney (1820-1898) know him only as the stern chaplain of General "Stonewall" Jackson and the author of a classic biography of the general. Yet, after the War Between the States Dabney became one of the most intransigent and impressive American critics of industrial capitalism of the late 19th century. During his lifetime his acerbic criticisms were widely read and debated, if not readily embraced.

On April 1865, after four years of bloody conflict, the South, which in many ways had politically dominated the American nation for much of its first seventy-five years, lay defeated, disenfranchised, and ruined. The triumphant Republican Party had eliminated Southern influence and weight in the Federal union, and by so doing, had imposed its view of the American Founding. Through Reconstruction policies and financial dominance, the Republicans and newly-empowered central government would seek to remake the defeated South in a new image. With support from some prominent Southerners, a "progressive" South would arise in the 1870s and 1880s, advocating change, industrialization, and turning away from older ideas of a patriarchal and agriculture-based society. It was Dabney's role during those years, holding fast to his understanding of the principles of the American Founders, to question the values of this "new South," as well as the foundations of triumphant capitalism.

Historian David H. Overby has said of Dabney that after the war he "possessed the shrillness of a scorned prophet." And, indeed, Dabney completely and caustically rejected the new progressivist creed which was being accepted by so many of his fellow Southerners. "I am the Cassandra of Yankeedom," he exclaimed late in his life in 1894, "predestined to prophesy truth and never to be believed until too late."

During the last thirty years of his life Dabney would become the South's — and one of the nation's — most aggressive critics of industrialism, corporate monopoly, educational "reform," and religious liberalism. Of course, these had existed long before the Confederacy's defeat in 1865. But prior to the war, plantation agriculture had been dominant in the South, shaping the region's politics and cultural outlook. Defeat had given rise to strong doubts concerning the basis for Southern society and culture. In the recent conflict the Northern states apparently had proven the importance of industrial society. Many Southerners now echoed the view of former South Carolina planter Ben Allston: "We must begin at the beginning. We must make a new start."

The Birth of the New South Creed

Already in the years immediately following the war at least one prominent Southern magazine advocated a reorientation of Southern society towards industrialism. *DeBow's Review of New Orleans* had championed a policy of Southern economic nationalism and industrial development before 1861. For editor J. D. B. DeBow (1867), the war confirmed the necessity of leaving behind the old agrarian South: "We have got to go to manufacturing to save ourselves.... Every new furnace or factory is a nucleus of a town, to which every needed service is sure to come from the neighborhood or from abroad. Factories and works established establish other factories and works."

DeBow was soon joined by other Southerners in recommending an economic cure for the problems of Confederate defeat, most notably Edwin DeLeon in *Harper's* magazine, Henry Watterson in his *Louisville Courier Journal*, and Bishop Atticus Haygood in his widely distributed sermons. But it was the young Henry W. Grady, editor of the *Atlanta Constitution* in the 1880s, who became the real prophet and symbol of the "new South" creed. Grady, from a unionist family, studied at South Carolina College and Rensselaer Polytechnic Institute (in New York), working later in Northern iron mills. Paul Gaston in his volume, *The New South Creed*, says of Grady: "Commercial in its essence, young Grady's world was built on bristle, energy, and shrewdness, and he experienced none of the genteel leisure allegedly characteristic of the planter class which had led his region into the war."

As a chief prophet of the new creed, Grady was joined by two other individuals of almost equal importance — Richard Edmonds, editor of the *Manufacturer's Record* of Baltimore, and North Carolina publicist Walter Hines Page. For these "new" Southerners industrialization and educational reform were the keys to future success. The fate of the South was inextricably linked to the growth of big industry and commerce. The South could offer the manufacturer natural resources and raw material, cheap labor, and favorable legislation. In turn, the manufacturer would bring jobs, diversification, and, above all, cash wealth. New railways, new businesses, and new (Northern) immigrants would stream south to take advantage of these opportunities. The South must show itself ready and eager for what Grady termed "progressive development" and Northern capital. Most significantly, the South would have to discard its conservative and patriarchal ways when these conflicted with modern ideas and innovation.

For former Congressman James Phelan of Tennessee this meant not only rapid industrialization, but also such innovations as free public education. Other leaders, including Virginia superintendent of public instruction, William H. Ruffner, agreed, and initiated broad programs to transform Southern education by implementing a broad program of state-supported public schools. For them education was to become the base of a permanent prosperity. The child, educated at state (taxpayer) expense, would pay the state back later with his talents and expertise.

For the proponents of the "new South" creed there was literally no place (except perhaps in sentimental novels) for "the antebellum ideal of the leisured gentleman who scorned manual labor." He was, as Paul Gaston states paraphrasing Grady, a "relic that has no place in the new age." And to confirm the moral superiority of the new commercial man, even religion lent its blessings. Episcopal bishop William Lawrence of Massachusetts echoed a widely held sentiment when he proclaimed: "In the long run, it is only to men of morality that wealth comes. Godliness is in league with riches.... Material prosperity is helping to make the national character sweeter, unselfish, more Christ-like." To which Mark Twain, in his sardonic remarks on these proponents of the postwar capitalist creed, responded: "Brisk men, energetic of movement and speech; the dollar their god, how to get it their religion."

Robert Lewis Dabney: His Early Years

Moral uncertainties never afflicted Robert Lewis Dabney. He had been reared in a staunchly Calvinist "Old School" Presbyterian home in Louisa County, Virginia. Born of aristocratic Piedmont parents in 1820, Dabney never lost an inherited sense of social hierarchy. As a student at Hampden-Sydney College and the University of Virginia in the early 1840s, he was, according to Virginia historian Francis Butler Simkins, "the Virginia gentleman par excellence, who did not let righteousness interfere with exquisite manners in the presence of ladies." Ordained and licensed to preach by the Union Theological Seminary then on the Hampden-Sydney campus, Dabney led an active life as a pastor in the Shenandoah Valley before the war. His prominence as a minister and thinker brought him back to Union in the 1850s, where his influence as a teacher of young Southern men was profound. During the war he served as chaplain to "Stonewall" Jackson, and it is through his eloquent biography of that legendary commander he became known throughout the South and the union.

In 1867 Dabney published his famous *A Defense of Virginia [and Through Her, of the South]*, one of the most unreconstructed apologies produced in defense of the old South. He would take the arguments elaborated in *A Defense of Virginia* and during the next twenty-five years develop and extend them into a comprehensive critique of the "new South" creed.* It was if he were still riding at "Stonewall" Jackson's side. But Dabney's "ride" in the post-war period would be a lonely one. Only a small group of conservative, mostly Presbyterian divines, would accompany him in his critique of the "new South" and industrial capitalism.

Dabney's views owe much to his orthodox Presbyterianism. As his biographer Thomas Cary Johnson has pointed out, Dabney "was a servant of God first and primarily." Preaching, teaching, and writing tomes of theology and philosophy were his major concerns. His volumes *Practical Philosophy* and *Sensualistic Philosophy of the Nineteenth Century* and his membership in the Royal Philosophical Society of Great Britain attest to his expertise and international fame. In 1883, finding Union Theological Seminary too liberal for him, Dabney moved to Texas, where he assumed the chair of Mental and Moral Philosophy at the University of Texas.

Industrialism, Monopoly, Oligarchy

Dabney actually first attacked the growth of "industrialism" in the South in 1868. But it was in 1882, at Hampden-Sydney, he first gave a fully developed overview of his thoughts on the topic. In this prepared speech, "The New South," Dabney methodically critiqued the ideas of Grady and his followers. He began by restating his firmly held belief in state sovereignty, strict constitutional construction, and natural social hierarchy. "But this century has seen all this reversed," he exclaimed, "not because the old forms were not good enough for this day, but because they were too good for it."

Striking directly at the "new South" doctrines, Dabney warned the chief temptation confronting the South was "to become like the conquerors." Many of the South's leaders seemed bent of converting the cities below the Potomac to industrial replicas of New York. For Dabney the South must not sacrifice its heritage and character for what he termed the "Yankee spirit" that, he declared, was "like the tawdry pyrotechnics of some popular feast, burning out its own splendors into ashes, darkness and the villainous stench of brimstone." The South must strive to retain "all that was true or ennobling in its principles."

For Dabney the defeat and turning away from those principles after 1865 had as a result the rise of what he termed three major "adverse conditions."

First, the true relation between God and man had been distorted by egalitarianism. There was no such thing as real human equality, Dabney repeated, and to attempt to impose it was to violate the laws of God and nature. The effects of such efforts were disastrous to society. Dabney explained (in a later commentary):

... one must teach, with Moses, the Apostle Paul, John Hampden, Washington, George Mason, John C. Calhoun, and all that contemptible rabble of 'old fogies,' that political society is composed of 'superiors, inferiors, and equals'; that while all these bear an equitable moral relation to each other, they have very different natural rights and duties; that just government is not founded on the consent of the individuals governed, but on the ordinance of God, and hence a share in the ruling franchise is not a natural right at all, but a privilege to be bestowed according to a wise discretion on a limited class having qualification to use it for the good of the whole; that the integers out of which the State is constituted are not individuals, but families represented in their parental heads; that every human being is born under authority (parental and civic) instead of being born 'free' in the licentious sense that liberty is each one's privilege of doing what he chooses; that subordination, and not that license, is the natural state of all men; and that without such equitable distribution of different duties and rights among the classes naturally differing in condition, and subordination of some to others, and of all to the law, society is as impossible as is the existence of a house without distinction between the foundation stone and the cap-stones.

The second adverse condition Dabney attacked was the growth of financial oligarchy. Here Dabney drew a comparison between the United States of 1789 and ninety-three years later, in the 1882. In the former year no one city, no one or two states, no handful of corporate giants controlled the nation's wealth. But in 1882 New York City had become "the commercial mistress" of the whole nation and a handful of industrial and financial barons dictated policies to presidents. Asked Dabney: "Can a sensible man persuade himself that political independence and individual initiative shall remain in a land where financial despotism has become established?"

Dabney continued: "the transfer of wealth and power into the hands of a few, and the marvelous applications of science and mechanic art to cheapen transportation and production" were causing not just the transformation of the South, but a massive change in all of American society. Centralization and monopolization in industry meant a vast reorientation in manufacturing, with far-reaching effects socially and culturally. What happened to independent small businessmen and craftsmen who were now overwhelmed by monopolies, mergers, and crushing competition? When capital was controlled by the few, and the powerful barons of industry commanded the masses at their bidding, individual liberty soon disappeared.

This brought Dabney to his third adverse condition, the destruction of true republican government and the establishment of what he saw as a political and managerial oligarchy.

In the old pre-war South most states had some sort of suffrage requirement, usually a freehold requirement, which meant only men who had a real interest in society (usually property) could vote. These requirements had been wisely included in the constitutions of the original states by their founders. Post-war Reconstruction constitutions did away with these in the name of "democracy." But the destruction of suffrage requirements did not bring a real victory for "democracy." Rather, on-the-make politicians could now make all sorts of promises to the enfranchised masses without the old limitations and safeguards to protect the system from serious abuse and corruption. Concentrated wealth provided almost unlimited opportunity for a powerful few to sway and manipulate the public. In post-war America it was but an easy step to observe that the oligarchies of wealth would now control politics, as well. "Is it Washington or Wall Street," exclaimed Dabney, "which really dictates what platforms [of the political parties] shall be set forth, and what candidates shall be elected, and what appointments shall be made? For certain it is not the people of the states."

Dabney in Texas

At the University of Texas Dabney expanded his critique of industrialism and the "new South" creed. Perhaps his most significant essay of his later career was "The Philosophy Regulating Private Corporations," in which he closely examined the whole idea of "incorporating" modern and national (and international) super-businesses. A modern corporation was "an artificial person, created by the law, usually of many individuals, and clothed by its charter with certain rights of personality, and with a continuity of existence outlasting the natural life of each of its members." Private corporations once in the years before the war had been "the only expedient of the weak as against the strong." But now, said Dabney, it was "too often the partial and usurping artifice of equals against their fellows — of the strong against the weak.... A new aristocracy, armed by law with class privileges and powers more odious than feudal" was the result. Such manipulation was "a flagrant natural injustice" to the public, and especially to "the honest working man." Who could not fail to see the error of the "ill-advised species of legislation" that permitted all shades of corruption in chartering such establishments? State legislatures, both North and South, seemed "to meet mainly to register the edicts of railroad presidents and coal barons," Dabney continued.

Perhaps worst of all was the corrosive influence that these monopolies and super-corporations had on the virtue of the citizens, the stability of families, and the independence of small businessmen. The new giants of industry and commerce undermined "the domestic and personal independence of the yeomanry," many of whom were driven off their farms in desperation to look for work in the bustling new cities of the South. The man of the country did not want to be a part of "the multitudinous mass proletariat, dependent on the corporation for his work, his wages, his cottage, his kitchen garden, and the privilege of buying the provisions for his family." Yet, that was precisely what was happening. Such a condition was incompatible with the principles of true, older republicanism, as the Founders had foreseen it.

In 1891-1892 Dabney authored two more important contributions, "The Labor Union, the Strike and the Commune" and "The Depression of American Farming Interests." Dabney distrusted unions and disliked strikes. To him they were "a forcible attempt to invade and dominate the legitimate influence of the universal law of supply and demand. This law instructs us that generally the relation of supply to demand in any commodity must regulate its price." Nevertheless, Dabney was "not oblivious to the plea that skilled labor is entitled to higher remuneration." It was true that many working men did not get a fair shake from their employers, especially from the new corporate monopolies.

The growth of Populism disturbed Dabney, not because he was unsympathetic to the plight of American farmers, but for the very reason that appeared so attractive to many: the Populists' simplistic approach to issues, especially concerning "free silver." In a letter to his son Charles in 1894, Dabney expressed his dismay that "the whole Southern Democracy, mislead by a parcel of shysters and demagogues … have gone mad after this free silver nonsense." Silver currency was not the cure to the nation's economic doldrums. Rather, wrote Dabney, the economy had become unbalanced by the over-expanding weight of monopolies which violated the equitable functioning of the law of supply and demand. The burden of rural taxation — a "crushing weight" — was grossly unfair. The "protective system" effectively cushioned the "monopoly rings and combinations" from the check of local and home competition. On one point Dabney did share views in common with many Populists: he strongly supported the repeal of all class legislation and laws unfairly favoring monopoly corporations at the expense of small entrepreneurs.

Dabney and Education

When he was not excoriating the financial capitalist doctrines of the "new South" creed, Dabney made periodic assaults on other new ideas. His running debate with Virginia's first superintendent of public instruction, William H. Ruffner, over state supported schools, is a case in point. Dabney began the controversy with his February, 1876 article, "The Negro and the Common School," in *Planter and Farmer* magazine, in which he clearly stated his opposition to the "Yankee theory" of free public education, especially for freedmen. For him the former slaves were wards of the South to be guided slowly and paternally through difficult years of adjustment. To promise the Negro immediate rights and an education that could never be his was dishonest and disingenuous; only through an extended period of tutelage could the Negro advance in Southern society.

In four successive articles published in the *Richmond Enquirer* Dabney attacked Virginia's plan for free public education as elaborated by superintendent Ruffner. General and free education sought to impose an unnatural equality on all, he insisted. "Providence, social laws, and parental virtues and efforts, do inevitably legislate in favor of some classes of boys," he declared. "If the State undertakes to countervail that legislation of nature by leveling action, the attempt is wicked, mischievous, and futile." Indeed, Dabney questioned "whether the use merely of letters is not education, but only one means of education, and not the only means." True education involved more than simply the use of letters. The laboring classes had traditionally found education through their various professions, a training of the "moral virtues by the fidelity and endurance" with which they earned their livelihood. The laboring man "ennobles his taste and sentiments by looking up to the superior who employs him. If to these influences you add the awakening, elevating, expanding force of Christian principles, you have given the laborer a true education … a hundred fold more true, more suitable, more useful, than the communication of certain literary arts, which he will almost necessarily disuse."

Mentioning the distinct danger of the new public schools being used by "demagogues, who are in power for a time, in the interests of their faction," Dabney moved on to his most serious indictment of public education: what happens to religious instruction if the state takes over the teaching of children? Given the status of post-war relations between church and state and changing constitutional interpretations, the state could not endorse one religious belief over another. State-sponsored education tended to become secularized. But if education were not Christian, then it would inevitably become anti-Christian. "He that is not with his God is against Him," Dabney repeated. Could education really be education if it educated "the mind without purifying the heart?" Dabney answered: "There can be no true education without moral culture, and no true moral culture without Christianity." All basic issues in life were at their core religious and ethical issues. To ignore this fact was to open the door wide to anti-Christianity.

Dabney felt the Virginia school system should be reformed "back towards the system of our fathers just as fast as possible." The old system — one of semi-private and private institutions, many controlled by families or religious interests — was much preferable to the new one. It would be economical, avoiding unnecessary taxation. It would solve the problem of religion in the schools by "leaving the school as the creature of the parents, and not of the state…. This old system evinced its wisdom by avoiding the pagan, Spartan theory, which makes the

State the parent. It left the parent supreme in his God-given sphere, as the responsible party for providing and directing the education of his own offspring."

Dabney and the Future of the South

When it came to suggesting remedies for the problems he saw implicit in the "new South" capitalist creed, Dabney does not elaborate in great detail. Generally, he writes, "the nation should return to a firm and just administration of the laws, coupled with wise and equitable commercial and industrial legislation and the propagation of industry ... economy and contentment among the people by means of Christian principles."

In his time Dabney's prescriptions appeared outdated to his contemporaries even before he presented them. Yet, the themes he kept alive have resonated throughout the subsequent history of the South (as well as in the nation). Only thirty years after his death, in the midst of the worst depression in American history, twelve prominent Southern writers — the Southern Agrarians — came together to produce the volume *I'll Take My Stand*, a call for the South to reassert its traditions, its culture, and its distinctive economy, echoing strikingly Dabney in a number of ways.

Contemporaneously in England, Catholic essayists G. K. Chesterton, Hilaire Belloc, and others developed a similar approach, Distributivism, advocating economic and political decentralization, regionalism, a return to the land, and a renewed emphasis on community, family, and church. Both Agrarians and Distributivists contributed in the 1930s to Seward Collins' journal *The American Review*, and subsequent essays appeared in two seminal volumes: *Who Owns America?* and *Attack on the Leviathan*. Despite efforts to translate these ideas into action, the South (and the nation) headed in an opposite direction.

In recent years a few Southerners and other Americans have begun to rediscover Robert Lewis Dabney. In our age of faceless managerialism and rootless international corporations who owe no allegiance to locality or community, when only money and power seem to sway politicians, and where hidden elites and "inside-the-beltway" think-tanks preside over what was once a republic, in this age Dabney perhaps has something to say.

In his fiery essays Dabney makes few concrete suggestions for reform. Nevertheless, his critical analysis — now after the sordid history of the twentieth century — is in many ways prophetic. For those who give up their heritage and abandon their principles, Dabney has a warning: you forfeit your birthright at your own peril. For those willing to fight for their beliefs, however forlorn the cause may seem, Dabney offers encouragement. For Robert Lewis Dabney, to paraphrase James Branch Cabell, history is not a matter of record; it is a matter of faith.

*Dabney's social, political, theological, and philosophical essays were collected by editor C. R. Vaughan, *Discussions (1890-1897)*, 4 vols. Mexico, Missouri, 1897, and have been republished. Volume 4 contains his "secular" essays. Thomas C. J. Johnson's 1903 biography, *Life and Letters of Robert Lewis Dabney*, remains the standard reference biography. The essays cited above are contained in volume 4.

(*The Unz Review*, October 19, 2014, at: www.unz.com/article/robert-lewis-dabney-and-his-attack-on-progressivism/)

Mel Bradford and the Defense of Southern Conservatism
→ Chapter 28 ←

This past May 8, 2014, would have been the late Melvin E. Bradford's 80th birthday. That the anniversary passed without much, if any, commentary is not surprising, given the intellectual tenor now prevalent in American society. Bradford — Mel, to his friends — was an incredible and fluent scholar, extremely well versed in the literature of the American South. He was a superb historian of the founding of the United States and arguably the dean, along with Clyde Wilson, of a group of brilliant Southern intellectuals who refused to accept the increasing veil of political correctness that strangles discussion and stifles legitimate investigation into the complex history of the South.

As a professor at the University of Dallas for many years, Bradford established a national reputation for his excellence in teaching. Several of his books remain testaments to his erudition and intellect, including: *A Better Guide Than Reason: Studies in the American Revolution*; *A Worthy Company* (brief biographies of the American founders); *Generations of the Faithful Heart* (on Southern literature); and very notably his study of the framing of the American Constitution, *Original Intentions: On the Making and Ratification of the United States Constitution* (1993). His essays appeared in publications ranging from *National Review* and the *Sewanee Review*, to the *South Atlantic Quarterly* and the *Wake Forest Law Review*. Many of these have been collected in various edited volumes. An appreciation of his accomplishments, *A Defender of Southern Conservatism: M. E. Bradford and His Achievements* (University of Missouri Press, 1999), is well worth exploring, and includes moving tributes by both Eugene and Elizabeth Fox-Genovese.

Beginning in the early 1970s and continuing on for twenty years, Bradford engaged in an ongoing conversation — a scholarly debate, mostly printed in the quarterly journal *Modern Age* — with Harry Jaffa, professor at Claremont McKenna College in California, over the philosophy of Abraham Lincoln and his role in American history. It was this long-running series of exchanges that eventually got Mel into trouble with newly-dominant neoconservatives who were rapidly establishing their control over the "conservative movement." The defining watershed came with his candidacy to become head of the National

Endowment for the Humanities (1981) under President Ronald Reagan.

Starting with George Will and descending on down into the realms of less fluent neocon writers, Bradford was attacked mercilessly, for the most part because he did not worship at the shrine of Abraham Lincoln, but also because he represented a threat to the then-growing neoconservative ascendancy in the ranks of movement conservatism. After that, when his name was mentioned as a candidate for Archivist of the United States, he was similarly torpedoed, again by the same group of intellectual terrorists.

For twenty-three years, Mel was a dear and close friend. On several occasions while researching books over at University of North Carolina, at Duke, and at the N.C. State Archives, he stayed with me. I shall always remember the last time we spent some time together: it was in Savannah, at a confab of former Richard Weaver Fellows in early 1993. In little more than a month he was dead, and the traditional South had lost an elegant and informed voice, a grand historian and commentator, a man steeped in Southern literature and history, whose writing will forever remain a model of written discourse and elegant communication. Perhaps above all, Mel exemplified what it was to be a Southern gentleman, a gentle soul, who brought together all the virtues our ancestors possessed and hoped to pass on. He "lived" the South, its traditions, its people. He possessed what Burke called, "the unbought grace of life." That is why the shameful and vicious attacks upon him and his character when he was up for the NEH position in 1981 and later were so despicable and inexcusable.

Mel took all these slings and arrows with equanimity and the kind of spiritual understanding that most of us lack. He continued to write and speak, and his later publications — his seminal volume on the American Founding, *Original Intentions*, and his edited and annotated volume of Elliot's Debates — remain a supreme testimony to his superb intellectual gift and labors. And since his death several volumes of his insightful essays have also appeared, not to mention appreciations by such distinguished historians as the late Eugene Genovese.

There is perhaps no one better qualified, then, to give definition to what exactly "Southern Conservatism" is and entails. Certainly, such a view of life, its traditions and heritage, are under very severe attack today, and not just from the politically-correct historical establishment. Indeed, millions of immigrants from other parts of the country have decided the nicer climate in the South and the lower taxes and nicer folks make it a good retirement or stopping place; after all, who really wants to live in colder climes when a nice home, usually much less expensive, and lower taxes can be had in north Raleigh, Charleston or Marietta?

But that isn't the only challenge; no, many of those graced with being born in the South, having received that inheritance and legacy, now shun it or are ashamed of it. "Maybe people will look down on me if I put a Confederate license plate on my car?" "Maybe they will think I'm a hick or redneck!" It is the abject and miserable ignorance and pusillanimity of such natives which always manages to try my patience. Failure of our schools? Yes! Failure of our media? By all means! But also, failure of my generation to pass on the grace of life the late Southern author and poet Donald Davidson illuminates and speaks of in his epic poem, *Lee in the Mountains.*

Mel Bradford loved the last lines of Davidson's marvelous narrative poem, one of the finest works of Southern poesy written in the twentieth century, and indeed, one of the finest works of poetry ever written in the English language. Here is Davidson remembering the past and recalling that, in the words of Faulkner, for the true Southerner, "The past is never dead. It is not even past."

> Young men, the God of your fathers is a just
> And merciful God Who in this blood once shed
> On your green altars measures out all days,
> And measures out the grace
> Whereby alone we live;
> And in His might He waits,
> Brooding within the certitude of time,
> To bring this lost forsaken valor
> And the fierce faith undying
> And the love quenchless
> To flower among the hills to which we cleave,
> To fruit upon the mountains whither we flee,
> Never forsaking, never denying
> His children and His children's children forever
> Unto all generations of the faithful heart.

Mel Bradford understood and lived Davidson's summons to resilience. He embraced his inheritance and wrote well of it. And he challenged us to embrace our heritage and intelligently defend it, passing it on to faithful generations who follow.

(Abbeville Institute, July 17, 2014, at: www.abbevilleinstitute.org/blog/mel-bradford-and-the-defense-of-southern-conservatism/)

A Partisan Conversation: Interview with Eugene Genovese

↣ Chapter 29 ↢

Eugene D. Genovese is a remarkable man, a conundrum, a man who challenges all of our predispositions. Consider just a few of the contradictions in terms he embodies: he is an objective Marxist, a leftist scholar and a Yankee gentleman.

Of course, Professor Genovese would argue there should be no surprise in the linking up of such terms. And his argument would carry the heavy force of logic, the light touch of a good natured wit and always the impeccable credentials of a scholar of the first class.

In his books (for example, *The Political Economy of Slavery, The World the Slaveholders Made, Roll, Jordan, Roll*), in hundreds of speeches and essays, Genovese has the remarkable gift of seeing events through the eyes of the people who lived and acted 130 years ago. And while members of the academic left delight in lashing the South, Genovese has generally resisted the moralistic ritual.

Professor Genovese granted this special interview to *Partisan* senior editor Boyd Cathey.

PARTISAN: How did you come to be interested in the South and in the study of it?

GENOVESE: More or less by accident. I was an undergraduate student at Brooklyn College majoring in history, particularly American History. Not unusually, I was particularly interested in secession and the War because, after all, that's what happened in American History. But in the course of working at it, I had an opportunity to do an honors paper with Professor Arthur C. Cole, who was one of the outstanding historians of that period.

I told him I was interested in doing something on Southern thought from the Revolution to the Civil War. He didn't laugh. He said that was fine but it was a bit broad. He went through a list, and I picked economic thought after narrowing it several times; and the next thing I knew I was doing a paper on agricultural reform. I didn't know the difference between a horse and a mule, but I just plunged in. And in the course of working on it for the better part of a year I got hooked.

PARTISAN: In your work, you describe the existence, under slavery, of a considerable degree of Black dignity and independence through their development of personal relationships with their masters. This seems to contradict the charge put forth by Stanley Elkins and others that slave society was little better than a concentration camp. Could you elaborate?

GENOVESE: Certainly, I started writing *Roll, Jordan, Roll* and also *In Red And Black* as a reaction to Elkins. I must confess until I read Elkins I had never intended to write a book on the slaves; I was primarily interested in the masters. But Elkins' book shook me because it seemed to me to be logically irresistible. He took U. B. Phillips and Stampp and the whole received literature, transcended their specific disagreements and demonstrated there was a general agreement that slavery had rendered the blacks in some way or another "Sambos." Now in the case of the older, more Abolitionist literature this was couched as "the nature of the blacks." In the neo-Abolitionist literature, which Stampp's book epitomizes, it was projected as the dreadful outcome of a horrible social system.

Now, I read Elkins carefully; I had studied Latin American history with Frank Tannenbaum at Columbia. And I just didn't buy it. First of all, I really thought he was wrong in much of what he said about the Latin American side of it. Second, I looked at his argument and said this is a brilliant exposition of the logic of slavery, but there are too many countervailing forces he's not taking into consideration.

Nevertheless the book haunted me; and like many scholars, younger and not so young at that time, I began to study the question seriously. I owe that to him and so do a lot of other people. I must confess when I started out I thought I was going to do my book on slaves in about two years and that it would be a little book, an extended essay. It wound up taking about 10 years in the course of which I learned what l knew abstractly but came to know very specifically: if you want to understand the masters you really have to make an effort to understand the slaves and vice-versa. These people's lives were too closely bound up together.

PARTISAN: You are well-known as a practitioner of a Marxist methodology in historical research. I take this to mean you are interested in movements of people — the "masses" — rather than grand personages, presidents, elections or battles, as history's working material. Yet some of the more strident voices on the American Left tend to be hostile or unfriendly to you. Why do you think this is so?

GENOVESE: First of all, since I think I am a real conservative, I must insist that I have a *Marxist* method and not a *methodology*. But really what I want to express is this: I regard myself as a Marxist and I do not think that being a good Marxist means treating Marx's own work or any part of Marx's work as canon. I think that with the development of any point of view, once you do that, you're dead.

In any case, I interpreted the Old South from the beginning as a unique society based on the master-slave relation. Of course, I know perfectly well that most of the Southerners were not slaveholders and that many qualifications need to be introduced, but my central argument has been that slavery permeated that society on all levels of thought, of feeling and action. And that this gave the Old South a unique quality in the modern world, radically different from the other great slaveholding societies in Brazil, Cuba and Jamaica.

In any case, what I have argued from the beginning is that Southern society existed within, inexplicably, the modern capitalist world and that internally it had many of the attributes of a bourgeois society. But the master-slave relation carried it psychologically, materially, politically in quite a different direction, and this is the formulation that I have used and that my wife and I tried to develop in our book *Fruits of Merchant Capital* — that the South was in but not of the modern capitalist world. That has gone down very hard with many people on the Left.

PARTISAN: What do you think of Marx's observations on the War Between the States? Do they influence your thinking?

GENOVESE: Marx himself treated the Old South as a particularly vicious kind of bourgeois society and in *Fruits of Merchant Capital* my wife and I took up his argument and argued against it explicitly. One of the things we said (which some of my Marxist friends did not want to hear) is that Marx didn't know anything about the Old South. I mean, you know, he read Olmsted and he read a few newspapers and most of his generalizations about the Old South were actually based upon his knowledge of slavery in the Caribbean about which he knew a lot more. So to put it bluntly, I really don't give a damn what he said about the Old South. What difference does it make?

Of course, I think his theoretical work on history is very useful for understanding the development of Southern Society. If I didn't think that I wouldn't be a Marxist. You know, his observations on the War itself reflected a partisan hatred for slavery, but he was by no means uncritical of the North. You'll find in those writings some very hard criticisms of the kind that a lot of Southerners at the time might have said "Amen" to.

PARTISAN: Recently the *Raleigh News and Observer* attacked you as an "economic determinist" and you responded by a letter to that paper that this was a false reading of your work. Would you like to explain this in a little more detail?

GENOVESE: Well, if I had wanted to be really rude I would have said it was a stupid interpretation. I'm willing to listen to any kind of criticism of my work, but I don't see how anybody who reads it could call me an "economic determinist" of any kind. And, you know, Marxism is inherently hostile to economic determinism, although the confusion arises even among honest people.

Marx is primarily concerned with the centrality of social classes, and we define social classes in relation to the means of production which can narrowly be seen as an economic category. But this can't bear such a simple formulation. Social classes are a product of much more than their economic interests.

By the way, may I come back to one thing we left hanging? In an earlier question you said that as a Marxist, I was interested in the "masses" rather than grand personages, presidents, elections, battles, and so forth. May I comment on that? I wouldn't say it that way. My wife and I also took this theme up in T*he Fruits of Merchant Capital*. We don 't believe (and I think many historians from Right and Left would agree) that you can understand great historical changes, which to us are basically political, if you simply concentrate on the formal trappings of politics or high culture. What you may badly call "the masses," lumping together all kinds of people, are actors in history. Consequently historical changes are products of the constant tension between what is being generated below, as it were, and what is being generated above.

PARTISAN: Looking at whole societies, then, what differences do you see between the Antebellum South and the North, particularly New England? And have those differences persisted in your view?

GENOVESE: You know, this is a question which is battled out among historians, incessantly and with great heat. Of course, it depends upon how one sets things up.

For me, the essential question comes to this: Did the South and North diverge in a deep cultural sense, as well as politically and institutionally, to a degree that made secession and war understandable, not as a historical tragedy but as the outcome of a historical process? Under any circumstances the War would have had tragic dimensions, the mere fact that members of families fought on both sides, and so on.

Now, here I don't see the point of merging the South and the North at all, and I say that with full awareness that Louisiana was not South Carolina and Mississippi was not Virginia. Nonetheless, because the South developed as a slave labor society whereas the North developed as an essentially bourgeois society, these people became separate in sensibility as well as interests.

That does not preclude enormous regional variations on either side. It suggests a common range of behavior and much overlapping, but with a very different locus. And in this sense, I think that those Southerners who perceived themselves by the 1850s as being in the process of forging a separate nationality and as being a people apart were right. I think this was one of the great difficulties in the way of any kind of a compromise. Northerners from their perspective had to see the country as one; Southerners had to see themselves increasingly as a separate people who were trying to negotiate a coexistence.

This is reflected, it seems to me, in the difference in Constitutional perception. For Southerners, the Union was a compact; they put it in States' Rights terms and that meant something very real to them. I don't underestimate it. But at the bottom of that (and I think this can be demonstrated in their own testimony) was the notion that the Constitution made possible the political co-existence of two radically different social systems.

And that therefore from their point of view, the Constitution was a way to live and let live. From the Northern point of view it was much closer to being a national document. They never accepted the notion this was a solemn compact between two equal social systems. They may have been willing to tolerate slavery in the states as a States' Rights phenomenon, but they never acknowledged that therefore the Constitution sanctioned slavery and put that social system on an equal footing with their own.

PARTISAN: What kind of differences continue today between the regions?

GENOVESE: Well, I must confess the one thing about Southern history which continues to surprise is the staying power of much of the culture and sensibility that I would have thought would have eroded very quickly with the demise of the old regime. Now, to some extent I think the race question and the long period of segregation acted as a functional substitute, and I am skeptical of the continued staying power of much of what is called traditional in the South.

On another aspect of culture, my wife Betsey and I are doing a book on the master class. Central to that book is a thesis which we have taken up from Southern conservatives that the Old South should be understood fundamentally as a religious society. We take that very seriously. We are enormously impressed and moved by our work on the slaveholder, family by family, person by person. We've been digging into family papers for many, many years to do this project in a very specific way, and we're discovering in our study the efforts to develop not only the churches *per se* but the schools, the old-field schools, the academies, the female institutes, the colleges — all of which were permeated by religious values and largely either directly sponsored by religious institutions or by people who very much saw education as religiously grounded.

In our study, we say the intense religious quality of Southern life sets it apart from the North in two ways: First, and less firmly, we strongly suspect Southern culture was more deeply religious than Northern. But that's awfully hard to establish, especially since there are different qualities of religious experience. But second, and this is more important and easier to nail down, the religious quality of Southern society carried with it very specific social and political consequences.

Let me put it this way: Southerners were overwhelmingly convinced the Bible sanctioned slavery. Incidentally, while we are not Biblical scholars, we'll go out on a limb and say the Southerners won that argument against the abolitionists. These were people who were very close to the Book, that was true of the Presbyterians, even of the Episcopalians and certainly of the Baptists and Methodists and the smaller sects.

Now under the circumstances, what we think we can demonstrate is the defense of slavery was religiously grounded and not only that, the fundamental political and social thought of Southern society was religiously grounded. Where I think we can demonstrate the divergence from the North is that, over time in the North, religion was weakening even in the bastions of Old Puritanism in New England. It was increasingly being watered down by liberal religion and increasingly losing its hold on the discourse. In the South, it was being strengthened. In the North, politicians could appeal to God and the Bible in some fashion; after all, they still do. In the South, it was impossible to make any kind of a political or social statement without grounding your arguments firmly in a religious discourse and knowing full well that you were speaking to people who knew exactly what the touchstones were.

Look at James Hammond of South Carolina, a brilliant man but hardly the epitome of a good Christian, or Henry Wise of Virginia. Take the most opportunistic of people, the depths of whose religion one could suspect, yet these guys, in speaking about great social questions and political principles, knew they had to begin in the same way their deeply religious colleagues did. That was the discourse.

Now that was no longer true of the North. The discourse in the North was increasingly secular with God thrown in occasionally in a somewhat deeper way. But in the South I don't think you could find serious social and political arguments beyond the level of stump tactics that were not religiously grounded and didn't operate within a discourse that was steadily disappearing in the North.

PARTISAN: This is an interesting insight. Are you aware of anybody else who has brought this point up?

GENOVESE: Well, look, we've come to this in two ways. First of all, we formulated the hypothesis primarily by reading conservative defenses of Southern tradition: Allen Tate, for all of his feelings that the South wasn't a good Roman Catholic society as it should have been, the people from *I'll Take My Stand*, Richard Weaver, M. E. Bradford, and others who formulate it very sharply.

One of the things which has amazed me is that I've worked on these Antebellum Southerners now for a long, long time, but it wasn't until I started to go back and reread the conservative interpretations and defenses of Southern tradition that the full force of that hit me, the force of what it might mean.

And also ironically I was led in writing *Roll, Jordan, Roll* to place great emphasis on the centrality of black religion. Given my own biases, I was dragged kicking and screaming to that vantage point. But that's where my evidence led me and when I started to reflect on it I finally said, "You know this is absurd." You could not have this kind of a deeply religious black community without its white counterpart or vice-versa.

For Betsey this was a lot easier because she came in to Southern history late, without my prejudice and she saw it right away. She said, "My God, you cannot read the family letters of these people, what they write to the public, what they say to themselves privately, without being struck by the centrality of religion to Southern life. She's coming out with a book on Southern women and that realization will be up front because she saw it all over the place when she started this study.

PARTISAN: What about your future plans? We know now about your book on religion in the Old South.

GENOVESE: Well, let me say the book will be on the slaveholders, but religion will be central to it. It's not a separate study of Southern religion. And this study is going to take some years to complete. My guess is five or six. I'm 55 now and my wife is eleven years younger. She has a number of projects that she's been working on and will be completing both on women's history and related stuff.

As for me, I try to be realistic about these things. I figure by the time the book appears I'm going to be on the other side of sixty. I hope in good shape and not about to quit. But this book will probably be the last large-scale thing I do. It takes an enormous amount of time and physical energy doing in-depth research, and the older you grow the harder it gets. You have to be sensible about that. If I lived in the South it would be easier because I want to stay with Southern topics.

I've made a tentative decision that what I would like to do after that is the opposite of what usually happens. I don't want to use the next ten years, which I hope God gives me, to try to work on broad theoretical questions. Maybe because I did a good deal of that when I was younger and got it out of my system. My critics might say I ran off at the mouth a lot. But what I really would like to do (and what I think would give me enormous pleasure) is to follow the example of people like E. Merton Coulter, whom I never met but whose work I admired not withstanding gagging on his racial views.

What I would like to do is something that would be very ambitious and would require physically moving some, here and there. Certain aspects of Charleston, for example in the 1850s, interest me. But in any case, I'm thinking smaller and smaller past this book. There's a case to be made for that kind of work to be done by people who have already been in the field for 40 years instead of just starting out. So that's what I'm thinking for the future.

(*The Southern Partisan*, Fall, 1985, volume V, number 4)

Rejecting Progressivism by Recovering the Fullness of the American Past: Senator Sam Ervin
❖ Chapter 30 ❖

Too often we are so wrapped up in the swirl of contemporary politics and the endless debate and bitter back-and-forth which dominates our national conversations we lose context and forget those basic principles, those constitutional foundations that informed the American republic at its inception. It is a gross understatement to say that when it comes to understanding the genius of the American Founding and what our Founders and the Framers intended, ignorance — some of it purposeful — rules the day, and not only among those on the Left, but also among many conservatives and Republicans.

One of the objects of this series has been to attempt to disentangle those principles from the modern confusion which distorts them. Thus, many of these commentaries have offered short historical accounts and descriptions with the specific goal of arriving at a better and clearer understanding not only of our collective past, but also how that past, that legacy, has been corrupted and displaced from much of the public square.

Since at least the second half of nineteenth century we have been facing a seemingly unstoppable and victorious historical movement — the Idea of Progress — which demands of each generation that it enact changes, and those changes, which it calls "reforms," are always to the definable ideological Left. Most importantly, this "movement" has engendered a certain overarching mindset, a certain way of thinking and looking at things and issues, so even if you oppose a specific revolutionary advance or "reform," you must do so using the same language and same long-range posited goals that are established and within the limited parameters and eventual goals of this movement. Almost everything in our lives, even the most mundane, is governed by this mindset and its accompanying narrative.

Thus, literally almost no one will openly oppose the nebulous concept of "equal" or "civil rights," which has become a totem, a kind of talismanic term, under the cover of which all sorts of expanding mischief have been injected into American society and into the American body politic. From women's suffrage in the early 20th century we have moved on to equal "civil rights" for black Americans, to the expansion of "civil rights" defined to include abortion, same sex marriage, and the latest aberration, "gender fluidity." Yet, amongst even those most intrepid defenders of more traditional belief, their arguments usually acknowledge *pro forma* the inviolability of civil rights, perhaps declaring that while the "civil rights" bills of the 1960s and early 1970s were justified and necessary, somehow what confronts us today is different.

It is unfortunately a slippery slope. Until the Progressivist intellectual template, its ingrained mindset and basic outlook, and its language we employ to express our goals and hopes, is discarded — until the idea of inevitable progress, which always moves Left, is rejected and the expression and intellectual framework of our ancestors recovered, we shall remain imprisoned, fighting the ongoing culture war with one hand tied behind us.

One extremely valuable means of recapturing our inherited legacy and beginning the journey of throwing off the accumulated dross of decades of suffocating Progressivist indoctrination, is to read the writings and texts of those great figures who went before us. Such a journey not only nourishes us with a better, first-hand knowledge of their principles, but repairs and ennobles our language and expression, itself. It represents, in fact, a defiant refusal to go along with the tawdry pablum and encrusted filth we are constantly told we must accept. Certainly, we should know about that narrative which does with its awful stench dominate in our contemporary society; but we don't have to — and must not — support it. And this is the very same admonition we must inculcate in our children.

Growing up my father would read to us children each night — frequently from the *Arabian Nights*, or from Joel Chandler Harris, or some of the Grimm fairy tales. As we got older, my sister and I read some of those classics for ourselves, and then there was Dickens, James Fennimore Cooper, Jane Austen, and mostly all before high school. Not only did that preparation inspire a desire to read more, but it also assisted, along with a loving and Christian family, to shape our thinking process and forms of expression. Older relatives, many of whom were born in the 19th century, offered the richness of a strong family oral tradition, stories from the past about ancestors, about the hard times of post-war Reconstruction, about love of country and of place and of family, and of the community in which all that took place.

As I boy and a young man, before the advent of Jesse Helms, I greatly admired Senator Sam Ervin of my home state. A Bible-quoting, story-telling and supremely-well educated conservative Democrat from Burke County who rose to be North Carolina's senior U.S. senator, "Senator Sam" was an archetypal "Southern conservative," yet today he is remembered, if remembered at all, as the "Watergate senator" who "helped bring Richard Nixon down." Yet, he was considerably more than that — indeed, to go back and read his superb speeches or his autobiography, *Preserving the Constitution*, is like unto a journey back into the mind of the Framers and a vision of the American republic and American society which is sorely lacking in today's environment of Harvey Weinstein, Frederica Wilson, or Nancy Pelosi.

How far we have descended! How much is our need for the wit and conservative wisdom of Senator Sam!

(My Corner by Boyd Cathey, October 23, 2017, at: http://boydcathey-reviewofbooks.blogspot.com/2017/10/october-23-2017-my-corner-by-boyd.html)

The South Out West: Randolph Scott, the Man from North Carolina
⇢ Chapter 31 ⇠

Tar Heel actor and Western movie star Randolph Scott never forgot his North Carolina and Southern roots. His final trip back to Charlotte came in March 1987, when he was buried in historic Elmwood Cemetery, with family friend Reverend Billy Graham conducting the service.

Scott had left Charlotte for Hollywood to try his luck at acting in 1928 yet returned fairly frequently while his mother remained alive. From the 1930s until the early 1960s, he was one of Hollywood's most respected actors, and one of its leading Western stars. A few years after the release of Scott's final film, *Ride the High Country*, in 1962, he seemed like a distant memory, and the America he had portrayed so well in film seemed relegated to the distant past. For generations of Americans in the 1930s, 1940s, and 1950s, Scott's characters had epitomized an older, traditional South of honor and duty, strong family values, and a belief in the triumph of good over evil. But by the mid-1970s, more than a few considered Scott to be "out-of-date." But technological access to Scott's films during the 1980s and 1990s via satellite, cablevision, and home video and DVD, and a growing critical re-appreciation of his cinematic oeuvre have helped reestablish his reputation as one of the film industry's finest Western actors.

George Randolph Scott was born January 23, 1898, in Orange County, Virginia, while his parents were visiting family. His mother, Lucy Crane Scott, was from an old and established Charlotte family, and it was in the Queen City that Scott spent most of his childhood. His father, George Scott, was a textile engineer and expected his son to study engineering at Georgia Tech. As a Yellow Jacket, Randolph Scott also played football, but a back injury eliminated any hopes of pursuing a sports career. He served honorably in World War I, and still destined to follow in his father's footsteps, he finally finished his university studies at the University of North Carolina.

Fascinated by acting, he persuaded his father to give him a letter of introduction to Howard Hughes, a friend of the family, and shortly afterward, off to "the city of lights" he went. At first struggling to make a go of it, he acted in several stage plays at the Pasadena Community Playhouse, before securing some bit parts, and finally, a contract with

Paramount to star in a well-produced series of Zane Grey Westerns in the 1930s. As an actor he adapted to other genres, as well, with starring roles in such fine dramas as *She* (RKO, 1935) and *Roberta* (RKO, 1935, with Fred Astaire and Ginger Rogers), and in historical epics such as *So Red the Rose* (Paramount, 1935, based on Stark Young's novel of the War Between the States) and *The Last of the Mohicans* (United Artists, 1936). During World War II, Scott, now in his mid-forties, turned out several well-received patriotic movies, including *To the Shores of Tripoli* (Fox, 1942), *Corvette-K225* (Universal, 1943), and *Gung Ho!* (Universal, 1943).

But it was in Westerns Randolph Scott made his mark in American cinematographic history. Twentieth Century Fox studio co-starred him in its immensely successful color spectacular, *Jesse James*, in 1939 (with Tyrone Power and Henry Fonda) and followed that with leading roles in director Fritz Lang's block-buster, *Western Union* (1941), and in another War Between the States epic, *Belle Starr* (1941).

Scott loved playing Confederates, especially those confronted by overwhelming odds and apparent defeat. His character would meet those challenges heroically and, if possible, overcome them. And always he would defend the Confederate cause with nobility and grace. In the big box Warner Brothers production, *Virginia City* (1940), co-starring Erroll Flynn and Humphrey Bogart, he portrays Vance Irby, a Confederate agent charged with securing gold from the mines around Virginia City for the Confederacy. Unlike most Scott Westerns, he is killed in this major production.

In the largely fictionalized *Belle Starr* he plays Captain Sam Starr, husband of the famous eponymous associate of the "James-Younger Gang" (played by Gene Tierney). Although at first motivated largely by plunder, Captain Starr finally gives in to Belle's pleas for civility, restraint, and a return to dedication to the Southern cause: in the final scene he presents himself to the Yankee commander, Major Crail (played by Dana Andrews), offering his sword in surrender. Both had loved Belle. Scott's act is consistent with his promise to Tierney and his honor as a Southern gentlemen.

Perhaps Scott's best "Southern" Western of the 1950s, at least before the partnership with director Budd Boetticher late in that decade, was *Hangman's Knot* (1952) in which he again plays a Confederate commander out West (Matt Stewart), this time leading a desperate mission to Nevada in search of Yankee gold and treasure, relenting only when he learns of the war's end. The film is enlivened by an over-the-top performance by Lee Marvin as one of Scott's (unruly) troopers.

After 1946 Scott preferred to play Western roles. He enjoyed doing them, he once remarked, because they fit his personality; and he said, there was money to be made. Beginning with *Abilene Town* (United Artists, 1946), Scott in sixteen years made thirty-nine Westerns, all successful at the box office and several now considered classics. From 1950 to 1952, the Motion Picture Herald Top Ten Poll included Scott as one of the top-ten box office moneymakers. With the advent of television during the 1950s, Scott's persona (along with John Wayne's) not only kept the cinematic Western alive but also defined it.

In 1956 John Wayne's production company, Batjac, offered Scott the starring role in *Seven Men from Now*, under the direction of Boetticher (Wayne had wanted to do the role, but commitments with the film *The Searchers* prevented it.) With a crackerjack screenplay written by Burt Kennedy, *Seven Men from Now* (Warner Bros., 1956, also with Lee Marvin) was a resounding success and began a creative and professional relationship among Scott, Boetticher, and Kennedy that produced six more superior oaters. In short succession, the team produced such cinematic gems as *The Tall T* (Columbia, 1957, co-starring Richard Boone), *Decision At Sundown* (Columbia, 1957), *Buchanan Rides Alone* (Columbia, 1958), *Ride Lonesome* (Columbia, 1959, with Lee Van Cleef and James Coburn), and *Comanche Station* (Columbia, 1960, with Claude Akins). These generally short films presented Scott as a hard-edged but highly principled loner, often driven by unattainable goals.

By 1960, Randolph Scott was ready to hang up his holsters, but he waited long enough to star in a fitting swan song for him and for the traditional Western genre, itself. Co-starring with fellow old-time Western actor Joel McCrea, Scott played the good/bad role of Gil Westrum in director Sam Peckinpah's elegiac *Ride the High Country* (MGM, 1962). *Newsweek* and *Film Quarterly* selected it as the best film of 1962, and many film critics now consider it to be one of the greatest Westerns of all time. Years later, Scott stated that he retired from acting because "the motion picture industry is in a steadily declining state, what with nudity and the like flagrantly displayed in films today."

Happily married to (Marie) Patricia Stillman since 1944 (an earlier marriage had been dissolved), Scott had two children, Christopher and Sandra. During retirement, he enjoyed playing golf and reading the financial pages of *The Wall Street Journal*. Politically, he was a staunch conservative Republican in a Hollywood which was becoming more

Democratic by the year. Scott's long and successful acting career and his successful investing in land and oil wells made him one of Hollywood's richest men. Scott was also a deeply religious man. According to Christopher, his father "was less an actor and more a man who simply portrayed himself. He lived by and believed in his own convictions." Perhaps director Budd Boetticher best described Scott: "If the Confederate cavalry had one hundred 'Randolph Scotts,' the South would have won the Civil War. There never has been such a Southern complete gentleman in the long history of the motion picture industry."

Twelve years after Scott's retirement, the Country-Western musical group, The Statler Brothers, scored a major hit with their song, "Whatever Happened to Randolph Scott?" In it they evoked in a popular and accessible manner what Scott had symbolized when alive and what in death his passing intimated was occurring in America, and also in his native South:

> *Everybody knows when you go to the show you can't take the kids along*
> *You've gotta read the paper and know the code of G P G and R and X*
> *And you gotta know what the movie's about before you even go*
> *Tex Ritter's gone and Disney's dead and the screen is filled with sex*
> *Whatever happened to Randolph Scott ridin' the train alone*
> *Whatever happened to Gene and Tex and Roy and Rex the Durango Kid*
> *Oh whatever happened to Randolph Scott his horse plain as could be*
> *Whatever happened to Randolph Scott has happened to the best of me. …*

At the age of 89, Randolph Scott died on March 2, 1987. For his contributions to American film, he was awarded a star on the Hollywood Walk of Fame, and in 1975 he was inducted into the Western Performers Hall of Fame in Oklahoma City.

But that was not the end. More than thirty years after his death his films are esteemed and his memory is still fresh: his films, after a period of laying on dusty studio shelves, now can be seen regularly on several major satellite and cable networks, and inexpensive sets of them have shown up on DVD. A new appreciation of his work has emerged, in particular of the seven short films he made with Budd Boetticher in the late 1950s.

Above all Randolph Scott yet serves as a model of probity — that Southern gentlemen dedicated to duty and honor — for those who care to notice. And that is a reason for hope.

BIBLIOGRAPHY

Jefferson Brim Crow, *Randolph Scott: The Gentleman from Virginia* (Carrollton, Texas, 1987);
Phil Hardy, *The Western* (London, 1983);
Robert Nott, *Last of the Cowboy Heroes* (Jefferson, North Carolina, 2000);
Lee O. Miller, *The Great Cowboy Stars of Movies & T.V.* (New Rochelle, 1979);
Christopher Scott, *Whatever Happened to Randolph Scott?* (Madison, North Carolina, 1994);
Garner Simmons, *Peckinpah: A Portrait in Montages* (Austin, 1976);
Jon Tuska, *The Filming of the West* (New York, 1976).

(*Southern Partisan*, volume IX, 1989; revised 2011)

On Abraham Lincoln and the Inversion of American History
↣ Chapter 32 ↢

Back in 1990 in Richmond, Virginia, as part of the Museum of the Confederacy's lecture series, the late Professor Ludwell Johnson, author and professor of history at William and Mary College, presented a fascinating lecture titled, "The Lincoln Puzzle: Searching for the Real Honest Abe." Commenting on the assassination of Lincoln now 150 years ago, here is a portion of Dr. Johnson's prepared remarks:

[After his death] *for many, Lincoln became a symbolic Christ, for some, perhaps, more than symbolic. They could scarcely help themselves, the parallels were so striking. He was the savior of the Union, God's chosen instrument for bringing the millenium to suffering humanity, born in a log cabin (close enough to a stable), son of a carpenter. ... He was a railsplitter (close enough to carpentry), a humble man with the human touch, a man of sorrows and acquainted with grief, called by his followers to supreme greatness, struck down by Satan's minions on Good Friday.*

Said one minister in his Black Friday sermon: 'It is no blasphemy against the Son of God and the Savior of Men that we declare the fitness of the slaying of the second Father of our Republic on the anniversary of the day on which he was slain. Jesus Christ died for the world, Abraham Lincoln died for his country'. ... Another spoke of his 'mighty sacrifice ... for the sins of his people.' Yet another proposed not April 15, but Good Friday be considered the anniversary of Lincoln's death. 'We should make it a movable fast and ever keep it beside the cross and grave of our blessed Lord, in whose service for whose gospel he became a victim and a martyr.'

For years after the war the rumor persisted that Lincoln's tomb in Springfield was empty. Lincoln was also frequently compared to Moses, who led his people to the Promised Land that he was not allowed to enter, and, like Moses after viewing Canaan, was taken by death.

It is right and fitting, then, given the legacy now increasingly laid at Lincoln's feet, the resultant and seemingly unstoppable growth of the "Behemoth" managerial state which has occurred since his presidency, and the anniversary of his death, to examine again his actual meaning in the context of our history.

Probably too much has been written about Abraham Lincoln. Most school-age children know almost nothing about him, except "he freed the slaves," which, of course, is patently untrue: he freed not one slave. Yet, his looming presence as a preeminent national lodestar, his role as a kind of holy icon after death, and the radical task he accomplished in completely restructuring the original American nation the Founders created, remain constantly with us. In a real and palpable sense, as the text excerpted from Professor Johnson shows, Lincoln immediately became the founder and canonized "saint" of a "new" nation, in which the ideas of "democracy" and "equality" were enshrined as bedrock principles.

As the late Professor Mel Bradford illustrates abundantly in his signal volume, *Original Intentions*, with Lincoln and his successors, concepts rejected outright by most of the Founders and eschewed by the authors of the Constitution, replaced the original understanding of what this nation was supposed to be and represent. The Gettsyburg Address makes clear Lincoln based the American founding on the Declaration of the Independence ("Four score and seven years ago….") and on his shaky reading of that war time document.

As such, today the "high crimes and misdemeanors" which are the most heinous, the most grave, in our benighted land are "crimes" against "equality," whether committed against racial minorities, or against "women," or against homosexuals who want to force the rest of us to fully accept their lifestyle … and "crimes" against "full democracy," including voter IDs, and preventing illegals from full participation in all the goodies the Federal government can dole out.

This is not to say there is an unbroken, direct line connecting the "Lincolnian Revolution" of the 1860s with the public and private defecated culture and corrupt and managerial political system which engulf us today. Indeed, the history of the USA since 1865 is filled with vicissitudes and "curves and variations." It would be unfair perhaps to blame Lincoln directly for these present happenings. Indeed, more than likely, as a 19th century liberal, he would be offended and shocked by much of what besets us today culturally and socially. But Lincoln, like other leaders of 19th century Liberalism, opened the door to future, much more radical change. So, while it is assuredly not correct to hold him responsible for, example, same sex marriage, there is a torturous genealogy that can be traced without injury to the historical narrative.

Of those radical changes which came as a result of the Lincolnian Revolution and that directly affect us today, the cataclysmic effects of the (illegally passed) 14th Amendment must be highlighted. Indeed, one could suggest it is under the rubric of the 14th Amendment most all of our present decay and distress has occurred. If there had been no 14th Amendment, would most of the horrendous court decisions we've seen have been rendered? Yet, the 14th Amendment grows directly out of the consequences of Southern defeat in 1865, in a War begun by Abraham Lincoln.

Certainly, there are those who would argue, erroneously, that the "Reagan years" or even the 1920s represented respites in this ongoing revolution. Nevertheless, the general and overwhelming propulsive movement, the historical dynamic, has been in just one direction. In sum, the triumph of the Lincolnian Revolution in the American nation was, in fact, the real triumph of the 19th century "Idea of Progress" and the belief in the inevitable and continuing liberation and enhancement materially and intellectually, of human kind.

It is interesting, I think, to focus the great Iliad of the Confederacy in the context of the brutal and vicious universal war between the forces of 19th liberalism and the forces of tradition and counter-revolution. The Confederacy, the old South, played a not unimportant role in that conflict, and, even if most Southerners did not recognize that context at the time, many European traditionalists, Legitimist royalists, and Catholics most certainly did.

In my research over the years I have been struck by the fact that almost without exception, all 19th century traditional European conservatives, Legitimists, and Catholics not only favored the Confederacy in its crusade against the North, but they did so enthusiastically, to the point that thousands of European traditionalists found their way to cities like New Orleans to volunteer to fight for the Confederate cause. Perhaps between 1,000 and 2,000 soldiers of the old Bourbon Kingdom of Naples (Two Sicilies) arrived in Louisiana in early 1861 to offer their services to the South after their defeat by the arms of the liberal Kingdom of Piedmont-Savoy. Volunteers from the Carlist traditionalists in Spain came by way, mostly, of Mexico. According to Catalan historian, David Odalric de Caixal, as many as 1,000 to 2,000 Carlists enlisted in Confederate ranks, many in the Louisiana Tigers (see M. Estella, "Un historiador investiga la presencia de carlistas en la Guerra de Secesion," *El Diario de Navarra* [Pamplona], December 9,

2011). French Legitimists (the "ultra-royalists" who opposed the "democracy" of the Citizen-King Louis Philippe) also volunteered, mostly notably the Prince Camille Armand de Polignac, a hero of the battle of Mansfield.

The recently exiled (1860) duke Francesco V of the Italian Duchy of Modena (called by modern writer and historian Sir Harold Acton, "the most conservative ruler in all of Europe"), from his exile in Trento, actually recognized the Confederacy. And Pope Pius IX, in his correspondence with Jefferson Davis, offered *de facto* recognition to the Confederate cause, and his sympathies were quite open, as were the Confederate proclivities of the official publication of the Vatican, *La Civilta' Cattolica*. The Crown of Thorns, a relic long associated with Pius IX and President Jefferson Davis, remains in a museum in New Orleans, along with a supportive and precious personal message from the pope to the Confederate leader.

And who can forget the favor given by and collaboration of the Habsburg emperor of Mexico, Maximilian? It was to his empire many Confederate soldiers fled after Appomattox and Palmito Ranch. (Recall the John Wayne classic, *The Undefeated*, and other cinematic representations of that relationship?)

The traditionalist press in Europe openly believed the Confederacy was part of a much greater conflict, a universalized war, to halt the advance of the effects of the French Revolution, and to — if possible — reverse the worst aspects which resulted from the opening of that Pandora's Box. And in particular, they visualized the Confederacy as a co-belligerent in the effort to stop the growth of "democratism" and "egalitarianism."

Certainly, one can debate if this vision by European traditionalist conservatives was completely valid, or mere fancy. But the reasons supporting it, given our subsequent history, are strong in an *ex post facto* way.

What we are talking about is, then, the triumph in the 19th century of a radical transformation in the way our society and our citizens look at history and change. Indeed, the result was the enthronement of the "Idea of Progress" as the norm, such that movement in history always is "progressive" or, better described, "*a la sinistra*"— to the Left. And, given this template, does not the ongoing Leftward —"progressive"— movement of both Democrats AND many Republicans in the US, as well as both Socialist and establishment "conservative" political groupings in Europe, make sense?

Until this narrative — this sanctified and blessed "progressivist" idealization — is overturned and reversed, we shall continue to be at the mercy of faux-conservatives who continue to lead us into more Revolution, even if by a slightly different route from the hardcore revolutionaries.

Thus, Professor Johnson's account of the apotheosis of Lincoln and the enshrining of the "Lincoln Myth" go hand-in-hand with the mythologization of Garibaldi in Italy, or of Louis Blanc in France, as symbolic of what happened to an older, pre-Revolutionary civilization … and to the "exceptional" American nation along the way.

In the USA it really began in earnest, as Dr. Johnson recounts, almost immediately after Lincoln's death, with his declared "martyrdom" and veritable "canonization," and it continues full force today.

(Abbeville Institute, April 17, 2015, at: www.abbevilleinstitute.org/blog/on-abraham-lincoln-and-the-inversion-of-american history/)

Victor Davis Hanson:
Demonizing the South to Purify the Nation
⇢ Chapter 33 ⇠

Victor Davis Hanson is one of the most lauded and applauded historians of the "conservative establishment." Honored by President George W. Bush, a regular writer for *National Review*, spoken of in hushed and admiring tones by pundits like Rush Limbaugh and Sean Hannity, Hanson is rightly regarded as a fine classicist and military historian, especially of ancient warfare. But like other authors who tend to cluster in the Neoconservative orbit, Hanson strays far afield into modern history, American studies, and into current politics — fields where his fealty to a Neocon narrative overwhelms his historical expertise.

And like other well-regarded writers of the Neocon persuasion — the far less scholarly Jonah Goldberg (in his superficial and wrongheaded volume, *Liberal Fascism: The Secret History of the American Left, from Mussolini to the Politics of Meaning*) and Dinesh D'Souza (in his historical mish-mash, *The Big Lie: Exposing the Nazi Roots of the American Left*) — Hanson when he writes of contemporary politics or modern American history, writes with an agenda. But, unlike them, his arguments are usually more firmly based and less fantastical.

Like Goldberg and D'Souza and other putative Neocon historians, Hanson is at pains to create a "usable past," to construct a history and tradition which buttresses and supports current Neocon ideology. Thus, he strains to defend the concept of an American nation conceived in and based on an idea, the idea of equality and "equal rights." And because of that, like D'Souza and Goldberg, he must read back into American history an arbitrary template to demonstrate that premise.

It follows that, as for other Neocons, the Declaration of Independence becomes a critical and underlying document for this historical approach. The words —"We hold these truths to be self-evident, that all men are created equal, that they are endowed by their Creator with certain inalienable rights"— become irreplaceably essential. Avoiding the contextual meaning of the phrase and the meaning clearly intended by the Founders, which was aimed specifically at the British parliament and the demand for an "equal"— just — consideration for the colonists from across the pond, the Neocons turn a very practical bill of grievances into a call for 18th century Rationalist egalitarianism, which it was not. As the late Mel Bradford and more recently, Barry Alan Shain, have convincingly demonstrated, such attempts to read current ideology back into the Founding, runs aground on factual analysis.

But facts have little to do with Neocon ideology. What is demanded is a usable past to support present practice and to give legitimacy to the current narrative. It follows: if the American nation was founded on the "idea" of equality, then any successive deviances and variations from that idea are wrong and immoral, and, therefore, in some way, "anti-American." Thus, those Southerners who "rebelled" against the legitimate — and righteous — government of the sainted President Lincoln are become "traitors," who not only engaged in "treason" against the legitimate government of the Union, but through their defense of slavery, were enemies of the very "idea" of America — equality.

How many times in recent days in the debates over Confederate monuments and symbols have we heard echoes of such a refrain from the pages of "conservative" publications like *National Review* or *The Weekly Standard*? Or from certain pundits on Fox News?

And, more, those Southerners — more specifically, Southern Democrats — who opposed the "civil rights" legislation of the 1960s, who questioned various Supreme Court decisions on that topic (beginning with the atrociously-decided Brown decision), who enforced those evil "Jim Crow" laws, are not and never could have been real defenders of the "American [egalitarian] idea," and therefore, never could be considered "conservatives."

Confronted by unwashed, rednecky "Southern conservatives," most Neocons seek desperately to protect their left flank from criticism from those of the farther Left. They continually and in "*alta voz*" protest of their *bona fides*, of how strongly they supported Martin Luther King's crusade for equality (King was actually a "conservative," you see), of how they stood on that bridge in Selma with the noble demonstrators — well, at least in spirit! — against the "fascist" Billy club-armed police of "Bull Connor, and how they really do support "civil rights" for everyone, including "moderate" affirmative action, "moderate" feminism, yes to same sex marriage, and yes to transgenderism. Their fear of being called out as and associated with anti-egalitarians far outweighs their fear of confirming the cultural Marxist template, which, in their own manner, they both sanctify and thus, assist to advance.

The Neocon narrative stands history on its head. Not only does it fail as competent history, it simply ignores inconvenient facts, historical context, and the careful investigations and massive documentation of more responsible chroniclers and historians of the American nation, if those facts and documentation do not fit a preconceived narrative. All must be written, all must be shaped, to demonstrate the near-mystical advance and progress of the Idea of Equality and Human Rights in the unfolding of American history. Thus, the incredibly powerful and detailed contributions of, say, a Eugene Genovese (for example, his *The Mind of the Master Class: History and Faith in the Southern Slaveholders' Worldview*, and various other studies), go basically for naught.

Victor Davis Hanson, in a recent essay, adds his own contribution to this historical rewrite, examining what he calls Hollywood's irrational fascination with what he labels "Confederate Cool."

It is not the first time he has offered criticism of the Confederacy and Confederate history. In 1999 he authored a strenuous defense of "Sherman's March" to the sea and through the Carolinas, declaring: "As for the charge that Sherman's brand of war was amoral, if we forget for a moment what constitutes 'morality' in war and examine acts of violence *per se* against Southern civilians, we learn that there were few, if any, gratuitous murders on the march. There seem also to have been less than half a dozen rapes, a fact acknowledged by both sides. Any killing outside of battle was strictly military execution in response to the shooting of Northern prisoners. The real anomaly seems to be that Sherman brought more than sixty thousand young men through one of the richest areas of the enemy South without unchecked killing or mayhem."

These comments are as outrageous as they are untrue. Hanson ignores the findings of the very detailed and scholarly study, commissioned by the state of North Carolina, *Sherman's March through North Carolina*, by Drs. Wilson Angley and Jerry Cross (North Carolina Office of Archives and History, 1995), as well as W. Brian Cisco's impressively researched, *War Crimes Against Southern Civilians* (Pelican Publishing, 2007), and Karen Stokes' *A Legion of Devils–Sherman in South Carolina* (Shotwell Publishing, Columbia, South Carolina), plus contemporary accounts, which give the lie to his cavalier dismissal of pillage and savagery by Northern troops along the march.

In his most recent foray into Confederate bashing, "The Strange Case of Confederate Cool," his argument goes, if I may summarize it, as follows:

— Throughout the 1920s until at least the 1960s (and even beyond), Hollywood and the entertainment industry were kind, even partial, to the South, and in particular, to the Confederacy;
— But Hollywood and the entertainment industry are on the Left;
— Therefore, there were obviously certain elements of the Confederacy and the Old South which were consistent with a Leftist worldview.

Here is the kernel of his argument in his own words (I quote):

Can Shane and Ethan Edwards [The Searchers] remain our heroes? How did the Carradines and the Keaches (who played Jesse and Frank James) survive in Hollywood after turning former Confederates into modern resisters of the Deep State?

The answer is a familiar with the Left: The sin is not the crime of romanticizing the Confederacy or turning a blind eye to slavery and secession per se. Instead what matters more is the ideology of the sinner who commits the thought crime. And how much will it cost the thought police to virtue-signal a remedy?

Folksy Confederates still have their charms for the Left. All was forgiven Senator Robert Byrd, a former Klansman. He transmogrified from a racist reprobate who uttered the N-word on national television into a down-home violinist and liberal icon. A smiling and avuncular Senator Sam Ervin, of Watergate fame, who quoted the Constitution with a syrupy drawl, helped bring down Nixon; that heroic service evidently washed away his earlier segregationist sin of helping to write the Southern Manifesto.

Progressives always have had a soft spot for drawling (former) racists whose charms in their twilight years were at last put to noble use to advance liberal causes — as if the powers of progressivism alone can use the kick-ass means of the Old Confederacy for exalted ends....

Literally, it would take a fat book to unravel Hanson's farrago of misplaced asseverations.

First, in impressionistically reviewing American film history in the 1930s until the upheavals of the 1960s, he makes an assumption that Hollywood was dominated and controlled by the same ideologically cultural Marxism that owns it today. That assumption is not exact. Indeed, there were Communists and revolutionary Socialists working and prospering in the Hollywood Hills during that period — the "Hollywood Ten" and Communist writers and directors like Dalton Trumbo stand out as prime examples. And during World War II, such embarrassing and pro-Communist cinematic expressions as *Days of*

Glory (1943) and *Mission to Moscow* (1944, and pushed hard by President Roosevelt), proliferated.

The fiercely anti-Communist studio bosses back then, Jack Warner (of Warner Brothers Studio), Carl Laemmle (Universal Pictures), Howard Hughes (RKO), Herbert Yates (Republic Pictures) and Walt Disney, were anything but sympathetic to the far Left. They were much more sympathetic to the power of the almighty box office dollar.

And the Hollywood Screen Actors Guild (SAG) — especially under the leadership of Ronald Reagan — attempted to root out Communist influence. It was not uncommon to find dozens of prominent actors supporting conservative or Republican candidates for public office until the 1960s. For instance, during the 1944 election campaign between Roosevelt and Governor Tom Dewey of New York numerous celebrities attended a massive rally organized by prominent director/producer David O. Selznick in the Los Angeles Coliseum in support of the Dewey–Bricker ticket. The gathering drew 93,000 attendees, with Cecil B. DeMille as the master of ceremonies and short speeches by Hedda Hopper and Walt Disney. Among those in attendance were Ann Sothern, Ginger Rogers, Adolphe Menjou, Randolph Scott, Joel McCrea, and Gary Cooper, plus many others.

A majority of entertainment personalities did support FDR, just as did a majority of the American voting public, in those years. But, significantly, it was not considered a "social crime" or "cultural sin" for a famous actor back then to openly support a conservative or a Republican.

Hanson views an earlier sympathy of Hollywood for the South as the expression of some Leftist fascination — and a certain identification — with the South's agrarian, anti-establishment, and populist traditions, and its opposition to an oppressive Federal government. Thus, he asserts the songster Joan Baez could make popular "The Night They Drove Old Dixie Down," and more recently, post-Vietnam, director Walter Hill could, in *The Long Riders* (1980), turn "the murderous Jesse James gang … into a sort of mix of Lynyrd Skynyrd with Bonnie and Clyde — noble outlaws fighting the grasping northern banks and the railroad companies." And, torturously, he draws out a Leftist meaning.

He misunderstands the history. Hollywood's fascination with the Old South and its more or less successful effort sixty or seventy years ago to portray the Confederacy with some degree of sympathy reflected the general tenor of the times then, of the desire for a united nation, of binding up old wounds — and especially when the nation was apparently threatened by external forces: Nazism and Communism.

But that desire for unity and respect for the Confederacy and Confederate heroes would begin to evaporate in the 1970s.

And the nature of the Hollywood Left would also significantly change. The cautious leftward movement of the 1950s — which mostly did not affect Hollywood Westerns (most studios had their own separate "ranches," separate from any main studio "contagion") — was transformed by the growth of a fierce and all-encompassing cultural Marxism in the '60s and '70s, just as academia and society as a whole were radically transformed. The modern anti-Southern, anti-Confederate bias and hatred emitted by Hollywood and by our entertainment industry today must be seen in that light, and not as simply the seamless continuation of an older ambiguous relationship with the South.

Constructing this narrative permits Hanson and other Neocons to write off the older, traditional South and the Confederacy, while defending their precious narrative of the egalitarian idea of America: "See," they tell us, "the far Left actually identifies with that anti-democratic, anti-American Southern vision which undermined our progress towards greater unity and progress and"— of course —"equal rights." The Neocon narrative and version of history is, thus, kept unsullied and ideologically pure, while the attempts by the farther Left to lump them in with associated "neo-Confederates, racists, and the extreme right" are repelled.

The problem is — that view actually undermines a clear understanding of our history and perverts the American Founding and the intentions of those who cobbled together this nation. It is a myth built on a poorly-constructed and poorly-interpreted bill of historical goods. Or, as they say in eastern Carolina, "that dog don't hunt."

(Abbeville Institute, October 19, 2017 at: www.abbevilleinstitute.org/blog/demonizing-the-south-to-purify-the-nation/)

PART V

REVIEWS AND REVIEW ESSAYS: FILM AND BOOKS

This section includes reviews and short review essays of books and films with Southern and Confederate themes which have appeared in recent years. There is no logical order in these pieces, except they attempt impressionistically to link efforts to illustrate the culture of the South by examining films and books on topics related to the War for Southern Independence, the events politically and constitutionally leading up to it, and its far-reaching results.

The first item included here ("Kirk Still Leading the Charge") is the first piece that I wrote (1983) which I include in this anthology. It is a review of the late Russell Kirk's book, *The Portable Conservative Reader* (1982), an annotated and edited collection of essays by various conservatives. It appeared originally in *The Southern Partisan* (Spring 1983, volume 3, number 2). It was my first article for that much-lamented journal; ten additional pieces would follow in the *Partisan*, several of which appear in this current collection. Kirk (1918-1994) had been my mentor and close friend for twenty-seven years, and his love for and interest in the South and for its history and heritage were notable.

Following the Kirk review are two review essays printed in the *Confederate Veteran* magazine examining recent releases on DVD of classic films which should be of interest to Southerners and, in fact, to Americans, in general. It goes without saying that, with a few notable exceptions (e.g. *The Conspirator, Ride With the Devil, Gettysburg, God and Generals*), Hollywood is not kind to the Confederacy or the South these days. Not only are Confederates portrayed as racist bigots, but Southerners, in general, come across as redneck hayseeds. Yet, it was not always that way, as an examination in the first two reviews of DVD releases indicates. The first item is a review essay titled, "Classic Confederate Hollywood," which takes a panoramic view of Tinseltown when the South was not demonized, examining specifically four great films which now appear in good transfers on DVD. The second piece is a review of the new DVD release by Olive Films of *The Sun Shines Bright*, a superb film directed by the legendary John Ford. Ford once was quoted as saying this film, a remake of his earlier 1934 opus, *Judge*

Priest (starring Will Rogers), was his favorite of all the films he directed (a distinguished list that includes *Grapes of Wrath, Stagecoach, She Wore A Yellow Ribbon, The Quiet Man,* and *The Searchers*).

I include one additional film review, a critical look at Dinesh D'Souza's *Death of a Nation*, which attempts to portray Abraham Lincoln as the great savior of the American union who preserved the nation against those "racist" and "fascist" Southerners. Needless to say, D'Souza's latest cinematic excursion fails as history and demonstrates the parlous state into which filmmaking has descended these days, not just on the Left but on the so-called Neoconservative Right.

The six remaining book reviews include commentaries on several fine volumes of interest not just to Southerners, but also to all readers interested in excellent military history, classic novels, and comprehensive considerations of events surrounding the War for Southern Independence. Among these are several scholarly studies: David Loy Mauch's fine volume on the Constitution and how most Americans viewed it, including secession, up until the outbreak of war in 1861, W. Davis Waters' superb and comprehensive biography of General Gabriel Rains (with excellent technical support, charts, and appendices by Joseph I. Brown), and Walter Donald Kennedy's *Rekilling Kennedy* which re-discovers and evaluates the prescient writing of a number of fascinating authors and profound intellects of the nineteenth century. Also reviewed are Howard White's concluding volume in his impressive *Bloodstains* series and Charles A. Jennings' volume, *Cultures in Conflict*, specifically examining the heinous depredations inflicted specifically on Southern churches and burial yards, a volume which confirms and illustrates in horrid detail the findings of such researchers as W. Brian Cisco and Drs. Wilson Angley and Jerry Cross, these latter two who were commissioned by the state of North Carolina to catalogue and detail the ravages inflicted on North Carolina during Sherman's March from Savannah.

Finally, there is a review of the superb historical novel, *Souls of Lions*, by R. E. Mitchell, one of the finest works of historical fiction I have read in recent years, and a book which gave life to characters who once did exist and suffer for their home state and for a cause they thought just. The variety of subjects addressed and the quality of the writing by these authors demonstrate the literary and historical traditions of the South continue to flourish.

Review Essay: Kirk Still Leading the Charge
❖ Chapter 34 ❖

Thirty years ago Russell Kirk wrote *The Conservative Mind*, and the American body politic has not been the same since. An entire generation was enabled to rediscover the perennial vitality of a Burke, a Randolph and a More. The influence Kirk has had on young minds, in particular, cannot be over-estimated. I think of my own case, born in rural North Carolina, I first became aware of Russell Kirk through a book of essays entitled, *What Is Conservatism?* My 1965 Christmas gifts included *Beyond the Dreams of Avarice, Old House of Fear, A Program for Conservatives*, and, of course, *The Conservative Mind*. I remember the relish I experienced when I literally devoured the contents of those tomes; the relish has never left me. When later I started corresponding with Dr. Kirk, and finally, after beginning my graduate education, went to be his assistant, I considered myself — as I still do — one of the most fortunate young men in America. From Mecosta to Spain and Switzerland and back to North Carolina, I have carried that experience, with its rich educational and humane benefits, with me. Much may have happened since then, but nothing so determining.

This most recent volume, *The Portable Conservative Reader*, is a carefully selected and edited collection of essays which, to my mind, serves ideally as a companion to *The Conservative Mind*. As the earlier Kirk volume traces the train and development of the somewhat amorphous body of Anglo-American conservative thought during the last two hundred years, so *The Portable Conservative Reader* includes generous excerpts from the writings of many of the lead characters who make their appearances in *The Conservative Mind*. A finely-chiseled introduction sets the tone and describes the limits and goals Kirk intends for the volume.

As in *The Conservative Mind*, Kirk restricts himself largely to English and American conservatism. I admit that in most studies of conservatism, in the anthologies, and so on, this has always been one thing which has bothered me. Conservatism, as that adherence to the natural and moral law and to the teachings of the Church, the defense of tradition, and the love of place, is something quite universal. Indeed, Kirk says as much himself: "something that we may call the conservative impulse or the conservative yearning does exist among all peoples.

Without this instinct, any society would fall to pieces. ... In that sense, a kind of universal conservatism may be glimpsed." (p. xxxv, Introduction). But it is clear that if we consider the American experience as our measure, it is the Anglo-American variety which affects us most.

For much of the last two hundred years an identifiable English conservative tradition, incarnated in the Conservative Party, has enjoyed a dominant position in English society. Its leaders have included Canning, Wellington, Disraeli, and Churchhill. Its antecedents reach back to Magna Carta, to the medieval Schoolmen, and, in a later period, to a Richard Hooker and a Sir Thomas Browne. The American conservative tradition is much more illusive. Some writers have gone so far as to deny an American conservatism has ever really existed at all. Louis Hartz and others have maintained the American nation was founded on the Rationalist principles of the Enlightenment. For them, any kind of conservatism on this side of the Atlantic tended to conserve basic principles which were "liberal" to begin with. Beginning with the Declaration of Independence, America was shaped in a liberal mold which successive generations have only continued.

Undeniably there is some truth in this. Yet the strands of continuity between the American experience and the Old World are stronger than the dissimilarities. Conservatism is not dependent on the alliance of throne and altar — one does not have to be a monarchist to be a conservative. Kirk's oft-repeated "six canons" of conservatism are present in any number of diverse climes and historical situations. In the United States such a discernible conservatism has manifested itself throughout our history. So Kirk points out, John Adams, Gouverneur Morris and John Dickinson were men of conservative temperament and *The Federalist Papers* and the Constitution, itself, reflect this same temperament. In his basic lineaments the American conservative "is a person who believes strongly that the old pattern of American society ought not to be much altered. Typically, such a person holds by the Constitution, maintaining that it should be strictly interpreted; he endeavors to oppose the drift toward political centralization; he dislikes organizations on the grand scale, in government, in business and industry, in organized labor; he is a defender of private property; he resents the heavy increase of taxation and many of the transfer payments of the welfare state; he is unalterably opposed to the Communist ideology and the aspirations of the Soviet Union; he sighs, or perhaps shouts, *O Tempora! O Mores!* at the decay of private and public morality." (p. xxviii).

It is perhaps in the Old South that American conservatism finds its most notable exemplars: men like Calhoun, Randolph (both represented by ample selections in the *Reader*), Nathaniel Macon and George Fitzhugh, plus an intense attachment to the land and to custom, and a belief in a transcendent God, helped make the South the most conservative of America's regions. It is true, as Kirk says, the "catastrophe of the Civil War dealt a grim blow" to conservatism. But the sense of tragedy and defeat, together with a profound understanding of human nature, have, if anything, reinforced the Southerner's conservatism. Only the South could produce a Harry Byrd or a Richard Weaver.

The conservatives Kirk features in this *Reader* are refreshingly free of cant so often associated with an economically centered conservatism. Through its adherence to transcendent moral norms and its rejection of utilitarianism and unrestrained individualism, their high-minded conservatism refuses to make economics the measure of man. It is uncomfortable with those who think the dollar or the "American way" synonymous with civilized society. While defending the right to property, conservatism asserts property should be used as a means in life and not as the end. A conservatism of mere possession, Fafnir-like, is at the mercy of destructive ideologies. Robert Lewis Dabney, unreconstructed Confederate that he was, saw this clearly one hundred years ago when he scathingly denounced the hierarchs of the "New South" who wished to tum the South country into a little Pittsburgh.

In some of his other works, Kirk talks of the moral imagination, one of the distinctive characteristics of a truly reflective conservatism. It suffuses the selections in this volume. Whereas conservatism has suffered some serious defeats, politically, since the days of Burke, it surfaced victoriously in the world of letters. Many of the great writers and poets of our age illustrate this. What a serious examination of the course of events since Burke's time reveals is that it has been the vision of poets which reminds us of what we have lost and what needs to be passed on to posterity.

Is it any wonder that men of imagination reject out of hand the vacant drabness of Marxism and the moral bankruptcy of liberalism? English poet Laureate Sir John Betjeman recoils in poetic horror from *The Planster's Vision* (p. 545):

I have a vision,
> *of the Future, chum,*
The worker's flats in fields of soya beans
> *Tower up like silver pencils, score on score;*
And Surging Millions hear
> *the challenge come*
From microphones
> *in communal canteens*
"No Right! No Wrong!
> *All's perfect, evermore."*

The conservative experience is a lived experience, grounded in the rich soil of time-tested norms. I recall a good friend of mine in northern Spain, not a wealthy man materially, but certainly one of the most complete persons I've ever met. A Carlist volunteer against Spain's Socialist republic at the age of sixteen, he works now in a potash mine where Communist influence is predominant. But he refuses to flinch in his defense of Spanish tradition. He once single-handedly ejected five Communist agitators who were illegally attempting to organize the miners. He assists Mass daily, he studies his catechism assiduously, and he greatly enjoys that finest of Spanish products, tinto wine. Since his creed is orthodoxy, he doesn't spend half his waking hours trying to "find himself." His feet are firmly planted in normative canons of life as old as Spain itself.

The Portable Conservative Reader includes several pieces from contemporary conservatives, among them Robert Nisbet and Malcolm Muggeridge. Nisbet published his epochal *The Quest for Community* in 1953, continuing the great tradition of social philosophy begun by Frederic Le Play one hundred years ago. The selection included is from *Twilight of Authority*, a defense of the variety of subsidiary organs in society. Malcolm Muggeridge speculates in a scintillating essay on what he sees as the death-wish of liberalism

Three representative women writers, Freya Stark, Phyllis McGinley, and Jacquetta Hawkes, find niches among their masculine counterparts. It would have been nice to see something from Flannery O'Connor, but then, if Kirk had included much more in his *Portable Reader*, it would have soon ceased to be "portable."

Our age has been called "Post-Modern" by Romano Guardini and John Lukacs. The ideologies of the last two hundred years seem bankrupt and in headlong retreat. In such a case there is a grand opportunity for a renewed conservatism to capture the imagination of men. And it will be reflective conservatives like Russell Kirk who lead the charge.

(A review of Russell Kirk, editor, *The Portable Conservative Reader*, in *The Southern Partisan*, Spring 1983, volume 3, number 2)

Review Essay: Classic Confederate Hollywood
→ Chapter 35 ←

Recent releases of four classic films should gladden the hearts of patriotic Southerners and those viewers not yet infected by the currently-raging virus of political correctness and multiculturalism.

A few years back Warner Brothers inaugurated an Archive series and began releasing hundreds of classic films which had, in most cases, never shown up previously in any commercially released video format. Warner began releasing these movies in the DVD-R format, copies of which could basically be made on demand. Very soon other studios, including MGM/United Artists, Sony/Columbia, and Fox initiated similar projects. The result is that inveterate viewers of classic films — and films about the Confederacy and the Old South — now have much greater choices in viewing.

Fortunately, several good War Between the States films from the 1930s-1950s have been included in these releases. Two of them on Fox DVD-Rs are highly entertaining, and would amply repay the investment of a few dollars. First, a real gem: *The Raid* (1954), starring Van Heflin, Anne Bancroft, and Richard Boone, detailing the famous Confederate raid on St. Albans, Vermont. *The Raid* is a superb war film, a model in its genre, in colour, with a good script, fine acting, and superior direction by old Hollywood pro, Hugo Fregonese. In particular, Lee Marvin, as the fractious Confederate trooper who hates Yankees (and can't always hold his liquor), stands out. But *The Raid* also puts a human face on war, with Heflin's Confederate officer character illustrating both nobility and admirable Southern honor. Fox has issued a re-mastered version, and it can be easily ordered using Amazon.com (in particular, Amazon's marketplace feature).

A second Fox release is the 1938 Technicolor classic, *Kentucky*, showcasing Loretta Young, Walter Brennan, and Richard Greene. Beginning with depredations committed by a neighbor Yankee officer (Douglas Dumbrille) against a pro-Confederate landowner and horse-breeder in old Kentucky, the film then jumps up to the 1930s and a new generation competing in horse flesh and racing. Walter Brennan plays the crusty and irrepressible Peter Goodwin who had seen his father cut down by Federals during the War and who remains highly suspicious of the grandson of his hereditary enemy who begins to have designs on Brennan's granddaughter, played by Loretta Young. With flair Young and Greene interpret the roles of the scions of the rival families, whose racing competition ends up in romance. Like other films produced before the advent of political correctness and the post-1960s trend of hatred of anything Confederate, Kentucky epitomizes the period when national harmony and respect of Southern tradition seemed to dominate. The acting, especially by Brennan, is fine and the colour photography — rare for 1938 — is excellent. As I said, *Kentucky* is not politically correct, and its portrayal of blacks has offended some reviewers, whose vocabularies seem always limited to the word "racism." But it is much more than a contextual view of race relations; it's a heartwarming film which will appeal both to adults and the whole family.

A third recent release has shown up on Olive Films in both regular DVD and Blu-Ray formats (in a fine black and white print). Perhaps the finest movie about Reconstruction ever made and directed by one of the finest cineastes in the history of the film industry, John Ford, *The Sun Shines Bright*, is a sheer delight, combining all of the wonderful characteristics of Ford's famous movie-making. As usual the "Ford actors ensemble" works extremely well together. Thus, Grant Withers, Jane Darwell, Russell Simpson, John Russell, James Kirkwood, Trevor Bardette, and other Ford regulars show up, playing off each other with ease and grace.

The story, taken from Irvin S. Cobb's tales of Old Kentucky, details life towards the end of the 19th century, with the little community of Fairfield split between partisans of the South and those who appear to be mostly carpetbaggers or scalawags. In a role assumed by Will Rogers twenty years earlier (in another Ford classic, *Judge Priest*), Charles Winninger is simply perfect as Confederate veteran and bugler Billy Priest, now judge of Fairfield County. Winninger heads up a diminishing encampment of the United Confederate Veterans. And Milburn Stone — *Gunsmoke's* Doc Adams — takes the role of Horace K. Maydew, the Republican attorney who hopes to replace Judge Priest at the next election.

As with most of Ford's films, humour plays a central role. Add strictly comedic roles with Stepin' Fetchit, Slim Pickens, and Francis Ford, and the traditional Ford magic takes off from the first scene and never ceases until the final credits. Fetchit is Judge Priest's "boy," an integral and beloved part of his household who keeps him abreast of all the gossip and news circulating in Fairfield, but also insures that the old judge gets his "rheumatiz" medicine every morning to, as he says, "get my heart started."

Early on there is a rapturous scene in Judge Priest's courtroom when a young black man is brought in for vagrancy (as charged by attorney Maydew). Stepin' Fetchit reveals that the boy can superbly play the banjo and asks him to begin "Dixie." He does, and every UCV member in the small town hears it and makes his way to the courthouse to join in. It's as if the whole town, both white and black, is celebrating "old times there are not forgotten."

Yet, despite its boisterous humour and rhapsodic flow, *The Sun Shines Bright* also offers the spectator some wonderful insights into human nature, loyalty, justice, love of tradition and devotion to one's native land. The final moving scene, with Judge Priest disappearing past a series of opened doors, was adapted by Ford years later for the final scene of his masterpiece, *The Searchers*.

Originally released by Republic on VHS cassette, *The Sun Shines Bright* has now been licensed to Olive Films who have released it both on DVD and Blu-Ray disc. For a birthday, an anniversary, or for any occasion, this film is a must for any Southerner and any lover of great filmmaking. John Ford, reportedly, said *The Sun Shines Bright* was the favorite of all his superb films. That is high recommendation indeed.

The fourth recent release of a War-related film from the 1950s is a new re-mastering of *Drums in the Deep South* (1951). This movie has long been available, both on VHS cassette and DVD, but always in sub-standard and poor quality, with bad color separation and smudgy video reproduction. I can recall many years ago seeing it on television, and even then the Super Cinecolor process looked bad. But, finally, VCI Entertainment has found an acceptable master copy and restored it. The Super Cinecolor is still a bit washed out (as most Cinecolor films are), but the colour separation is far superior to other editions and the copy on DVD is sharp, and does not detract from the story line. And the film can be had from sources like Amazon.com for under ten dollars.

James Craig stars as the Confederate officer charged with inhibiting Sherman's march from Chattanooga to Atlanta, and his close friend, Guy Madison (not yet into his Wild Bill Hickok role), assumes the role of Craig's Yankee nemesis. The action is plentiful and the attention to both historical and military detail is very good. The last scene, as James Craig decides to sacrifice his life for the Cause, is memorable.

Final credits include the obligatory statement about a re-united nation, "indivisible," but this should not deter purchasers.

Academy Award winning film composer Dmitri Tiomkin provides a lush and lyrical score. The result is another product those devoted to Southern history, the War Between the States, and good cinema should snatch up without hesitation. Amidst the clutter of contemporary attempts by Hollywood to produce politically-correct films on the history of the War Between the States period (with such ahistorical examples as *Abraham Lincoln: Vampire Hunter* and *12 Years a Slave* now typical), exploring films of an earlier era in American history serve as an antidote to the infectious brew that both pollutes our minds and warps our judgment.

(Abbeville Institute, July 30, 2014, at: www.abbevilleinstitute.org/blog/classic-confederate-hollywood/)

Review Essay of John Ford's *The Sun Shines Bright* on DVD
⇝ Chapter 36 ⇜

On March 26, 2013, Olive Films released the classic John Ford-directed film *The Sun Shines Bright* on DVD and Blu-Ray disc. This superb, but little-known, Ford work has been fully restored to its original 101 minute theatrical release length, and the transfers are spectacular. For some time now this lyrical portrayal of life in post-Reconstruction Kentucky has been one of my favorite films.

Normally, I wouldn't write a review of a DVD release, certainly not about a film which has languished in relative obscurity for sixty years. But with this particular film things are different. There is a great deal of fascinating ancillary history connected with *The Sun Shines Bright*, some of which continues to this day. Based on three short stories of old Kentucky by Irvin Cobb, *The Sun Shines Bright* was released by Republic Pictures in 1953. The film was, for Ford, a remake of his better-known *Judge Priest* (1934) starring Will Rogers. And for Ford, the justly famous director of such classics as *My Darling Clementine, Stagecoach, The Searchers, Rio Bravo*, and *The Man Who Shot Liberty Valance*, it was by all accounts his favorite film.

Unlike his other non-Western classics — *The Grapes of Wrath* or *How Green Was My Valley* — it was received by some critics at the time of its release with decidedly mixed reviews. Part of the reason, evidently, was its avowedly pro-Confederate viewpoint, and what a few critics perceived at the time as a "patriarchal" view of race in the South. After all, it was 1953 and the Brown vs. Board of Education decision was right around the corner. Even more so, in recent years the film has come in for criticism as defending "racial stereotypes" and "celebrating the myth of the Lost Cause." Yet, even in 1990, Leonard Maltin, in his *TV Movies & Video Guide*, praised it and gave it very high marks, remarking on the "fine array" of Ford regulars as principal actors.

In the starring role of Judge William Pittman "Billy" Priest is the inimitable Charles Winninger, who had been a fixture in numerous Hollywood films beginning in 1915. Unlike Will Rogers' portrayal, Winninger projects Judge Priest as a kindly, rotund, avuncular patrician, who relishes a chance to engage in old-fashioned oratory (and a nip of the squeezins' occasionally, but only "to get his heart started!").

And as usual with Ford's characters, he really looks the part — always dressed in a white suit, with a cane or umbrella, flowing white hair, and possessed of a genteel Southern manner. His man-servant — his "boy Jeff" — is Stepin' Fetchit, who reprises the role he had in the 1934 film. By 1953 portraying black characters comically, or in caricature, as has been claimed by some writers about *The Sun Shines Bright*, was on the way out. Yet, Ford is able to convey the real affection and genuine camaraderie which existed among the races in that age which we are now told was so benighted and severe.

Other actors in the film include some of the finest in Ford's "stock company," including Jane Darwell (remember her from *The Grapes of Wrath* and *Wagonmaster?*) as the grand dame of the United Daughters of the Confederacy, Milburn Stone (he of later *Gunsmoke* Doc Adams fame) as the Carpetbagging attorney Horace K. Maydew, a young Slim Pickens, Russell Simpson (whose long acting career spanned from 1903 until 1959!), John Russell, James Kirkwood, and Arleen Whelan. There is definitely a feel of ensemble acting, as these players had worked together often in the past.

It is 1905, and it's election time in Fairfield County, Kentucky. Judge Billy Priest, the commander of the much-reduced UCV encampment, is up for re-election. He represents the traditionally conservative Democratic Party, defending the honor and legacy of the Old South and the Confederacy. He is opposed by attorney, Horace K. Maydew, the Republican, who boasts that, if elected, he will bring "progress," "science," and the "fresh wind of the twentieth century" to Fairfield. Under this rubric there are two interweaving plot-lines in *The Sun Shines Bright*: one involving Judge Priest's defense of an innocent young black man, accused of attempting to ravage a white girl, and the other, establishing the relationship between the old county patriarch, General Fairfield (James Kirkwood), and his granddaughter, Lucy Lee (Whelan), the adopted daughter of Dr. Luke Lake (Simpson). By defending the innocent black man, Priest may jeopardize his re-election chances, it seems. But his innate sense of right and wrong, and his Christian belief in justice, prevent him from taking a politically-expedient course. Just as Joel McCrea did in the heartwarming *Stars in My Crown* (1950), Billy Priest refuses to hand his prisoner over to the mob. In the end he will be proved right and rewarded for his stand.

Likewise, the return of General Fairfield's wayward daughter (Lucy Lee's mother) and her death in the residence of some "ladies of the night," causes initial scandal in the town, and threatens to be the nail in the coffin in the judge's election effort. Fairfield's daughter's last wish had been for a church funeral, and, despite the eyebrows raised, Judge Priest agrees to honor that request.

The conclusion of the film is one of Ford's finest cinematic successes. The triumph of Christian charity and justice, bathed in Ford's famous lyricism and ability to evoke deeper meaning, and his passionate love for American traditions and the very fabric of traditional society, are all in play. The final camera shot of Judge Priest entering darkening doors reminds us that this is the device Ford would use later so memorably in *The Searchers*.

And, as always, there is his comedic genius, established early on in each of his finely-delineated, often eccentric, characters. Ford knows well how to use humor to make his points. Yet, beneath their outward simplicity and *naivete*, and their comic foibles, his characters speak sympathetic volumes about our history and our journey as a nation, or, in this case, as a distinctive region.

So, despite the obvious lack of political correctness, *The Sun Shines Bright*, like Ford's *The Man Who Shot Liberty Valance* ten years later, evokes something profound about American character and history. Indeed, Ford captures, as no other cineaste of the period, genuine characteristics of those old Confederates who attempted to rebuild their society during the years after the conclusion of the War Between the States. He probes beyond the currently fashionable stereotypes that prevent us from seeing, rather than assist us to see, a people — and individuals — and how they coped, in many cases honorably, even admirably, within the context of an historical epoch. In so doing, Ford adds not just to his superb corpus of cinematic work, he opens a door to our collective history that few historians or novelists have ever been able to do.

In our age of oppressive multiculturalism, enforced political correctness, and hatred of anything reminding us of our Southern heritage, the release of *The Sun Shines Bright* is a small reason to celebrate, a chance to go back and enjoy top notch film-making thanks to the great directing of John Ford, and an opportunity to look deeply at an older America — the post-bellum South of "old Kentucky" — through the lyrical lens of a master.

Don't hesitate to snatch this one up; it may not be around for long.

(Olive Films release, 2013) (*Confederate Veteran* magazine, July/August 2013)

Review Essay of Dinesh D'Souza's Latest Film, *Death of a Nation*
↣ *Chapter 37* ↢

In case you haven't heard, there is a new "conservative" film out; it is titled *Death of a Nation: Can We Save America a Second Time?*

It's director and screenwriter is Dinesh D'Souza, the somewhat pompous, word-measuring figure who occasionally shows up on Fox to talk in pious tones about "conservatism." He is the movie producer who, by his own admission, has done as much as anyone to shape (in an almost ahistorical manner) perceptions about American history and the Founding Principles that have supposedly guided this country. And, in his latest cinematic adventure he stunningly compares the "triumph of America and its values" under that "great president and martyr" Abraham Lincoln to the crisis facing President Donald Trump. Like Lincoln, Trump is saving America "for a second time."

Here is the film's official blurb from D'Souza's web site:

Not since 1860 have the Democrats so fanatically refused to accept the result of a free election. That year, their target was Lincoln. They smeared him. They went to war to defeat him. In the end, they assassinated him. Now the target of the Democrats is President Trump and his supporters. The Left calls them racists, white supremacists and fascists. These charges are used to justify driving Trump from office and discrediting the right "by any means necessary." But which is the party of the slave plantation? Which is the party that invented white supremacy? Which is the party that praised fascist dictators and shaped their genocidal policies and was in turn praised by them? Moreover, which is the party of racism today? Is fascism now institutionally embodied on the right or on the left? [www.dineshdsouza.com/films/death-of-a-nation/]

Thus, the president who refused all compromise (and torpedoed negotiations) with Southerners and Confederates (who were, as D-Souza assures us, no better than "racists" and "fascists"), the president responsible for the most egregious violations of *habeas corpus* and constitutional liberties in American history, the president who in effect unleashed a vicious conflict which took the lives of at least 620,000 Americans and maimed and handicapped for life hundreds of thousands more, the president who by military force radically altered the original American Constitution and set the stage for the growth of powerful and unchecked government, and the emergence of the managerial Deep State … that president is D'Souza's model … and his analogy for Donald Trump.

And Lincoln, that noble opponent of "racism?" D'Souza omits Lincoln's contradictory statements on American blacks and his repeated desire that blacks be sent back to Africa. And he conveniently fails to cite Lincoln's declaration to *New York Tribune* editor Horace Greeley, August 22, 1862, scarcely three months prior to the formal issuance of the Emancipation Proclamation:

> *If I could save the Union without freeing any slave, I would do it, and if I could save it by freeing all the slaves, I would do it, and if I could save it by freeing some and leaving others alone, I would also do that. What I do about Slavery and the colored race, I do because I believe it helps to save this Union, and what I forbear, I forbear because I do not believe it would help to save the Union.*

The one very significant fact which becomes clear in his latest cinematic screed is that D'Souza is ignorant of American history, and he is an ideological and historical fabricator who seeks, in the name of defending his adopted nation, to bend and mishandle its history to fit a preconceived narrative which satisfies his Neoconservative task masters. For him history becomes a cudgel, a weaponized arm to further the Neoconservative agenda of "equality" and "liberal democracy," both against the "farther Left," but also, very significantly, against the traditional Right and traditional conservatism … and, as well, against Southern conservatives who would dare defend their heritage and traditions.

His narrative is essentially a leftist one, and like other Neoconservatives, he partakes of the basic philosophical views of the post-Communist Left, emphasizing politicized constructs of race and gender, and equality and democracy, projecting them back to incorporate all of American history. Thus, so it goes, echoing Marxist historians like Eric Foner: "the South had slavery, therefore it was a racist society. Racism had to be opposed at all costs and by all means. And that is what Lincoln did."

The equation says too much, and leaves out too much. Four slave states did not leave the union, and Lincoln's reasons for attacking the Southern states were far more economic and power-driven than not, with his later appeals to abolitionism seen by most observers then, as well as by many historians since, as desperate propaganda appeals to war-weary Northerners, to gin up the sagging war effort.

As noted economist Frank Taussig has detailed in his classic study, *Tariff History of the United States* (1967 edition), tariffs were the chief revenue source for the Federal government. The Morrill Tariff more than doubled American tariffs and greatly expanded the list of taxable items. Abraham Lincoln had campaigned vigorously on a platform of strong support for the Morrill Tariff. While the South would be paying nearly 80 percent of the tariff, most of the revenues would be spent in the North. With the Southern states seceding, such a loss of revenue would be devastating to the Federal treasury and could not be allowed to stand.

There is another major critique which must be made: despite D'Souza's claims, it was the Republican Party in 1860 that was, by every measure, the radical party, the party intent on destroying the original Constitution and transforming the union, not the more conservative (at that time) Democrats. D'Souza projects a political genealogy that simply will not stand up to serious historical investigation. The outbreak of war in 1861 did not come about due to Democrats who "went to war to defeat [Lincoln]." As historian William Marvel, in his *Mr. Lincoln Goes to War* (2006), relates, the conflict must be laid squarely at the door of the Lincoln administration: "It was Lincoln, however, who finally eschewed diplomacy and sparked a confrontation. He backed himself into a corner from which he could escape only by mobilizing a national army, and thereby fanning the flames of Fort Sumter into full-scale conflagration." (p. xvii) Thus, it was the intransigence of the Lincoln administration that literally provoked war.

Even D'Souza's supposedly hated Marxists recognized Lincoln and his actions furthered their program and ideals. In 1864 Karl Marx sent Lincoln a famous "Address" from his "workingman's group," in which he declared "victory for the North would be a turning point for nineteenth-century politics, an affirmation of free labor, and a defeat for the most reactionary capitalists who depended on slavery and racial oppression," that is, one more critical step in the projected Marxist historical dialectic. The American ambassador in London, Charles Francis Adams, responded and "thanked them for their support and expressed his conviction the defeat of the rebellion would indeed be a victory for the cause of humanity everywhere." [www.jacobinmag.com/2012/08/lincoln-and-marx]

Like his supposed enemies over on the farther Left, Dinesh D'Souza employs the same faulty historical template, and, even if his arguments appear, at times, attractive or useful to conservatives, the end result is certain: you do not triumph historically or argumentatively using the same essential propositions, albeit less outrageous, as your opponent. Once you accept his grounds for debate, the battle — the war — is over.

No: stay away from this cinematic fraud … like tasty ice cream infected with poisonous venom, it might taste good at first, but the poison is sure to work its effect.

(*My Corner* by Boyd Cathey, August 5, 2018, at: http://boydcathey-reviewofbooks.blogspot.com/2018/08/august-5-2018-my-corner-by-boydcathey.html)

Review of David Loy Mauch. *This Constitution Shall Be the Law of the Land*
❖ Chapter 38 ❖

David Loy Mauch, the author of *This Constitution Shall Be the Law of the Land*, is an Arkansan, a former state legislator, a fellow of the Society of Independent Southern Historians, and an active member of the Sons of Confederate Veterans. More significantly, he is a facile writer and researcher who has produced a book which could well be a primer for those searching for that one accessible source on the real meaning of Constitutional liberties, states' rights, and what the Framers actually intended, but also — at times, a searing indictment of those forces that continually have perverted the Founders' Constitution and destroyed not only the prescribed rights of the States, but also the liberties of the citizens of the United States.

Author Mauch examines the history of the American "experiment" in constitutional government largely chronologically, beginning with the Constitution, itself. He assembles ample and overwhelming testimony that "the United States of America" was the creation of the free and separate states who had won their independence from Great Britain. The Constitution the thirteen independent states eventually adopted delegated certain very specific and limited powers to a Federal government, reserving the vast majority of rights and self-government to the states. Both the 9th and 10th Amendments — part of the Bill of Rights — make this reservation of powers explicit. Indeed, Mauch cites extensive proof from *The Federalist Papers* and from James Madison to show the explicit intent of the Founders in this regard.

During the ratification period, even Federalists like Alexander Hamilton were loathe to claim what exponents of powerful managerial Federal government centralization assert today. And the bizarre theory that Abraham Lincoln put forward, that it was the central government which somehow actually preceded and created the states, doling out parsimoniously to them only the rights that it deemed acceptable, is so foreign to the thinking of the Framers that it beggars the imagination.

The originalist belief continued to underlie constitutional considerations during much of the Antebellum period. As Mauch illustrates, the U.S. Supreme Court, in an 8-1 decision in the *The Bank of Augusta vs. Earl decision* (1839), clearly enunciated this accepted theory:

The States between each other are sovereign and independent. They are distinct separate sovereignties, except so far as they have parted with some of the attributes of sovereignty by the Constitution. They continue to be nations, with all their rights, and under all their national obligations, and with all the rights of nations in every particular; except in the surrender by each to the common purposes and objects of the Union, under the Constitution. The rights of the States, when not so yielded up, remain absolute. (p. xxi)

And such views of the powers and authority of the several states were not restricted to those states below the Mason-Dixon Line. Indeed, as Mauch details, at various times, including during the War of 1812 and the Mexican War, states in New England seriously considered seceding, leaving, the Federal Union. And most constitutional writers and authorities of the time agreed. Indeed, famed jurist William Rawle's volume, *A View of the Constitution of the United States* (1825), states clearly: "The secession of a State from the Union depends of the will of the people of such State. The people alone as we have already seen, hold the power to alter their constitutions." (p. 90) Rawle's text was used as the official text on the Constitution and constitutional interpretation at West Point prior to the War Between the States.

In particular, Mauch offers a breath of fresh air and needed clarification in his discussion of the famous *Dred Scott vs. Sanford* decision by the Supreme Court (March 1857). In a lopsided 7-2 decision, Chief Justice Roger B. Taney, delivered for the court a decision just about everyone on the current political scene today condemns. Yet, as Mauch carefully documents, Taney's decision was entirely consistent both with the Constitution and with congressional statutes. A slave escaping to a free state could not, then, assume the rights of a citizen and sue in court, for the Constitution had explicitly excluded such a possibility. Agree with the law or not, Taney stated, it was the law. The Constitution provided a process for change: passing a constitutional amendment.

Mauch's discussion of interposition, nullification, secession, and the secession crisis offers a useful summary of arguments which will be familiar to many readers. Yet, it is valuable to have these points recapitulated concisely and persuasively. As he points out, interposition, nullification, and secession had been discussed widely prior to 1860; indeed, both Southern *AND* Northern States had implemented such actions. As late as the 1850s Wisconsin actually nullified the Fugitive Slave Law of 1850 (p. 55).

President James Buchanan, in his last message to Congress and the nation before Lincoln's assumption of the presidency in March 1861, made it explicitly clear that, as much as he regretted and disagreed with the secession of the Southern States, the Federal government had no power to coerce a state or force it to remain in the Union. Lincoln, of course, with his radical and revolutionary ideas of Federal supremacy would have nothing of that, and as historian William Marvel has pointed out (in his volume, *Mr. Lincoln Goes to War*), sabotaged and undercut every attempt at mediation and peaceful resolution prior to the outbreak of war.

Echoing writers such as Charles Adams (*When in the Course of Human Events*), Thomas Di Lorenzo (*The Real Lincoln*), and Greg Durand (*America's Caesar*), Mauch methodically details the severe economic hardships placed on the South as a major reason for eventual secession of the lower South, and the flagrant violation of the Constitution when Lincoln called for troops as the major reason for the secession of the upper South (and, more, the opposition of a large percentage of citizens above the Mason-Dixon Line, as well). Interestingly, several states when they had joined the Union had included specific language declaring that they could withdraw from it if conditions dictated. And this is what individual Southern states did: they rescinded their acts of union.

Certainly, the issue of slavery was discussed at the time; but the major concerns expressed by most Southerners were: (1) slavery is a question for the respective States to decide; and (2) it is a question of property legitimately recognized by the constitutions of the States AND by the Federal Constitution. Any eventual manumission would have to recognize these facts. Interestingly, Lincoln understood fully well that freeing the slaves was not an issue to rally Northern support for a war, and his appeals, certainly up to the Gettysburg Address, were mostly pleas to "save the union." His overriding concern was to defeat and control the South and empower the Federal government, whatever method was most useful. Recall his famous interview with Horace Greeley in late 1862 that if he were able to save the union and maintain slavery, he would:

"My paramount object in this struggle is to save the Union, and is not either to save or to destroy slavery. If I could save the Union without free-

ing any slave I would do it, and if I could save it by freeing all the slaves I would do it; and if I could save it by freeing some and leaving others alone I would also do that. What I do about slavery, and the colored race, I do because I believe it helps to save the Union."

As Mauch shows, the Lincolnian "revolution"— through the defeat of the South — removed the counterbalance to the growth in Federal and national managerial power. The 14th Amendment, passed illegally without the requisite number of states approving it, opened the door in the 20th century to the wide-open doctrine of "incorporation," that is, applying all types of radical and unthinkable (to the Framers) legislation to the States, when even the drafters of that amendment did not foresee such a process. One such result, clearly *NOT* foreseen, is the present state of affairs which permits an illegal immigrant, non-citizen female to simply cross the Rio Grande River and have a child on this side of the border and, there you have it, a new "American citizen." The 14th Amendment was directed to former slaves, and in no way to illegal immigrants. Clarification of this process is just one major item which needs to be addressed both by Congress and the Courts.

Mauch's final chapters treat a number of the consequences of the Lincolnian revolution and the virtual abolition of the Framers' Constitution. The Framers had written: "The Constitution shall be ... the supreme Law of Land." As he pleads with his readers, it is long past time for a counter-revolution and the recovery of what has been lost. Such will not be easy, certainly, but for the sake of our children and grandchildren it must be attempted.

North Charleston, SC: CreateSpace Independent Publishing Platform, 2014. Paperback; 371 pages, notes, addenda, recommended reading, index. (Available via Amazon.com)
(*Confederate Veteran* magazine, May/June 2016)

Review of Howard Ray White. *Bloodstains: An Epic History of the Politics That Produced the American Civil War: Volume 4: Political Reconstruction and The Struggle for Healing*

⇾ Chapter 39 ⇽

For those who have already acquired the first three volumes in Howard Ray White's important series dedicated to the first hundred years of the South in the Federal union (i.e., volume 1, "The Nation Builders," on the formation of the old Republic; volume 2, "The Demagogues," on events, personalities and the coming of the War Between the States; and volume 3, "The Bleeding," on the War itself), this final volume will be self-recommending. Employing his chronological method of relating parallel biographies of major players, White blends in a rich mixture of contemporary accounts, personal letters, quoted speeches, and newspaper articles. In so doing, he recounts a complex and engrossing history of initial despair immediately after the War, followed by recovery and the eventual re-emergence of a vibrant South, what historian Paul Buck once termed "the road to reunion."

Beginning immediately after the conclusion of the War, White offers short introductory chapters on two future major Southern figures of Reconstruction, Lucius Lamar of Mississippi and Wade Hampton of South Carolina. Both men would be instrumental in ending the horrors of the Reconstruction period. White then continues year-by-year until the election of President Grover Cleveland in 1884. In his "Afterword," he offers a fitting conclusion, finalizing his biographies of Lamar and Hampton, plus adding a moving and fascinating chapter on the last years of Jefferson and Varina Howell Davis.

The chapter on Davis interested me especially. When Davis' body was transported by funeral train to Richmond to be interred at Hollywood Cemetery, the train stopped in Raleigh, North Carolina. Historic photographs show a mammoth procession down Fayetteville Street. My grandfather Henry Johnson Perry, then a sixteen-year-old apprentice, stood along the street paying respects to Davis along with thousands of other Carolinians. Grandfather would, six decades later, recount that moving and indelible experience to me, his young grandson.

For readers new to Howard White's books, the format and structure differ from other histories or biographies readers may be accustomed to. The chronological style and parallel biographical discussions will be useful to those interested in researching information and pinpointing specific events during the decades following the War. As in his other works, White includes an index; but additionally, in volume 4 there is a bibliography of sources for all four volumes, keyed to in-text notes and specific citations. This makes it easy for readers to locate works he has used.

Howard White began this series back in 2002, and his labor represents a veritable lifetime of research and distillation of material and information. Much of White's narrative was once accepted as normative by our fathers and grandfathers. In the "road to reunion" most historians once included the facts that he highlights. But for the past fifty years there has been a practical "historical blackout" imposed by a new generation of radicalized and neo-Marxist historians. Thus, White's books serve as a kind of encyclopedia of the history and times, hopefully reminding us our inheritance and our legacy.

Our history — our traditions — do not really die. Sometimes they just remain dormant, to be re-awakened by new generations that re-discover them and the supreme importance that they have played, and can continue to play, in our lives, if we let them. Howard Ray White has done that, and he is owed our thanks for his labors.

Paperback; 530 pages; published 2012; available as a printed volume through Amazon.com and www.civilwarcauses.com, and as an e-book. (*Confederate Veteran* magazine, November/December 2014)

Review of Charles A. Jennings.
Cultures in Conflict: The Union Desecration of Southern Churches and Cemeteries
↠ Chapter 40 ↞

Cultures in Conflict, Charles A. Jennings' account of the depredations inflicted on Southern churches during the War Between the States, has now been reprinted in a third edition, and it also includes as additional sections in the present edition: "There Was Joy in the Camp: A Brief History of the Spiritual Revival in the Confederate Army," "Confederate Chaplains," and Jennings's essay, "The Twin Merchants of Destruction and Greed: Northern Abolitionists and Carpetbaggers."

Along with Walter Brian Cisco's *War Crimes Against Southern Civilians* (Pelican Publishing, 2007) and *Sherman's March through North Carolina*, by Drs. Wilson Angley and Jerry Cross (N. C. Division of Archives and History, 1996), Jennings' useful study offers documentation of the incredibly severe devastation Northern soldiers carried out during their brutal invasions and occupation of the South. However, Jennings' particular emphasis is on what can only be called "the war on Southern religion." Jennings has combed through older accounts, diaries, newspaper articles, and even contemporary photographs to illustrate his case. In so doing, be reveals a smoldering hatred many Northern soldiers, including high ranking officers, exhibited. Numerous personalized accounts from pastors and parishioners and striking photographic reproductions bolster his charges.

Underlying Jennings' work is the assumption, which he supports with discussion of some of the leading Northern advocates of total war against the South, that by 1861 the northern and Southern states in the Federal union were growing dramatically apart, not just politically and economically, but also religiously and culturally. In this he follows, in a more fragmentary and documentary style, the findings of such scholars as William R. Taylor (in his classic work, *Cavalier & Yankee*), Mel Bradford (in various essays), and Perry Miller (in his work on the New England Puritans): by the 1830s and 1840s, the South was becoming more conservative religiously and culturally, while in many areas of the North, the older Puritanism had evolved into Unitarianism and liberal evangelicalism. These different outlooks and philosophies shaped the societies and their views.

But how to explain the rage and sickening zeal of many Northern soldiers and the ravages they committed when they came South? In his Foreword to the book, Dr. Charles Baker attributes this lapse into what was basically barbarism to the collapse of orthodox Puritanism and the increasing dominance of liberal Protestantism. But as Bradford and Miller and other historians have indicated, the New England Puritan mind, itself, contained the seeds of unending revolutionary zeal, and the continuing desire to "remake the world." Traditional Christianity, which in the eyes of many Northern soldiers was incarnated in the old South, stood in the way of this insatiable desire for human perfectibility and Progress. Propaganda, religious tracts, and fiery anti-Southern sermons served the same purpose as the lurid (and untrue) charges against those horrid Germans bayoneting (or eating) poor Belgian babies at the outset of World War I.

The late Professor Eugene Genovese, in his extensive research on the old South, came to greatly admire perhaps the most notable Southern theologian of the antebellum period, James Henley Thornwell. With great prescience Thornwell came to understand the War of 1861-1865 was not just a "war between the states," but a war of two civilizations, one — the South — connected organically to the great stream of Western Christian civilization, and the other, a burgeoning new and "progressive" culture that, although protesting its "liberalism," could not abide dissent or opposition.

Thornwell described the conflict starkly:

"The parties to this conflict are not merely abolitionists and slaveholders — They are atheists, socialists, communists, red republicans, Jacobins, on the one side, and the friends of order and regulated freedom on the other. In one word, the world is a battleground — Christianity and atheism are the combatants and the [true] progress of humanity is at stake." (p. 98)

Jennings' dramatic documentary of the attack on and destruction of Southern churches, cemeteries, and religious institutions gives support to Thornwell's description.

Third Printing. Owasso, Oklahoma: *Truth in History*, 2012. Paperback; 173 pages. (*Confederate Veteran* magazine, January/February 2016)

Walter Donald Kennedy
Rekilling Lincoln
✧ Chapter 41 ✧

Many members of the Sons of Confederate Veterans will have read at least one, and probably several, books by the "Kennedy Twins," Walter Donald Kennedy and James Ronald Kennedy. Their published works include such popular titles as *The South Was Right!*, *Myths of American Slavery*, and *Nullifying Tyranny: Creating Moral Communities in an Immoral Society*. This latest volume, *Rekilling Lincoln*, by Walter Donald Kennedy, takes its title as a kind of counter-foil to another volume about Lincoln, but with a major difference: this one in many ways could be subtitled: "The Case against Abraham Lincoln."

And as a brief against Father Abe it is a very powerful indictment, indeed, employing a rich repository of historic texts and documentation by many substantial writers whom most historians have forgotten or ignored. But it is also written in an accessible style which invites reading and learning. In many ways, I found it to be one of the finest books by Walter Donald Kennedy, and one of the best on this topic.

Kennedy announces at the beginning, in the short Preface (pp. 7-15), how his book will proceed. He divides it into three main parts: "Exposing the Myths," "Witnesses Against Mr. Lincoln," and, finally, "Defenders of the Real America." For the next 280 pages he progressively and methodically builds an irrefutable case for the prosecution.

The first five chapters, "Exploring the Myths," examine in some detail the "Lincoln myth," with ample documentation concerning Honest Abe's reputation as "the freer of the slaves" (he did not free them), as "savior of the union" (he destroyed the Founders' conception of the American union), as "defender of the Constitution" (he violated it numerous times and set the precedent for the growth of a giant Federal bureaucratic state), as the "Christian president" (Lincoln was not a Christian), and, lastly, as a "humanitarian and friend of the common man" (his consistent actions belie that reputation). Kennedy mines the Lincoln bibliography, including a number of primary sources, to offer a convincing case that the Lincoln "myth," which continues to exert such a stranglehold over the public imagination, is built on sand, on falsehoods which have found their way into popular American culture. Quoting from those sources, including the words of Lincoln, himself,

Kennedy demonstrates "the Rail-Splitter from Illinois" was a crafty and amoral politician who was controlled by Northern commercial interests for much of his career, and who was devoid of the high moral principles often attributed to him. And, rather than the caring "father" figure so often portrayed, he demonstrated a calculating and insincere (and insecure) character on more than one occasion.

His views on slavery, despite his renown as "the Great Emancipator," are a prime example of his calculating mindset. From pushing for emigration of blacks back to Africa, to his solemn promise not to interfere with slavery during the 1860 presidential campaign, to his nominal support for the first "13th Amendment" (1861), which would have enshrined slavery into the Constitution, and much more, to Lincoln's use of the slavery issue to win support from staunch Abolitionists when the Northern war effort seemed to be sagging, his views were amorally political and dictated by his overriding desire to defeat the Southern constitutionalists, who threatened to undo his conception of America and a centralizing American government.

The second section of *Rekilling Lincoln* is subtitled "Witnesses Against Mr. Lincoln," and offers detailed, critical and damning testimony on both Lincoln and his ideas about the Constitution, from several of his 19th century contemporaries: Congressman Clement Vanlandingham, President John Tyler's Secretary of State Abel P. Upshur, eminent Constitutional scholar William Rawle, "Founding Father" St. George Tucker, and Marylander Francis Key Howard, grandson of Francis Scott Key. Vanlandingham is better known than the others, as he was arbitrarily exiled by the Lincoln administration for his opposition to the Northern invasion and its violation of the Constitution. Reading the long citations that Kennedy offers from Upshur, Rawle, St. George Tucker, and Howard demonstrates that these men were extremely thoughtful and profound in their understanding of our Constitutional system. Rawle authored the significant pre-war text on the Constitution and its meaning: *A View of the Constitution of the United States* (1825), a volume which was used at West Point for many years and considered standard. Upshur, who had died seventeen years prior to the outbreak of hostilities, authored the largely — today — unknown study, *A Brief Inquiry into the Nature and True Character of our Federal Government* (1840), reprinted after the war in 1868 as *The Federal Government: Its True Nature and Character*. Originally, a response to the constitutional theories of Justice Joseph Story, Upshur's tract is an amazing and thorough "pre-answer" to the constitutional usurpations of Lincoln and his administration. Indeed, the impressive quotations and arguments that Kennedy cites were enough to send me searching for a copy of Upshur's book!

In his third section Kennedy assembles a diverse group of spokesmen, some better known than others, but each a superb defender of the Founders' vision of the Old Republic, and by extension, of the rights of the Southern states to dissolve their relationship with a union which had deviated seriously from the Constitution and the constitutional conception handed down to them by their fathers and grandfathers. Kennedy offers testimony from such disparate figures as author Paul Whitcomb, historian Claude Bowers, the great Southern writer and historian Mel Bradford, Lincoln historian Edward L. Masters, C. Chauncey Burr of Maine, and Governor Joseph Lane of Oregon, John C. Breckinridge's vice-presidential candidate in 1860. In each case his commentary is accompanied by substantial and illustrative quotes.

With twenty-four pages of helpful notes and a full index following nearly 300 pages of text, *Rekilling Lincoln*, offers the reader an overwhelming case — an historical and legal brief — against Abraham Lincoln. As such it takes its place alongside the works of Thomas DiLorenzo and others in the growing library of studies that hope to puncture the Lincoln myth, and, by so doing, begin the labor of restoring the Founders' Republic.

Pelican Publishing Company, Gretna, Louisiana, 2015. Hardback edition; 328 pages. Notes, Index. $28.95. (*Confederate Veteran* magazine, September/October 2017)

Review of W. Davis Waters (author) and Joseph I. Brown (technical consultant). *Gabriel Rains and the Confederate Torpedo Bureau*

↣ Chapter 42 ↢

Among the numerous books and studies dealing with the War for Southern Independence, every once in a while there appears a biography of lasting historical merit, a volume which can be called definitive. W. Davis Waters' detailed study of inventor of the torpedo, the brilliant Confederate general and scientist Gabriel J. Rains (1803-1881), is such a book. He and Joseph I. Brown, his technical consultant and author of the highly analytical chapter VII, have produced a volume that not only is encyclopedic in covering their subject, but is also highly readable by those not so well-versed in naval and scientific marine terminology.

Gabriel James Rains was born in New Bern, North Carolina, one of eight children of Gabriel Manigault and Hester Rains. A younger brother, George W., would also serve as a lieutenant colonel in Confederate ranks, while Gabriel would reach the rank of brigadier general. Both men would survive the war; but it was the older Rains who would become one of the 19th century's most innovative military inventors and masters of the rapidly changing technology of warfare. His role is slowly being recognized, and Waters' study should do much to solidify that reputation. Nevertheless, one cannot help think that the old maxim about victors writing the history of a conflict holds true here, too. Had Rains been working for the Yanks, we might be seeing his name on various naval ships, bases, and elsewhere.

Rains is most noteworthy for three significant inventions. He invented three mines: the land mine ("subterra shell"), the keg torpedo, and the submarine mortar battery. Yet, getting his inventions approved for use was not always an easy task. During the war years he faced, at times, opposition from other Confederate leaders. Nevertheless, he usually had support from President Jefferson Davis, and that, certainly, made all the difference.

After the Battle of Seven Pines Rains served as Superintendent of Conscription and also Commander of the Torpedo Bureau. He spent much of his time perfecting new and very effective weapons to use against the invading Yankee hordes. His agents mined the harbors of Mobile, Charleston, Savannah and Wilmington. Through his efforts and then-novel inventions numerous Federal ships were sent to the bottom, and the life of the Confederacy was prolonged. At the onset of the final siege of Richmond, President Davis requested Rains mine the main roads leading to the Confederate capital. Again, his efforts gave time to the beleaguered Confederates … and one has to wonder if the efforts he expended in 1864-1865, had they been effected much earlier and with greater application, might have even changed the course of the war.

Waters and Brown have provided numerous illustrations, photographic representations, charts, and diagrams to give any reader ample information on the subject matter. The seven appendices include reports and essays by Rains, letters from Rains on torpedos and torpedo/mine technology, and a complete list of Federal vessels sunk by Rains' inventions (35) or seriously damaged by them (14) — not a bad war record!

Lastly, despite the detailed and well-presented technical aspects of his career, Waters gives flesh to Rains as a man, a man who cared about his country and his native state, who was dedicated and always went beyond the call of duty. Brilliant, determined, and courageous, Rains now has a fine study of his life and inventions. Waters and Brown have given us a superb biography of one of the 19th century's finest scientists, and one of the Confederacy's unsung heroes: Gabriel J. Rains.

Durham, NC: Monograph Publishers, 2014; 204 Pineview Road, Suite 1, Durham, NC 27707. Paperback; 162 pages, appendices, notes, illustrations, glossary of terms, acknowledgments; bibliography, index. $17.95. (*Confederate Veteran* magazine, January/February 2017)

Review of R. E. Mitchell
Souls of Lions
⇾ Chapter 43 ⇽

Very seldom do I review novels, even historical ones. But R. E. Mitchell's volume, *Souls of Lions*, after just a few pages, captured my attention and kept me glued to my couch seat for several days until I had finished it … and with its surprising and fascinating ending. At the end, tears swelled up in my eyes, as I bid goodbye to characters I had grown to know and whose eyes I felt that I could see through.

The plot basically concerns two brothers, George and Walsh Hawkins, both very young and from Person County, North Carolina, and several of their friends who are members of the 50th North Carolina Regiment during the last six months of the War for Southern Independence. George and Walsh actually existed, although Mitchell has recreated various situations and added imagined and fictitious dialogue.

We follow the 50th on its painful and gruesome march, many times as a rearguard unit against General Sherman's overwhelming numbers, from Savannah through ravaged South Carolina, to Averasborough and then to the fields of Bentonville, and at last to the final emotional farewells in Greensboro, where the Army of Tennessee, and particularly Hardee's command, lay down their arms and disbanded.

Through it all we get to know these two brothers, we see through their eyes, experience their unbearable suffering due to Yankee might, ruthless bummers, lack of provisions, and the very cruel winter of 1864-1865. Although author Mitchell conveys fully, at times, the desperation and hardships, we also see a true spirit of courage and incredible sacrifice and a real love of country, and, even more, a certain nobility that inhabits these poor farmer boys.

One of the excellent characteristics of Mitchell's narrative is the obvious research and attention to historical detail he incorporates. You can actually trace the march from Savannah to Bentonville using a good chronology — Mitchell knows his facts and geography. But even more, he is able to express both the sufferings and hardships, as well as the courage and, yes, even moments of simple joy.

Here is an example of his description of the despair that can afflict a soldier in such circumstances:

"An exhausted, starving man lives only for the moment. The past is meaningless, like a disjointed, noisy dream. It is hard to hold. There is a bit of something here, a piece of something there, all loosely joined memories held together by invisibilities. Of what point are they? Yet, they are the things every man has done, the commonplace. George had eaten thousands of meals, slept in bed countless times, all without giving it much thought. But now his desperation was a concentration of plain, simple memories, a singularity of infinite desperation, like struggling to draw a breath, and so the future had become everything." (p. 112)

And of the superhuman courage, emotion, and exhilaration that comes in the midst of contested battle, here is Mitchell describing a successful Confederate counter-attack by the 50th in the heat of Bentonville:

"The smoke had cleared enough for him [George] to see the [Yankee] skirmishers reforming. Several were kneeling, reloading their rifles. He charged them recklessly, swinging his rifle like a club until the enemy fled back into the brush. George charged after them and soon found himself back among his company. He was flying as though in a dream, destined to rule the world. There was nothing they could not do. They were invincible. Here at last there was glory and honor, not of this world, but of another dimension, where all his senses were compressed by time, an excitement so exhilarating, he felt immortal." (p. 135)

Tears came to me as Mitchell, speaking through his characters, recounts the death of young Willie Hardee the general's only son, aged only sixteen. Learning of young Willie's wound, George asks: "How serious is it?" And his compatriot's reply: "Mortal, they say. I guess the general finally gave in. I guess it was hard to say no when a lot of sixteen-year-old boys were fighting and dying. I guess they did some good … Anyway, we're asked to pray for the boy." Then, on hearing of Willie's death from Captain Van Wyk, George sadly exclaims: "I'm sorry … a lot of Willies have died in this war. A lot of fathers have lost their sons." (pp. 139, 143)

And, again, I felt the emotions as the news reaches their camp outside Raleigh that Marse Robert had surrendered at Appomattox: "The men tried all that day to understand the meaning of Marse Bob's surrender. Some denied it was true. It couldn't be true. Why, Lee had whipped Grant at the Wilderness and Spotsylvania and Cold Harbor…." (pp. 155-156) And then thinking about what surrender would mean, in one of the finest summations of what separated those valiant

Southern boys from their Northern counterparts, George declares:

"It [the war] will be our fault ... that is the way it will be told. We liked things the way they were. It was the Yankees who wanted to change things. They want to change the world. But when you think about it, I imagine that most folks are farmers same as us. When you think about it, that should be enough. But the Yankees want to lay up treasures on earth. The whole country will be belching smoke and puffing steam. A man will try to sleep at night to trains and the whistles of steam. I reckon now we'll see the kind of world they want to make. It ain't likely to include us." (p. 156).

The final laying down of arms and banners at Greensboro also captures the bursting emotions and the memories of men who, despite their seemingly infinite hardships and sufferings, had an incredible *esprit de corps* and composed an army scarcely paralleled in human history: "One by one, the regimental flags dipped and were surrendered. The men lowered their heads with the flags and wept. Tears flowed freely down every face. Not one could hold back the tears. To capture an enemy flag was a great feat, but to lose the colors, a disgrace." (p. 163) And at General Hardee's farewell, "[T]he soldiers cheered...They reached up to touch the general and shake his hand," and one companion of George and Walsh expressed their emptiness: "I feel like a hound with his teeth pulled.... At times I prayed for this day, but with a different ending. It just don't feel right." (p. 164)

There is also a heroine in *Souls of Lions*. Her name is Sally Jo, and she catches George's eye in the midst of what probably is the low point during the Carolinas campaign. It would be unfair to reveal details of their amazing romance, for it comprises a special ingredient which makes this novel so rewarding and heartrending. Needless to say, if you are like me, you will not have a dry eye after reading this volume.

At the very end, thirty years later in 1895, at a reunion of those now aged heroes of the 50th on the battlefield at Bentonville, "a band played, the Goldsboro Rifles paraded by the light of the campfires, and the Confederates commenced to sing the old songs. George listened for a while and then joined the singing. His voice cracked with emotion ... of sadness and joy, of sweet memories and bitter ones. He had known suffering but little joy, defeat and no victory, but through it all he had done his duty.... (p. 194)

Thus, with *Souls of Lions* Mitchell's vision, through the eyes of his larger-than-life characters, becomes reality. Through this stirring account of their pain, but also their unexcelled courage and heroism in defense of their country and a way of life, we can see what they saw and fathom what they felt.

Souls of Lions can be ordered through Amazon.com, or directly from the publisher: www.iuniverse.com, or, iUniverse LLC, 1663 Liberty Drive, Bloomington, Indiana 47403; telephone: 1-800-288-4677.

Bloomington, Indiana: iUniverse LLC, 2014). Paperback; 194 pages. $14.95. (*Confederate Veteran* magazine, March/April 2016)

PART VI

A FINAL ESSAY AND APPEAL TO THE VIRTUE OF HOPE

The final essay in this collection is another meditation which uses as its theme a major feast of the Christian calendar. It is "Reflections on the Future," a short piece which appeared in *The Carolina Confederate* in the November-December 2012 issue. It is a reminder to men of goodwill — to Southerners in particular — that the dreams and visions of our forefathers do not die; men die, but ideas —belief— can be and are revived in each age, despite the seemingly overwhelming obstacles, if we possess the resilience and the intelligence, and the faith, to raise the banner once again.

REFLECTIONS ON THE FUTURE
❖ *Chapter 44* ❖

One-hundred and fifty one years ago a Tar Heel soldier stationed in Virginia wrote to his wife in North Carolina that although life was hard and difficult at the front, he never lost hope — hope for his small family, hope for North Carolina, and hope for the infant Confederate nation. In December 1861 the prospects for the Confederacy looked relatively bright. The South had thrown back the Yankee hordes at Manassas, and throughout the Southland patriotism and enthusiasm for the new nation were at their zenith. A little more than three years later this same Tar Heel soldier had experienced unparalleled deprivation, several wounds, hunger, cold, and ultimately military defeat. He had watched as the tattered remnants of Lee's proud army were besieged and battered at Petersburg and Richmond. He had seen the carnage at Gettysburg, Spotsylvania and the Wilderness, the final valiant attack at Fort Stedman. Soon he would join the pitiably reduced regiments — the finest troops in all Christendom — on one last march, a retreat westward towards a small community in central Virginia, where his own war would end.

But before his final march, he had one last letter to his wife to write. It was a letter to wish her Happy Easter which fell that year on April 16. Interestingly, when he wrote his Easter letter in 1865 he linked that holy day to Christmas, for, as he wrote, "the two days are truly connected, as both the birth of Our Saviour and His Crucifixion brought Hope into the world and His blood then transformed us all." While the cause of Confederate independence had suffered much, the beliefs and view of life that motivated it would never die. All men who accepted Our Lord, he added, were given the special virtue of Hope. It was this Hope which inspired him and the men around him spiritually. And it was his deeply spiritual belief in the justice and rightness of the Confederate cause that always overcame discouragement and defeatism. Even in late March 1865, he wrote, the men not only believed in their cause, but they had hope that even if they suffered losses on the battlefield, the cause for which they fought was just and would somehow eventually triumph.

It was this same hope, this same serene certainty of the rightness of their cause that inspired General Stephen D. Lee many years later in New Orleans when he gave to the Sons of Confederate Veterans, their "Charge." In the darkest of times the "Charge" reminds us that temporary "victories" in this life may just be that: temporary. It was the great English poet and essayist, T. S. Eliot, who wrote some seventy years ago that there are in reality "no lost causes," that you can't extinguish truth if good men and women stand boldly for it. And Eliot was specific: it was not necessarily the vast armies of past conquerors who had secured lasting influence; after all Gideon's small army in the Old Testament defeated a force many times its size. Rather, it was dedicated and farsighted believers who were willing to make the necessary sacrifices, even if they personally did not live to see the triumph of their beliefs, who would achieve success.

There are numerous lessons we can gain from knowledge of our history. As we consider the American nation now, it is apparent it is factionalized and fractionalized, probably beyond repair. Our elected officials, achieve office by appealing to the lowest and basest instincts of pressure groups, minorities, and special interests. Moneyed interests put down millions of dollars to make certain their voices are heard; but at the same time, the voices of most citizens are rendered inaudible. Money and power talk. James Madison in *The Federalist Papers* warned us two-hundred and twenty odd years ago that "democracy" was impossible on a large scale and republican government could not exist in a nation torn asunder by radicalized "factions."

How does a tobacco farmer from Johnston County, North Carolina, who has worked all his life on the farm, who has raised a God-fearing family, who obeys the just laws of man and God, who believes government should leave him alone basically to live his life — how does such a man communicate with, for example, the Hollywood leftist who advocates a virulent form of Cultural Marxism, who believes in same sex marriage (or no marriage at all), who believes the Federal government should dictate almost every aspect of our everyday lives? To follow Madison further, when a nation devolves in such a fashion, unity becomes illusory, and to keep the nation together more and more force and coercion will be required. The national government must become more intrusive, more dictatorial. To paraphrase T. S. Eliot again: "If you will not have God (and He is a jealous God), then you must pay your respects to Mr. Stalin or Mr. Hitler."

Southerners have always been patriotic. Even after our defeat in the great crusade of 1861-65, our people came back from their heartbreaking reverse, and in the Spanish-American War, World War I, World

War II, Korea, Vietnam, and in the deserts of the Middle East, offered the world unforgettable examples of courage, heroism, and patriotism. Certainly, those boys were fighting for beliefs and values they believed undergirded our nation. But in our day is this still so?

The Sons of Confederate Veterans and other heritage organizations have a long history of recalling the memory of ancestors who fought, suffered, and died for beliefs they knew were right and just. Despite the horrors of war and Reconstruction, they never despaired. They left for us not just a memory, but actual remnants of our history, living traditions, beliefs, a view of life which connects us to generations long past. It was, and is, a sacred trust. It is something we must pass on solemnly to our children and their children. We live in times of crisis, critical times. Large portions of the American nation no longer accept the basic beliefs which gave birth to this nation. We face discouragement and feel helpless. The media, the entertainment industry, politicians, our educational system, at times our very culture, seem arrayed against us. Yet, we, too, must embrace the hope the Tar Heel soldier had in 1861, but also in 1865. That is something no one can take from us. Certainly, we can abdicate, give it up; but then we turn our backs on our ancestors, our traditions, our home, our beliefs. Are we prepared to do that? I don't think so.

During this very special and holy season, let us think about our heritage, about the rich traditions and legacy entrusted to us. We may be few, but if we are committed, if we work intelligently and skillfully, each one of us doing what best he can do, then we can change the course of history, starting here and now.

(*The Carolina Confederate*, November/December 2012)

That admonition may appear like no easy task. At times, it seems, despair reigns, and the questions arise: Why even try? Why attempt to reverse the apparent and irreversible movement — the tide — of history? And the response must come from deep within us: Because God is still in control of history — because we do not know what may happen — even the best laid plans and the surest theories and most predictable outcomes often do not materialize.

We can recall many such instances throughout recorded history. Who among respected observers and diplomats in July 1914 would have thought that in a little more than four short years three great European empires, dating back hundreds of years, would disappear from the face of the earth? Indeed, few predicted in 1923 that a jailed and obscure German war veteran and failed artist would, in less than eighteen years, come to dominate the European continent, if only for twelve years. Who would have dreamed in 1916 that Vladimir Lenin, in lonely exile in Switzerland, would in one short year become dictator of the world's largest nation? And, then, who would have thought that the Communist system he created would suddenly expire ignominiously in a few short months in 1991, to quote Eliot again, "not with a bang, but with a whimper?"

These lessons and many others spread out before us and offer a cautionary tale: history is not written by the pusillanimous or by timid souls, but by those who, even woefully outnumbered and seemingly destined for failure, seize the initiative and, like General Bedford Forrest, "get there first with the most," those who keep high the standard of faith and conviction, those who believe that they can succeed and continue trying until, with God's good help and His grace, they do succeed. In the process, the path may be littered with the bodies of martyrs much like what happened to the great general Aetius — the last true Roman — and his legion on the plains of Gaul and in the valleys of the Rhone River in the waning days of the Roman Empire. But the prize is certainly worth it. To quote the Spanish philosopher, Miguel de Unamuno in his volume, *The Tragic Sense of Life*, "Our life is a hope which is continually converting itself into memory and memory in its turn begets hope."

About the Author

Dr. Boyd D. Cathey, retired registrar of the North Carolina Office of Archives and History, is an eleventh-generation Tar Heel. He graduated from Pfeiffer University, earned a Master's degree in American history at the University of Virginia, where he was a Thomas Jefferson Fellow, and earned his doctorate in history at the University of Navarra in Pamplona, Spain, where he was a Richard M. Weaver Fellow. He also worked with the late conservative writer and philosopher Dr. Russell Kirk. He has contributed chapters to several published books and published dozens of articles in several languages. He was chief of staff of the North Carolina Division of the Sons of Confederate Veterans, 2002-2009.

— Photo by Walton Photography